To our own families

THE FARM FAMILY BUSINESS

Ruth Gasson

Senior Research Fellow
Centre for European Agricultural Studies
Wye College
University of London
UK

and

Andrew Errington

Senior Lecturer
Department of Agricultural Economics and Management
University of Reading
UK

CAB INTERNATIONAL

CAB INTERNATIONAL
Wallingford
Oxon OX10 8DE
UK

Tel: Wallingford (0491) 832111
Telex: 847964 (COMAGG G)
Telecom Gold/Dialcom: 84: CAU001
Fax: (0491) 833508

A catalogue entry for this book is available from the British
Library

ISBN 0 85198 859 8

Typeset by Solidus (Bristol) Limited
Printed in Great Britain by BPCC Wheatons Ltd, Exeter

CONTENTS

INTRODUCTION   1
   Justification for the Study   1
   Studying the Farm Family Business   3
   Scope of the Book   8
   Acknowledgements   10

1 DEFINING THE FARM FAMILY BUSINESS   11
   The Function of Definitions   12
   The Farm Family Business as an Ideal Type   13
   Components of the Farm Family Business   23
   Issues Arising from the Definition   36
   Summary and Implications   39

2 THE IMPORTANCE OF FARM FAMILY BUSINESSES TODAY   42
   Current Importance of Farm Family Businesses   42
   Historical Trends   49
   Summary and Implications   56

3 FAMILY FARMING, CAPITAL AND THE ROLE OF THE STATE   57
   Introduction   57
   Past Predictions   58
   Penetration by Capital   59
   Slow Capital Penetration in Agriculture   64
   Rival Perspectives   69
   Family Farming, the Small Farm and the Role of the State   77
   Countervailing Power   83
   Summary and Implications   84

4 OBJECTIVES, GOALS AND VALUES IN THE FAMILY FARM   88
   Introduction   88
   Objectives, Goals and Values   88

Objectives of the Family Firm   90
Evidence on Farmers' Objectives   97
Developing Ideal Types   102
Farmers' Objectives under Capitalism   104
Objectives of Other Family Members   107
Coping with Multiple Objectives   110
Summary and Implications   112

5   LABOUR USE IN THE FARM FAMILY BUSINESS   114
     Introduction   114
     The Demand for Labour in the Farm Business   115
     Sources of Labour Available to the Farm Business   118
     Family Labour: Demand and Supply   120
     The Advantages and Disadvantages of Family Labour   125
     Empirical Studies of the Farm Family Workforce   132
     The Management of Family Labour   134
     Summary and Implications   143

6   MARRIAGE AND THE ROLE OF THE FARMER'S SPOUSE   145
     Introduction   145
     Marriage among Farmers   146
     Backgrounds of Farmers and Wives   148
     The Nature and Extent of the Wife's Contribution   149
     Manual Work   150
     Administration, Management and Decision-making   157
     Hours of Work   162
     Other Contributions to the Farm Business   164
     The Wife's Role in Reproduction of the Farm Household   166
     Ideal Role Types   169
     Rewards, Remuneration and Recognition   173
     Trends in the Wife's Contribution   176
     Summary and Implications   179

7   PATTERNS OF SUCCESSION AND INHERITANCE   182
     Introduction   182
     Defining Terms   183
     The Need for a Successor   184
     How many Farmers have Successors?   186
     Patterns of Inheritance   189
     Partibility or Impartibility: The Key Determinants   198
     Patterns of Succession   203
     Summary and Implications   208

8   THE PROCESSES OF SUCCESSION AND RETIREMENT   210
     Introduction   210
     Identifying the Successor   211
     The Succession Ladder   211
     Retirement from the Farm Family Business   220
     Do Farmers Ever Retire?   222
     Sources of Retirement Income   225
     The Importance of Psychic Income   228
     Retirement Housing   229
     Managing the Processes of Inheritance, Succession and
          Retirement   231
     Summary and Implications   237

9   THE FUTURE OF THE FARM FAMILY BUSINESS   240
     Introduction   240
     Strengths and Weaknesses of the Family Farm   241
     Macroeconomic Trends   243
     Patterns of Adaptation   246
     Synthesis of Household Responses   249
     Conditions for Survival   250
     Farm Household Reproduction under Subsumption   257
     Continuity of Family Farming   259
     Conclusion   266

REFERENCES   268

INDEX   282

INTRODUCTION

> Clearly there is need ... for investigations which take as their starting
> point the relationship between farmers as a social and economic group
> on the one hand and the land they occupy on the other.
>
> (Williams 1973: 116)

Farming as it is practised in the United Kingdom and other market industrialized countries is predominantly a family business. The message of this
book is that the nature of the farm business cannot be properly understood
without reference to the family that operates it. Attention focuses not so
much on the farm family or the farm business *per se* but on the interaction
between them. How are farm structure and performance influenced by
family ownership, control and transmission of the business? How are the
attitudes, aspirations and life chances of farm household members affected
by living and working on a farm? To what extent are family relationships
being redefined as farming is increasingly drawn within the orbit of
capitalist market relations? Are marital instability and the trend towards
greater autonomy for women and children threatening the future of the
family farm? First of all, though, we need to justify the study of farming as a
family business.

JUSTIFICATION FOR THE STUDY

> ... the family farm is as much ideological imagery as it is
> socioeconomic fact ...
>
> (Bennett 1982: 112)

The study of family farming can be justified readily enough on economic
grounds. More of the world's population has been, and still is, engaged in
farming than in any other single activity and most farms are operated as
family businesses. The scope of the book is confined to the most developed,
market industrialized countries of the western world, but even here farming

is mainly organized along family lines. Any exploration of the way in which the farm family relates to the farm business and how actions in either sphere serve to assist or constrain achievements in the other, must therefore have important implications for agricultural productivity and for human welfare.

Going beyond these practical considerations, 'family farming' is a concept imbued with emotional overtones. The myth of the family farm has never been as powerful in Britain as it has in the United States, a nation founded on the Jeffersonian ideal of the independent, self-sufficient family farmer, owning his land and relying on family labour. In other EC countries, too, the idea of 'saving the family farm' sways policy-makers to an extent unknown in the UK. One objective included in Article 39 of the Treaty of Rome is to ensure a fair standard of living for the agricultural community. The final resolution of the 1958 Stresa Conference, at which Member States compared their existing agricultural policies and formulated a statement of their resources and needs, provides a more coherent view of the Common Agricultural Policy. Given the importance of family holdings in European agriculture and a unanimous wish to safeguard them, it was agreed that every effort should be made to increase the economic and competitive potential of the family farm (Neville-Rolfe 1984). When, over thirty years later, EC Farm Commissioner Ray MacSharry put forward his blueprint for radical reform of the CAP, one of his prime objectives was that the maximum number of farmers should be kept on the land and particular reference was made to the maintenance of the family farm. Even in urban Britain where under two per cent of the population is engaged in agriculture, the idea of 'family farming' is still surrounded by a certain mystique.

Historically the family farm has been a stabilizing influence and thus valuable to governments, which helps to explain its political importance today. Stability arises from the fact that the family farm combines the four factors of production – land, capital, management and labour – in a single entity. 'If these four economic interests are normally antagonistic, to wrap them all up in a single unit is an ingenious device... Without exaggeration, it minimizes class conflict within agriculture' (Breimyer 1965: 71). During the depression of the 1930s, for example, family farms in Europe and North America were able to absorb some of the unemployed, thus helping to defuse tensions (Peterson 1990).

The emotional appeal of family farming may have the effect of blurring more hard-headed economic arguments for and against protectionist policies. To support their interests, farmers in market industrialized countries have successfully mobilized ideological arguments about the family farm, which do not always stand up to close scrutiny. The family farmer has sought and in large measure achieved political legitimacy by seeking to distance himself from 'capitalism' at the ideological level, while fully embracing it at the economic level (Friedmann 1986; Goodman and Redclift 1986).

If policy-makers seem anxious to avoid any sober factual analysis of family farming, it may stem from a desire to evade the fundamental issue, the inevitable conflict between increasing scale in agriculture and maintaining the maximum number of families on the land (Bennett 1982). In the EC this conflict has still not been resolved. To give but one example, the original MacSharry proposals for reforming the CAP, which would have given a significant advantage to the smaller family-worked farm, were modified at the last moment (partly at the insistence of the British Minister of Agriculture) so as not to discriminate against the larger farm. One of our aims is to 'demystify' family farming, to deal factually and objectively with the two-way relationship between the farm family and the farm business.

STUDYING THE FARM FAMILY BUSINESS

In this approach to family farming it is necessary to use the techniques and data of several disciplines, notably of the geographer, the economist and the rural sociologist.

(Williams 1973: 132)

The origins of this book go back to a conference of the Rural Economy and Society Study Group, held in Oxford in January 1985. At that meeting a number of researchers coming from different disciplinary perspectives presented papers on family farming. It was apparent to us that each researcher, working within a defined discipline, referring to a body of literature, using the concepts, models and tools of his or her own craft, had something original to contribute to the study of family farming. Yet none of us was really familiar with the approaches outside our own disciplines; we were generally unaware of the literature, not at home with the concepts and terminology, out of touch with current research, uneasy with some of the underlying assumptions. We felt there would be some value in meeting so that we might become better informed about the study of the family farm in other disciplines.

The first meeting took the form of an Agricultural Manpower Society workshop, at which the idea of collaboration across the boundaries of conventional academic disciplines was explored and its potential value endorsed by both academics and practitioners sharing an interest in family farming. A tangible outcome was an annotated bibliography, published with financial support from the Agricultural Manpower Society and the Economic and Social Research Council (Errington 1986a). A more ambitious project was the compilation of a review article, commissioned by the Agricultural Economics Society (Gasson *et al.* 1988). Its publication aroused a fair amount of academic interest, mostly it must be said from outside the United Kingdom. This exercise in collaboration brought home to us the differences in approach to the study of family farming between our respective disciplines – agricultural economics, farm management, rural sociology, political economy and social anthropology.

Agricultural Economics and Farm Management

By concentrating on the farm as a **family** business, we intend to counterbalance the emphasis given by the agricultural economics and farm management professions to farming as a **business**. Farm **business** management is now firmly established as part of the agriculture curriculum in British agricultural colleges and universities. The subject took off in the 1950s when the concern of British agricultural policy with increasing output at almost any cost gave way to a goal of increasing efficiency. At that time the farm management specialism was formally established within the state-run National Agricultural Advisory Service. Agricultural economists in university departments then began to develop techniques which the newly appointed advisers could use to analyse business performance and plan farm development (Lloyd 1970).

The whole thrust of teaching, extension and research in the agricultural economics and farm management professions is to reduce farm business problems to their bare essentials to which the universal laws of economics or tenets of business management can be applied. This approach is neatly exemplified in the introduction to Giles and Stansfield's book *The Farmer as Manager*:

> ... the book is about farming only in the sense that it is about the
> management of farms, and frequently it will be argued by us – while
> acknowledging that every industry has its own special technical
> problems, and farming may feel it has more than its share of them –
> that management is management wherever it is practised.
>
> (Giles and Stansfield 1990: 5)

Whether or not agriculture is a special case, there seems to be a perception among many mainstream agricultural economists and farm management specialists, of farming trailing behind other industries, being the last to apply rational business management practices and needing help to catch up with other, more enlightened sectors. A conference organized by the British Society for Agricultural Labour Science in the 1970s with the title 'Man Management – what can be learned from industry?' epitomizes this attitude.

It cannot be denied that farming has benefited enormously from the application of economic principles. The revolution which agriculture has undergone since the Second World War has been as much a triumph of economics and business management as of science and technology. Undoubtedly there is still much to be learned from the experience of industry and commerce. It is not our intention to deny the relevance of economic analysis and business management to the study of farms but rather to argue that the *family* dimension of these businesses should not be overlooked.

Farmers themselves are well attuned to the family dimension of their occupation. This was brought home by a recent survey in which farmers were asked to describe the most important changes that were likely to take place on their farms in the next five years. The bulk of respondents did not refer to the immediate crisis associated with reduced price support under the Common Agricultural Policy but to the kinds of perennial changes occurring in any family business – a son returning from college to be absorbed into the business, a father contemplating retirement, a son taking over the day-to-day management (Warren 1989).

Professional agricultural economists in Britain seem to be less aware of the relevance of family relationships to the business of farming. From time to time the dearth of studies on the farm family is remarked upon. In his presidential address to the Agricultural Economics Society, Hunt (1976) observed that 'It has never been judged proper amongst British agricultural economists to be actively concerned with the farm household'. Fifty years earlier one of his predecessors had made the same point:

> It is strange that the most important of the living things on the farm, the farmers and their families, the workers and their families, and the conditions of economic and human success for them have never been studied.
>
> (Ashby 1925: 16)

In the United States, 'the human factor' was included as a matter of course in early farm economics research but gradually it disappeared from view as the field of study moved closer to quantitative economic theory and methodology (Bennett 1982). The agricultural economics profession in Britain has followed the American lead. Among the founding fathers, Ashby and Orwin made notable contributions to the study of the family farm. In this tradition, some agricultural economists have not been afraid to acknowledge that the farm business may have objectives other than profit maximization and to highlight family issues (see for instance Harrison 1975; Fennell 1981; Peters and Maunder 1983). Giles has been influential in keeping family issues in focus in farm survey work, notably in studies of the role of farmers' wives and the contribution of very small farms (Buchanan *et al.* 1982; Ansell *et al.* 1989, 1990). Davies' pioneering work on farm tourism, although in the Farm Management Survey tradition, necessarily took a broader view of the economic contribution made by the farm household (see for instance Davies 1969, 1973). More recently Hill's analysis of farm incomes has drawn attention to the farm household and to the range of household members' activities, including some outside farming, which contribute to its well-being (Hill 1989, 1990, 1991, 1992).

The mainstream of development in British agricultural economics in the last thirty years has however been towards macroeconomic issues demanding econometric analysis and mathematical modelling, which have tended to take it further away from concerns of the farm household. The Japanese economist Nakajima (1986) has attempted to model the farm household but seems to have no British emulators. Farm family variables are sometimes included in econometric models (see for instance Dawson 1984) but by and large the current generation of British agricultural economists have kept the farm family at arm's length. Paradoxically those among them dealing with Third World countries often show greater sensitivity to family issues.

Rural Sociology

If the field of agricultural economics seems rather barren in its treatment of the farm family, other disciplinary approaches may prove more fertile. In sociology there has been a recent upsurge of interest in the farm household, which Redclift and Whatmore (1990) attribute to changes in the wider economy such as urban-to-rural migration and the growth of self-employment and homeworking. Rural sociologists may be more open than agricultural economists to the 'family' dimension of farming, but this is not to suggest that all sociological approaches should be accepted uncritically.

Orthodox Marxism is founded upon an opposition between family and work. Under capitalism, it is assumed that the two are spatially and functionally separate. They have therefore been studied in isolation, by far the most attention being paid to the sphere of work. In this area Marxism offers an intellectual challenge to agricultural economists of the neo-classical tradition, emphasizing the fact that most of the issues they discuss (e.g. price and income problems, structural policies) have a dimension of social conflict, either within agriculture or between it and other sectors of the economy (Petit 1982).

Orthodox Marxism is less satisfactory in its approach to the domestic sphere. The boundaries it has drawn between family/household and work/ economy reflect western assumptions deriving from the 19th century separation of home from work, which are far from universal. They do not represent the situation in pre-industrial times, nor that of much of the population in non-western countries today. They are not appropriate for the study of farm households nor of increasing numbers of other western households whose members make a living outside the wage economy (Pahl 1984; Redclift and Whatmore 1990; Whatmore 1991a).

Traditional Marxist analysis, then, has neglected the family, which was seen to be marginalized from the production process with the development of capitalism. The tendency to perceive family and market relationships as distinct and to interpret the growth of the modern farm business in strictly economic 'rational' terms has allowed sociologists to ignore the farm family as a central institution (Marsden 1984). The work of Newby, in the Weberian tradition, although it has contributed much to our understanding of British farmers in the class structure, has little to say about the internal workings of farm households. Those rural sociologists concerned with family issues have tended to concentrate on the changing position of the family farm within the capitalist economy, leaving its internal structure unexplored. The tendency has been to treat **the** family in general terms, assuming it to be a nuclear family where relationships are based on sentiment, the pooling and sharing of resources and an egalitarian distribution of power. This approach takes for granted what needs to be empirically investigated and assumes that one particular configuration of kinship/household relations applies universally (Whatmore 1991a).

> It is only through understanding household structure and composition, relationships between earners and dependants, and the disparities between individual members that any sense can be made of the individual and collective activities in the processes of production and reproduction.
>
> (Redclift and Whatmore 1990: 189)

Recent work by rural sociologists like Friedmann, Marsden, Nanneke Redclift, Symes and Whatmore, has provided a sounder theoretical basis for the study of family farming. Work is seen to be organized around relationships within the farm household which are structured by gender and age and are far from symmetrical.

Social Anthropology

The discipline of social anthropology also provides valuable insights. Detailed studies of farm households in defined localities shed light on the processes of family farming, notably the organization of work and inter-generational transmission of the property. The small sample sizes and qualitative methods used by anthropologists provide us with an under-standing of farming in a way that large-scale survey research cannot. The detailed work of Sonya Salamon in the United States, for instance, reveals how ethnic differences continue to shape farming patterns and land holding practices in the Corn Belt (Salamon 1992). Examples from the British Isles range from the classic studies by Arensberg and Kimball (1968) of farming families in County Clare in the 1930s and by Rees (1971) and Jenkins (1971) of Welsh farm life in the early twentieth century, to more recent work by Williams (1963) in Devon, Nalson (1968) in Staffordshire, Symes (1972, 1973) in County Kerry and Symes and Appleton (1986) in North Yorkshire. For present purposes these studies have some limitations. They are becoming dated and are largely confined to marginal farming areas in the upland north and west of the British Isles. In this connection the more recent work of Symes and Marsden (1983a) on Humberside and Hutson (1987) in Pembroke-shire, areas dominated by larger commercial farms, is especially valuable.

SCOPE OF THE BOOK

Two members of the original multi-disciplinary team who produced the annotated bibliography and the literature review decided to move on to the next stage of writing a book on the theme of the farm family business. This allows more space to present and expand on empirical material, develop arguments, weigh up the evidence, put forward personal views, speculate more freely on the likely implications and applications of the study. Here it needs to be pointed out that this is a work of synthesis rather than analysis. We have not carried out any new piece of research for the purposes of this book. We report a number of published studies, our own among them, to illustrate the concepts and issues which follow from our understanding of what it means to run a farm family business.

The main function of Chapter 1 is to define what we mean by a farm family business, to describe its component parts and to note issues arising from the interplay of the farm **family** or household and the farm **business**. Information on numbers of farm family businesses and historical trends is gathered together in Chapter 2. Most of the remaining chapters are concerned with the internal dynamics of farm family businesses; Chapter 4 considers business objectives, Chapter 5 the use of labour, Chapter 6 marriage and the role of the farmer's wife, Chapters 7 and 8 the processes of inter-generational transfer of family farms. Chapter 3 is more outward-looking, reflecting on the wider context within which farm businesses have to operate. It asks how the development of capitalism and intervention by the state constrain the family farmer's freedom of action. Subsequent chapters focusing on relationships within farm households need to be set against this background. How does continuing pressure to substitute capital for labour affect the farmer's choice of objectives, the use of family labour, the role of the wife, the sequence of inheritance and succession on the family farm? The final chapter returns to the wider context. Given the strengths and weaknesses inherent in family businesses, what can we say about the future of family farming within a capitalist economy?

Disciplinary boundaries are crossed freely, drawing on insights, borrowing concepts and using examples wherever we feel they are relevant. Inevitably this entails some loss of intellectual depth; it is not possible to do justice to highly detailed and complex debates in several different disciplines in the space available. On the other hand, by examining a familiar object (the farm family business) from a number of different angles we hope to add perspective and thereby deepen understanding.

Whilst we aim to use a multi-disciplinary approach, our own disciplinary backgrounds and biases ought perhaps to be made clear. Our first degrees were in agriculture and in politics, philosophy and economics respectively. Both of us currently hold positions in university departments of agricultural economics. One of us has leanings towards rural sociology, the other to farm management but we approach this project essentially as agricultural economists. We look outwards to other disciplines which may complement and supplement our understanding of the family farm which is grounded in our training as agricultural economists, and we look inwards to reappraise our own approaches and see where they might be strengthened, rounded and made more sensitive to the nuances of family and business relationships. It is our hope that the insights we have gained in the process of inter-disciplinary and inter-personal collaboration will be helpful to others who attempt to study, advise, train and guide farmers and farm families.

Most of our illustrations relate to the United Kingdom, with which we are most familiar. We believe, however, that the concepts and issues raised are universal, transcending national boundaries, cultural variations and differences in socio-economic structures. That is to say, certain consequences follow from farms being owned, managed and controlled by families and these consequences will hold wherever farming is organized on family lines – in other words, over most of the globe. We are confident that our conclusions apply in the market industrialized countries of the western world such as those belonging to the OECD and we draw illustrations from North America, the European Community, Scandinavia, Australia and New Zealand. As regards the former communist bloc and the Third World, we are on less sure ground. Our instinct tells us that many parallels could be drawn but we have not attempted to cover such a broad canvas here. There might be a value in using this book as a starting point for discussions with experts on Third World agriculture, to discover what is common and where there might be convergence or divergence.

Our background as agricultural economists studying farming in Britain may help to explain our particular stance regarding the farm family, aspects of which may be challenged by readers from other disciplines and other cultures. We understand first of all that ultimate responsibility for running a family farm will usually rest with one person, 'the farmer', who may be a sole proprietor or senior partner in the business. In the UK as in most market industrialized countries, 'the farmer' is usually a man, but we must not to overlook the fact that there are also women farmers. Second, we assume that on most farms there is a woman who plays the role of farmer's wife. We argue throughout the book that this role, often under-estimated and under-valued, is crucial to the success and survival of the farm family business. Yet we maintain that it is a distinctive role in its own right and understood to be so in British culture. One of our colleagues reviewing the manuscript asked a challenging question: 'If most women are involved in running the farm business, why are they not seen as farmers?' Our answer has to be that in our experience, partial as it may be, most women involved in farm family businesses in the UK are *not* seen as farmers nor do they describe themselves as such. Whether the situation is radically different in other western countries, remains an open question.

ACKNOWLEDGEMENTS

We should like to thank many individuals and organizations for their contributions to this project. The roles played by the Agricultural Economics Society, the Agricultural Manpower Society and the Rural Economy and Society Study Group have already been acknowledged. The other members of the original team, Graham Crow, John Hutson, Terry Marsden and Michael Winter, have made an invaluable contribution by participating in our earlier discussions and introducing us to areas of the subject previously unexplored. Each will recognize some of his own ideas here and if we have not given them sufficient credit elsewhere, may we do so now. We are much indebted to Mark Casson, Alan Harrison, Berkeley Hill, John Hutson, Norah Keating and David Symes for agreeing to comment on an earlier draft of the book and to Sue Errington, Richard Tranter and Frank Thompson for reading individual chapters. We are also grateful to Richard Crane for help with most of the figures and to David Merryweather for Fig. 1.2. A generous fellowship from the Centre for European Agricultural Studies, Wye College, allowed Ruth Gasson to spend several uninterrupted months working on the book, for which she is extremely grateful.

1

DEFINING THE FARM FAMILY BUSINESS

The precise nature of the family farm has troubled researchers around the world.

(Reinhardt and Barlett 1989: 204)

The family farm and **family farming** are terms which are widely used, yet which prove surprisingly difficult to define. Even the Smallfarmers' Association, a British pressure group set up to promote the interests of family farming, had some trouble agreeing what was meant by a family farm. The following extract from Galeski and Wilkening's book on family farming illustrates how difficult it is to arrive at an all-encompassing definition:

> While definitions of the family farm vary among the countries, it is generally regarded as a farm which is owned and operated by a family which may include one or more generations. Most of the land and capital is provided by the family, although additional land may be rented for expansion of the operation and capital may be borrowed for supplies, machinery, and improvements. Most of the labour is provided by members of the family living on the farm, but additional labour may be hired, most often on a seasonal basis.
>
> (Galeski and Wilkening 1987: 1–2)

The main function of this chapter is to define the farm family business. Economic and social behaviour in farm family businesses is likely to differ from non-family businesses because of the interaction between the two components, the farm business and the farm family or household. Salient features of these components are considered separately. The chapter then draws out certain characteristics of farm family businesses which result from the interaction of the two elements and highlights issues which they raise.

THE FUNCTION OF DEFINITIONS

A definition exists to serve a purpose. For purposes of raising awareness, a broad descriptive approach may suffice. For instance the notion of the **agrifamily**, the household unit of parents and children, plus additional relatives as required, who own and operate a production unit, the **farm firm** (Bennett 1982), conveys the essentials with commendable brevity. To be useful for analysis or policy-making, however, the concept needs to be defined with greater theoretical rigour and empirical precision. One method, the **taxonomic approach**, is to start from an empirical data base and devise a classification scheme, from which general principles may be derived (Whatmore *et al.* 1987a). For example, Furness applied the term 'small and family-worked farms' to the 100,000 UK agricultural holdings of between 4 and 24 ESU[1] which should theoretically be capable of providing work for one or two persons (Furness 1983). This allowed him to relate a large amount of statistical information about types of farming, regional distribution, output, labour use and income to the defined categories. It does however demonstrate some of the weaknesses of taxonomic classifications (Whatmore *et al.* 1987a). Observed relationships chosen as the basis of classification may have limited explanatory value. In this case, the ESU rating of a farm business has no direct bearing on the way it is organized; knowing that farms of a certain size *could* be operated on a family basis does not prove that they *are* run in this way. Another problem is that by concentrating on observable forms rather than underlying processes, the resulting typologies are likely to be static and ahistorical; business size as measured in one year gives no indication of the likely trajectory of that business over time.

The alternative is to begin with an abstract concept and devise Weberian **ideal types**. An ideal type is a hypothetical construct formed by emphasizing aspects of behaviour which can be observed in real life. The economist's notion of a perfectly competitive market is an ideal type. 'Ideal' in this case means 'pure' or 'abstract' rather than 'perfect' in a normative sense. Ideal types can be conceptually helpful without having to correspond exactly to empirical reality. Since the aim of this book is to raise awareness and discuss issues at a theoretical level, broad concepts and ideal types are appropriate. It is for policy-makers and future researchers to devise precise definitions and operationalize them as necessary for administering policies or analysing trends.

---

[1] This system applies Standard Gross Margins (SGM) to crop areas and livestock numbers on each farm. Total SGM for each farm is converted into European Size Units (ESU), one unit being 1000 European Units of Account of gross margin.

THE FARM FAMILY BUSINESS AS AN IDEAL TYPE

If a definition is devised to serve a purpose, the content of the definition and the measurement criteria used may change in response to changing policy needs. The family farm has never been a conscious target of agricultural policy in the UK, so the need to define it has never arisen. The situation is different in the United States, where both the purposes of study and the definition of the family farm have varied over time (Reinhardt and Barlett 1989). The early Jeffersonian ideal was of the self-sufficient family farmer owning his land, making all management decisions and relying on family labour. During the nineteenth century increasing market orientation reduced the need for self-provisioning, a growing workforce made it possible to hire labour and the closing of the frontier undermined the belief that family farmers had to own the land they operated. After the Second World War, all that remained of the earlier vision was that the farm family should control the operation and be able to earn a livelihood from it. A 1944 USDA publication defined the family farm as:

> ... one for which the principal source of labour is the family, and of sufficient size and productivity to pay expenses, including maintenance of the farm, furnish an income that will provide a comfortable living for a farm family, including food and shelter, medical care, education and recreation, and permit the accumulation of a reserve sufficient to meet the needs of old age.

In the UK the Smallfarmers' Association has taken a similar stance, laying stress on the family's dependence on farm income. In its inaugural conference, the 'family-worked farm' was depicted as

> a unit large enough to support two members of a family or one member of a family and one employee, possibly part time, with a standard of living fully comparable to urban occupations, but probably with a higher quality of life.
>
> (Buccleuch and Queensbury 1981)

Elsewhere it was suggested that the family-worked farm would enable

> an efficient family unit, plus some outside labour, to make a reasonable living using accepted modern techniques for the production of wholesome food or other products on a sustainable basis.
>
> (Hunter-Smith 1982)

Definitions like these are helpful in drawing attention to the interdependence of the farm business and the family unit, but beg the question of what is meant by a 'reasonable' living or 'comparable to urban occupations'. Moreover, increasing numbers of small, part-time farms raise the issue of whether to include households with other sources of earned income.

A compromise is to insist that farming be the *main* source of income, as suggested by Reid:

> By definition, family farms are those in which the working capital and the labour resources are mainly supplied by close members of the family, and from which family members obtain the main part of their income in the form of physical goods and services as well as cash.
>
> (Reid 1974: 50)

The definition of an agricultural household agreed for EC purposes is one in which independent (self-employed) agricultural activity on the holding is the main source of income of the entire household (Eurostat 1991). Other definitions have dropped the requirement that the farm should provide a livelihood.

The Labour Criterion

The most contentious issue in defining the family farm is the presence or absence of hired labour. The nature of family farming, as conventionally understood, hinges on the family furnishing all or most of the labour required at low cost (Bennett 1982). In Marxist terms, capitalism separates property and labour, with the monopoly of the means of production on one side and the sale of labour on the other. Returns to the enterprise have to be allocated between labour and capital. Within a family-worked business, the fundamental class cleavage between labour and capital is not present, so there is no need to divide the returns along these lines. As soon as the entrepreneur/farmer employs labour, though, she or he[2] begins to experience a change in the social relations of production; she has to pay *wages* out of *profits*. The presence or absence of hired labour therefore becomes the main criterion to distinguish family farms from capitalist enterprises.

In a strict sense, a family farm would be a holding occupied by a farmer and his family which is maintained as an economic unit without the use of any hired labour whatsoever (Williams 1973). This was the approach taken by Symes (1972) in his Irish study, where the family farm was defined as 'a commercially oriented agricultural enterprise almost entirely dependent upon the resident household for its labour resource'. This strict definition is not tenable in practice. At certain times in the family cycle, for example when children are young or at the 'empty nest' stage, outside labour may have to be employed. Thus Williams extended his definition to include holdings on which hired labour was employed *at certain periods in the family cycle*. Besides this, non-family seasonal, casual or contract workers have

---

[2]Most farm businesses are headed by men but to remind ourselves that there are female farmers too, we will alternate 'he' and 'she' when referring to 'the farmer'.

always been needed to help the resident family labour force over peaks of labour demand. In recent years British agriculture has become increasingly reliant on these short-term sources of labour. It is unsatisfactory to have such an ephemeral basis for a definition. Moreover it does not seem to correspond to the experience of farm people; Hutson (1987) describes going into the field at the start of his Pembrokeshire study, expecting to compare 'business' farmers employing wage labour and 'family' farmers relying on their own resources, and finding no such simple dichotomy existing in practice.

If the presence or absence of wage labour is not to be applied rigidly as a criterion, it becomes more difficult to distinguish between family and non-family farms; Bennett (1982) speaks of the family furnishing a 'critical' amount of the labour requirement, without defining how much is critical. Two alternatives suggested by Ghorayshi (1986) are the employment of a 'substantial' amount of labour and the ratio of paid to unpaid family labour. On the first count, Marx regarded capitalist production as beginning when each firm employed 'a comparatively large number of labourers'. He appeared to accept five workers as the minimum required for an employer to function as a capitalist. Employing at least five workers allows the farmer to make a living by appropriating surplus value rather than relying on his own labour or that of his family. Applying this measure to agriculture in market industrialized countries, however, means that a very small proportion of farms are classed as capitalist units; under 5 per cent in England and Wales and under 1 per cent in Canada, for example. A more appropriate threshold might be the employment of at least one man-year of non-family labour, all below this level being family farms. A problem with this approach is that most farm **families** supply more than one man-year of labour to the business, so that farms defined as capitalist could still be mainly dependent on family labour.

The ratio of hired to family labour is theoretically more acceptable as a criterion. Putting it into practice requires a reliable estimate of the family labour supply. In his analysis of farmers' incomes and business performance using FADN, the EC Farm Accounts Data Network, Hill (1991) distinguished family farms from those operated in other ways. Family farms were those on which unpaid (family) labour provided more than 95 per cent of the total labour input, intermediate farms those where it was between 50 and 95 per cent and non-family farms where the family contribution was less than 50 per cent.

Applying measures like these depends on having reliable information on hired and family labour inputs, which is not always available. British agricultural statistics, for instance, exclude the labour of school children and probably under-estimate the unpaid labour contribution of spouses (see Chapters 5 and 6). Standards may have to be used instead. A definition used by the USDA, for instance, refers to the farmer and family doing most (more than half) of the work. Nikolitch (1969) estimated that the average US farm family supplied approximately 1.5 man-years of labour. He therefore categorized any farm with a total labour requirement of three or more man-years as a larger-than-family farm, any family-managed unit requiring less than this amount of labour being a family-operated farm business. This method gives a rough estimate of numbers of farms using more hired than family labour but may not be valid in individual cases (for instance a farm with a total labour requirement of three and a half man-years operated by a farmer, spouse and two sons). Even if the methodological problems are solved, the theoretical problem remains that a large proportion of farms with more hired than family labour will employ fewer than five workers and will therefore not operate fully as capitalist units under Marx's law of value (Ghorayshi 1986).

Family Ownership and Management

Some definitions of farm family businesses take both labour and capital into account. One typology of US agriculture uses Marxist class analysis as the theoretical basis, relating the amount of land and capital owned by the farm operator to the amount of management and labour the operator and family provide (Figure 1.1).

In Figure 1.1 'family-type' farms are characterized by the unity of land, capital and labour. A large proportion of 'tenant-type' farms in this classification are former sharecropper enterprises on plantations in the southern states, though in other regions a livestock-share system or straightforward renting of land predominate. 'Larger-than-family farms', historically found in the south and west of the United States, are wholly or mainly owned by operators and their families but most of the work is done by hired labour. The 'industrial-type farm' is the polar opposite to the family farm with maximum separation beween ownership, management and labour; that is to say it has a resident manager who does not own the land, the capital or the

Amount of land and capital owned by operator	Amount of labour provided by operator	
	most or all	least or none
most or all	*FAMILY TYPE*	*LARGER-THAN-FAMILY TYPE*
least or none	*TENANT TYPE*	*INDUSTRIAL TYPE*

Figure 1.1. Typology of US agriculture. Source: Rodefeld 1978

business and is worked by hired labour with limited involvement in daily management decisions (Rodefeld 1978).

Other definitions stress the unity of business ownership and management and play down the more questionable labour criterion. Where Rodefeld defines four ideal types, Reinhardt and Barlett (1989) just distinguish between non-family and family farms on the basis of the way production is organized. The non-family unit is characterized by the separation of business ownership, management and labour, leaving aside the issue of land ownership. Owners of capital are not involved in farm work and may withdraw their funds if they perceive more profitable investment opportunities elsewhere. Day-to-day operations are supervised by a manager and carried out by hired workers, all of whom must receive the going wage for their labour. Distinctive features of the family farm, by contrast, are the centrality of kinship relations and the direct involvement of the farm owner in the daily work. These authors also see business objectives as a distinguishing feature. 'Capitalist agriculture' is undertaken as an investment and the unit can only survive if it earns at least the average rate of profit. Reinhardt and Barlett do not specify what the objectives of family businesses are, beyond the fact that they are more complex, and they concede that profit maximizing may be one of them. Goals and objectives, which are explored in Chapter 4, are perhaps better considered as contingent features than as a defining characteristic of family farms.

A family business can be characterized more simply as one in which productive efforts and rewards are largely vested in the family (Nikolitch 1972: 248). Following this concept, Nikolitch defined a family farm as 'one for which the operator is a risk-taking manager, who with his family does most of the farm work and performs most of the managerial activities'. A more recent official US definition characterizes family farms by 'the existence of an independent business and social entity that share responsibilities of ownership, management, labour, and financing' (OTA 1986). Friedmann (1986) lays more stress upon internal family relationships. Stripped to the essentials, she argues, two things are specific to family enterprises in a capitalist economy; the labour process and property relations. First, production is organized through kinship with a division of labour by gender and age, instead of through the labour market. Second, property and labour are combined where the capitalist economy is premised on their separation and the purchase of labour power by capital. Again, ownership is not equal but distributed according to gender and age. These indeed are the essential elements of the definition used in this book.

The Chosen Definition

There are six elements to our own definition of a farm family business:

1. Business ownership is combined with managerial control in the hands of business principals.
2. These principals are related by kinship or marriage.
3. Family members (including these business principals) provide capital to the business.
4. Family members including business principals do farm work.
5. Business ownership and managerial control are transferred between the generations with the passage of time.
6. The family lives on the farm.

We emphasize that this represents the 'ideal type' of farm family business, not a strict operational definition. It is not our intention to build a watertight construct for policy purposes. Our aim is to raise awareness of relationships and to highlight their consequences. The problems of operationalizing concepts, of having to compromise due to the availability of data, are not under-estimated, but they do not have to be addressed here. Taking this approach allows us to concentrate on principles without being sidetracked by having to explain exceptional cases. Such an approach has its dangers, for the exception may signal an emerging trend or a failure of theory. We believe that the danger can be minimized by using the results of empirical studies to support and illustrate the theory.

Most of the definitions discussed earlier stipulate that the family is the principal source of farm labour. Our chosen definition departs from these in not specifying what proportion of the total labour requirement is supplied by the family. Many UK farm families do in fact provide the greater part or 'a critical amount' of the labour used in farm production, but this is not seen as a crucial condition. More important is the combination of business ownership, management control and labour within a single family. We firmly believe that family ownership and control of the business has important implications quite apart from the use of family labour. Indeed, we suggest that in some ways family relationships may be *more* significant for the operation of the larger farm, for instance with regard to succession. We therefore include what Nikolitch terms 'family-owned businesses' within our definition. In Rodefeld's typology we would treat larger-than-family farms, wholly or mainly operated by their owners, as family businesses. Rodefeld's 'tenant-type' category would need to be split between family businesses with a full secure tenancy and an alternative category of sharecroppers who do not satisfy the condition of controlling the farm business.

The concept of the **farm family business** is therefore much broader than that of the **family-worked farm**. The farm family business is not limited by the labour which the family can provide, since for the reasons discussed above the labour criterion is felt to be unsatisfactory and no longer of crucial importance. As time goes on, capital (mainly in the form of machinery) is helping to overcome the limitations which reliance on family labour imposes on the family-worked farm. This is a crucial point. When the major inputs for agricultural production were land and labour, the scale and nature of activities on family farms were determined to a great extent by the labour the family was able to supply. Production was heavily dependent upon the number of children, stage in the family cycle, the age and health of the operator and spouse. Increased dependence on capital means that business size is no longer constrained by the family labour supply. Fluctuations in the quantity and quality of labour available over the phases of the family cycle can be significantly reduced by mechanization. The point was well made over sixty years ago:

> So these are the two principal types of family-farmer – the thrifty, frugal peasant-cultivator of the old world, spending himself in a round of endless toil upon a small plot of land, and the pioneer of the new world working, probably, at equal pressure, but harnessing to his hand every mechanical device by which he can extend the scope of his operations.
>
> (Orwin 1930: 84)

We recognize that the family is an important source of capital and management as well as labour. As capital replaces labour as the organizing principle of the farm business, the family's capacity to acquire and manage capital may be superceding its importance as a source of labour (Hutson 1987). At the same time there are dangers in relying on productive resources outside the immediate family or household. When the comparative advantage of the farm family business depended largely on access to the unpaid labour of family members, the uptake of hired labour was seen as a potential threat. Nowadays a bigger threat to the integrity of the farm family business is growing reliance on external sources of capital, a theme expanded in Chapter 3.

Marginal Cases

To move from this **ideal type** to a **definition** of the farm family business for purposes of policy or analysis would require decisions to be made about critical thresholds. What degree of kinship constitutes a 'relationship' between business principals? Where is the capital supply limit set among family members? How rigidly is 'working in the business' to be interpreted? More fundamentally, the approach embodies a number of assumptions which need to be tested. Is inheritance a necessary condition for a farm to be regarded as a family business? Must *all* family members be involved in farm work? Should a distinction be made between farm work and domestic work?

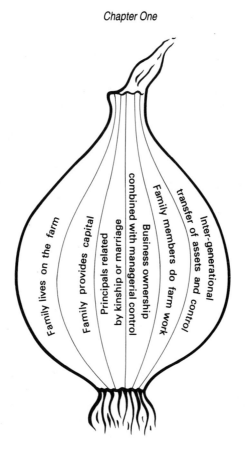

Family lives on the farm

Family provides capital

Principals related by kinship or marriage

Business ownership combined with managerial control

Family members do farm work

Inter-generational transfer of assets and control

Figure 1.2. The farm family business.

Must the family be resident on the farm to qualify? Does the concept of the family farm embrace the single farmer?

We have attempted to define the farm family business as an entity on its own, although characteristics of the non-family farm have been mentioned in passing. In practice it is not so easy to draw boundaries between family farms and non-family or sub-family farms. Official statistics do not usually indicate, for instance, how many farming companies are run for or by families. To sharpen the focus, we explore the boundaries of the ideal type in this section. Deciding what is *not* a farm family business may help to clarify what it *is*.

Figure 1.2 represents the ideal type of farm family business as a series of layers, like an onion. At the core are those conditions which are absolutely essential to the concept – business ownership combined with managerial control in the hands of business principals who are related. Towards the outside are conditions which, while typical of farm family businesses, are not absolutely essential – provision of capital and labour, inter-generational transfer, living on the farm. An onion lacking all the outer layers would not be much of an onion, but if one or two of the layers were missing, the onion would still be recognizable.

Kinship relations are central to the farm family business. This implies a minimum of two family members resident on the farm – cohabiting spouses, a parent and child, siblings or more distant relatives. A farm run by someone living alone – a widower or widow, an unmarried child of deceased farming parents – does not therefore conform to the ideal type in all respects. Some of the key issues, such as the division of labour by gender and generation, will not apply although others like retirement, succession and inheritance, are still relevant.

Crucial for the definition is that business ownership, management and labour are vested in the same family. Often all three functions are embodied in the same person, where the occupier of the holding is the sole proprietor of the farm business who also performs most of the manual work. At the other extreme we can envisage a case where grandfather owns the business, father manages the farm and the son does the manual work. It would cease to be a family business in our terms if the ownership or management functions passed out of family control, for example to a bank or to a hired manager.

Business ownership does not imply that the family owns all the capital tied up in the business; in fact this is unlikely to be the case for the assets may be considerable. Nor is it a requirement that the family owns the land it farms. Historically most British farmers were tenants and only since the Second World War has owner occupation become the norm. The crucial consideration is that the farm family *controls* the assets of the business, that is to say fixed assets like buildings and working capital of machinery, livestock, growing crops, milk quota and so on. The extent to which family farms are losing control of their enterprises through dependence on outside sources of capital, is discussed in Chapter 3. With regard to land, legislation over the last century has progressively strengthened the rights of the tenant farmer and weakened the powers of the landowner, to the point where the landlord can exercise very little control over the way the tenant farms. Under 1976 legislation even the right of succession was guaranteed to the tenant farmer's family, though that Act was subsequently modified. The typical tenant farmer in the UK thus controls the land and provides a proportion if not all of the working capital in the business, thereby meeting the requirements of the definition.

Being a tenant farmer has a different meaning in the United States and it is significant that Rodefeld's typology draws a distinction between 'family-type' and 'tenant-type' farms. Jefferson's belief in a democracy based on the self-sufficient farm family owning its land, had a particular resonance for peasant farmers emigrating to escape the more oppressive regimes of the Old World. In the US today a full tenancy is compatible with family farming since most tenants make day-to-day management decisions with little or no interference from landlords. The traditional southern sharecropper form of tenure, by contrast, lodges so much power in the hands of the landlord, that these particular tenants are more like employees paid with a share of the crop (Nikolitch 1972).

The requirement that 'family members including business principals do farm work', is fraught with difficulties. Many cases raise no problems, with some members of the household working full-time on the farm and all able-bodied members helping at the busiest times. At the very least, the entrepreneur must be involved in farm work, not necessarily manual work. It is not a condition that the farmer work *full-time* or *solely* on the farm; the growing army of dual-job farmers is not excluded from the concept of family farming. She must however do *some* work on the farm. A farm owner who makes decisions from a city office and communicates with farm staff only by telephone or fax, does not qualify under this definition.

It is not a necessary condition that other family members work on the farm. The EC definition of an agricultural household covers members who contribute no labour input to the holding; those persons may or may not have other occupations or sources of income (Eurostat 1991). A growing trend in market industrialized countries is for the farm operator to work full-time alone on the farm while his wife holds a job elsewhere. If farmers' wives become increasingly occupied off the farm, can the farm still be viewed as a family business? Is family farming being transformed into one-man farming? (Blanc and MacKinnon 1990). If a family farm is defined as one which gives full employment to the labour of the family, which in a modern context may mean just husband and wife, then a one-man farm must be regarded as something less than a family farm. In these terms the highly-mechanized one-man farm which no longer requires the labour of the farmer's wife represents a 'severance of the definitional bond of the family farm' (Djurfeldt 1992). The present study *would* however include such a household in the definition since business ownership and management are combined and at least one member works on the farm.

Not all farmers' wives do farm work in addition to domestic work, but Chapter 6 will argue that any boundary between productive and repro-ductive work in the farm household is artificial. Women's work in 'reproducing' the labour force – that is to say doing all that is necessary to service the productive workers and keep them in a fit state to work by feeding, housing and clothing them, caring for them in sickness and old age and raising replacements – is just as much an economic contribution to the farm family business as rearing calves or drilling wheat. As Long (1984: 8–9) puts it, 'Capital cannot operate without subsistence production since the goods and labour power it appropriates are based on previous expenditure of labour which takes place within the household'.

The definition requires the family to live on the farm. As in many other types of family enterprise like small retail businesses, workshops, hotels and public houses, 'living over the shop' is economical when the dwelling is an integral part of the business premises, convenient when the hours of work are long and unpredictable, saves the time and cost of journeys to work, helps to reduce the risk of theft and vandalism. In agriculture, having the family living on the premises assumes much greater importance because of the need to keep a watchful eye on livestock, react swiftly to avert danger from storm, fire, flood and frost, disease, pest attack and so on.

While the ideal type of farm family lives in a farmhouse in the midst of the farm, this has not always been the pattern historically and does not always apply today. Over much of lowland England, farmers only moved out of villages to dwell on their newly-acquired land following enclosures. In some parts of Europe, where plots are still very fragmented, farm families may live in nucleated settlements some distance from their fields. There are parts of Britain, too, where farm families tend to live away from the farm; in low-lying areas such as the Fens and Romney Marsh where 'ague' used to be prevalent, farmers and their families preferred to live in the healthier climate of settlements on the higher land and they continue to do so. Only the hired stockmen or 'lookers' actually dwelt on Romney Marsh in the past. Where the family does not live on the farm, certain characteristics of farm family businesses will not apply although in other respects the family may conform to the ideal type. On the other hand, many families live on farms but do not run farm businesses and these fall outside our definition.

With the ideal type there is a presumption that the business will be handed on to a member of the family. Sometimes this condition is not met in businesses which fulfil all the other criteria, due to a childless marriage, absence of suitable or willing heirs, termination of a tenancy and so on. Inter-generational transfer also implies that the present farmer succeeded to the business, a condition which may not apply on farms which are family-run today. Succession is therefore another characteristic of the ideal type which is not achieved in practice on every family farm.

COMPONENTS OF THE FARM FAMILY BUSINESS

The underlying assumption of this book is that farm family businesses are distinctive; they behave in different ways from non-family businesses, because they are **family** businesses. By the same token farm families differ from other types of families, even families running other businesses, because they run **farm businesses**. That is to say, distinct patterns of behaviour result from the interaction between the two components, the farm family and the farm business. Some issues arise directly from the 'chemistry' of this reaction, for example use of family labour and inter-generational transfer of the farm. Others are more in the nature of contingent factors, not defining characteristics of the farm family business but likely to follow from it, such as a high value being placed on intrinsic aspects of the farming occupation. Some of these topics are introduced in this chapter, to be developed later in the book. First, though, we will look more closely at the basic components themselves, the farm business and the farm family.

The Farm Business

The concept of a farm business used in this study is based on Harrison's working definition of a farm:

> . . . a separate business unit or farm, is defined so as to embrace such farming activities as fall within the compass of a given fund of capital. But it is not enough that a single person owns a number of establishments and that he should allocate capital between them, on a more or less continuing and regular basis. To count as a single business unit, there must be participation in a regular and at least annual assessment of the capital position with all sectors contributing to, and competing for, resources.

(Harrison 1975: 4–5)

A farm business is not synonymous with an agricultural holding, the unit of enumeration employed in official agricultural statistics. A holding is a discrete, identified parcel of land; a farm may consist of several holdings. From his national survey conducted in 1969, Harrison (1975) estimated the number of farms in England to be only 89 per cent of the number of holdings. Since that time the discrepancy between holdings and farm busineses is thought to have narrowed, as Ministry of Agriculture statisti-cians have identified most of the multiple-holding farms and persuaded the holders to return a single entry for agricultural census purposes.

The present study uses 'farm business' in preference to 'farm' to draw attention to the commercial nature of the activity. With the prevalent practice of 'lotting' farm property when it comes on the market, many new purely residential 'farms' are being created consisting of a farmhouse or converted farm building with a few acres. The farm family business as an ideal type does not exclude farm-based households mainly dependent on non-farm sources of income, but there must be a minimum of commercial farm production to qualify as a farm business.

One way of looking at farm businesses is to start by describing the structure – of holdings, capital and and so on. Another way is to start by describing farming itself. Farming may be regarded as a system through which inputs (sunlight, nutrients, water, labour etc.) are transformed into outputs (e.g. meat, eggs, cereals) using biological processes. The labour input is critical because the defining characteristic of farming is human intervention in 'natural' biological processes in order to tailor them to the satisfaction of human needs. Various revolutions in agricultural technology have tended to make these farming systems more 'open' since the new technologies have been embodied in both physical inputs (machinery, agrochemicals etc.) and services (advice, credit etc.) that must be purchased from the wider economy. This is necessary because the farm itself is not large enough to provide the scale of activity and investment required to generate these new technologies.

Farming becomes a business when the outputs of the farming system are no longer used simply to 'reproduce' the labour inputs but enter the wider economy through monetary exchange, thus drawing farming into a more open system. As the individual farming system opens up in this way, it moves further along a continuum which stretches from a pure form of subsistence production, where labour is the principal input and all the outputs are either consumed by the labour involved in their production, given away as charity or seized by others through coercion, to a pure form of commercial production where all inputs are purchased and all outputs sold. As the farmer engages in monetary transactions, selling outputs or buying inputs, his farm becomes a business; a farm which is not involved in any form of commercial exchange, does not constitute a farm business for our purposes.

Each business will have at least one principal, the entrepreneur, whose task it is to allocate the resources available to that business to their most effective use in achieving the objectives of the owners of those resources. In some cases, and typically in a small family business, the principal herself will be the owner of the resources but in other cases the authority to allocate resources may be delegated by the owner to someone else, such as an employed manager. The separation of ownership from managerial control is a notable feature of twentieth-century economic development (Cyert and March 1963). The farm family business, in which the farmer is both owner and manager, is distinctive in not having gone down that road.

Allocating scarce resources within the business to achieve pre-defined objectives involves the farmer in three major functions: planning, implementation and control. These functions are directed to four areas of action within the business, namely production, marketing, finance and staffing. **Planning** demands the prior review of alternative courses of action, both evaluating the alternatives and identifying the individual activities required to implement the one that is chosen. Planning may be **strategic**, involving major decisions about farm policy such as what to produce, whether to buy additional land, or **tactical**, relating to day-to-day, on-the-spot management decisions such as which job shall be done first today, which special offer on fertilizer to accept. Some of this decision-taking may be delegated to other members of the workforce or even to people outside the business (Errington 1984). **Implementation** means taking the course of action chosen by carrying

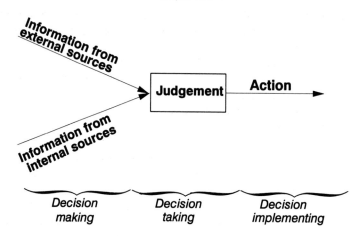

Figure 1.3. A model of the decision process. Source: Errington 1986b

out all the activities identified. Again, some of this responsibility may be allocated to persons outside the business. Finally, **control** involves the monitoring of the intermediate outcomes of particular courses of action to ensure that the objectives they are intended to achieve are actually being achieved. It also involves analysing reasons for any discrepancy between targets and actual performance in order to take corrective action if necessary (Errington 1986c).

The decision process, depicted in Figure 1.3, lies at the heart of these functions. For example, planning requires decisions to be made between alternative courses of action while the control function is not complete until an appropriate course of corrective action has been decided upon and implemented. Figure 1.3 illustrates the different components of the decision process, highlighting the judgemental act of taking the decision, having weighed up the likely consequences of the alternative courses of action which are contemplated. Information on the available options and their likely consequences comes from two distinct sources. First there is all the information external to the decision-taker and then there is the information currently already stored in the decision-taker's brain (and most commonly labelled 'experience'). The information from external sources can take a wide variety of forms. For example, in deciding whether to replace the farm's combine harvester, information may be gathered from the detailed records of past harvests, brochures and information from a variety of manufacturers, the views of neighbouring farmers, details of current charge-rates from local agricultural contractors, the comments of various members of the family, the reactions of the local bank manager and so on. Once the decision is taken it must be implemented, in this case perhaps by placing an order with the local machinery dealer.

It will be clear that different family members may be involved in the different parts of the decision process and that any assessment of the extent of their involvement will be hampered by the fact that the intellectual activity of **decision-taking** cannot be observed directly. It is well-nigh impossible to determine the weight which the decision-taker has attached to the information coming from the various sources.

A recurrent theme in this book is the locus of power within the farm family business. Insofar as power is construed as the authority to take decisions regarding the use of resources, close examination of the decision process provides the clearest indication of the locus of that power. And where the decision-taking authority of one individual becomes constrained by the wishes of others there is *prima facie* evidence that the locus of power has shifted. This movement may be voluntary (as when a farmer begins to pass the control of the business to his successor or delegates particular decisions to a marketing group) or it may be involuntary (as when he passes his plans to the bank for prior approval under threat of foreclosure on a mortgage).

The management of any business takes place within an ever-changing environment of physical and biological, economic, political, legal and social forces which can quickly overtake the best of plans. Identifying and responding to these changes is a fundamental challenge for the farmer who wants his business to survive and prosper.

The management of biological systems presents a particular challenge to the farmer because of the heterogeneity of some of the inputs (e.g. variations in soil fertility and structure, variations in livestock quality), the unpredictability of others (sunlight, rainfall etc.) and the interactions between them all. The complexity of these interactions reduces the predictability of outcomes, increases the risk associated with production and places particular emphasis on the control function of management. There is a continual need for intervention and adjustment in the production process, as when disease or pest infestation threaten to strike.

In many cases, the information required for control purposes, both to identify deviation from target norms and to analyse the reasons for this deviation, can only be gathered on the spot through the senses – smell, touch and sound as well as sight. Thus a good deal of farm management is concerned with the operation of informal control mechanisms while the farmer is engaged in manual work or merely walking round the farm (walking the crop, looking over the cattle). The need for continual direct monitoring, crucial where livestock are concerned, makes it necessary for the farmer to live and work on the farm; that home and workplace are usually synonymous for the farmer is not simply a question of pleasure or convenience but a necessity for effective management.

Changes in the economic, political, legal and social environment are clearly of immense importance to the farm business. There is not the space within this brief overview to describe and assess all the changes which are currently taking place in the farmer's environment and the interested reader is directed to the work of others such as Bowers and Cheshire (1983) and Marsh *et al.* (1991). However, it is important for the reader not familiar with UK farming to recognize some key aspects of the context in which the farm business currently finds itself.

At the most fundamental level are the consequences of Engel's Law which holds that, as incomes rise, an ever-smaller proportion will be spent on food. In the face of this Law, Britton (1990) and others have concluded that if average farm incomes are to keep pace with those in the rest of the economy, the number of farmers must fall. However, more recent research (Gasson 1988; Shucksmith *et al.* 1989) has recognized the role of 'pluri-activity' in enabling farmers to safeguard household incomes and their own farming future against the inexorable pressures of Engel's Law.

Other, more recent, changes in the farmer's environment have signalled a fundamental change in public attitudes and government policies towards farming. A whole series of seemingly unrelated changes have brought UK farmers increasingly under pressure. In particular, the 1980s saw a series of challenges to the case for agricultural support in all its forms, from intervention-buying to government-funded research. The critique of both the level and nature of government intervention appeared in a variety of media ranging from television and the popular press to academic journals and conference papers.

While the most obvious results to date are to be seen in the revision of grant schemes and various suggestions for reform of the Common Agri-cultural Policy, there seems little likelihood that Government will become fundamentally less interventionist in the future, and it is the nature rather than the fact of intervention that will change. Significant modifications to the legal and political environment are likely to continue to have a major impact on the farm business. Within the industry, the net effect will simply be to make the legal, political and economic environment as complex and unpredictable as the biological processes that farming seeks to manipulate.

The Farm Household

> 'The family' is an ideologically-loaded composite of kinship and
> household relations which is historically and culturally varied in form.
> (Whatmore 1991a: 43)

In common parlance, and in this book, the terms **farm family** and **farm household** are used interchangeably to refer to the group of kin normally resident on a farm. To be more precise, though, the family or kin group, the set of individuals related to one another through common ancestry and marriage ties, and the household or domestic group, the set of individuals sharing daily activities and living arrangements, are not necessarily governed by the same norms of behaviour. In practice the domestic group is usually organized along kinship lines but the criteria for family and household membership are different (Schwarzweller and Clay 1992). This section tries to tease out the concepts of kinship, family and household.

Kinship relations

Kinship relations, ties of blood and marriage, control the processes of bearing and raising children and determine rights of inheritance. They legitimize the distribution of power within the kin group and in a family business they also determine the relations of production. The dominant model of kinship is based on the notion of an ego-centred network of kinship ties among which a person can choose to recognize and activate some links and ignore others. Whom one regards as 'family' to whom the rights and obligations of kinship apply, is socially rather than biologically determined. In Ashworthy, Williams (1963) detected a strong element of personal choice in determining which kinship relations become intimate and which peripheral. Some kindred who are 'claimed' have no social relations with the person who claims them. Kinship ties which can be readily traced may even be denied by the persons concerned.

Kinship ties assume a particular importance in family businesses. Not only do they constitute the internal relations of the business but they also form part of the network of external relations and associations which help to buttress the individual small firm. Mothers and sons, brothers or cousins may farm independently but exchange labour or machines on a regular non-paying basis, helping one another with major tasks like harvesting or building projects. They may jointly own pieces of equipment or machinery, exchange advice and information, co-operate in purchasing requisites or in marketing produce. In other circumstances the informal network may consist of neighbours or friends rather than kin.

While the ownership and operation of farm family businesses are organized along kinship lines, there is not necessarily any correspondence between family type and mode of production. Two types of family system, nuclear and extended, are prevalent in the western world. In Britain as in other market industrialized countries, 'the family' is usually taken to mean the nuclear family of a married couple with immature children. Although this is the largest single category, not all families are nuclear families. One study of English rural areas found that only about one third of households were composed of parents and one or more children, the figure dropping to a quarter in the more isolated northern counties (Bradley 1987). Extended families of parents and adult children are thought to be more characteristic of rural and especially farming localities, yet they only accounted for between 7 and 17 per cent of Bradley's sample. Households incorporating blood relatives beyond the elementary kin group made up 6 per cent at most. Even the assumption that the nuclear family is the product of industrialization is challenged. Research by Laslett (1972) and others suggests that before the industrial revolution, large households may have consisted of wealthy small families with many servants (including children from other families of equivalent standing) rather than poor large families.

Although extended family and kin networks have historically been important sources of supplementary labour for the farm business, they may have become less important in many market industrialized countries with the increased availability of contractors and relief labour co-operatives and the declining importance of manual labour relative to capital inputs in the production process. Moreover, such networks have always had their drawbacks, as the Ashworthy farmers no doubt appreciated. Abrahams' study of farm families in Karelia suggested that

> Kinship is intrinsically a propitious base for active co-operation
> between farming families, but its equally intrinsic potential for conflict
> can easily counter this, and some farmers in fact seem to prefer to
> collaborate with good friends and neighbours.
>
> (Abrahams 1991: 153)

The household

The basic unit of subsistence, the household, can be defined as a group of people living under one roof and sharing meals, though large groups of people living together in institutions (religious houses, colleges and so on) are normally excluded. The relationship between kinship and household is variable. Although households are usually organized on the basis of kinship relations, the household is rarely coterminous with kinship but located within wider kin and community networks. A farm family business may incorporate members of more than one household, for instance parents and married children in separate dwellings. Households may include unrelated members such as living-in domestic help, lodgers and employees. Changing economic and cultural conditions may alter the basis of household formation. In the United States today, nearly a quarter of all households consist of only one person. Economic necessity dictates that many unrelated individuals share living accommodation, as for example in student hostels. Changing cultural norms have led the US census-takers to classify some households as 'POSSLQs' (persons of opposite sex sharing living quarters). Non-family households of single and non-related persons now account for 30 per cent of all US households (Schwarzweller and Clay 1992). This book is mainly concerned with the family household or more precisely with the **conjugal household**, a concept broader than the nuclear family household, centred on a heterosexual couple but covering all phases in the family cycle (Whatmore 1991a).

The household represents the arena of everyday life for most of the world's population. It acts as a buffer between the individual and the outside world:

> The 'household', we believe, stands as a sensitive and powerful social cushion, particularly in the poorer rural contexts, between the individual and the surrounding swirl of economic uncertainty, social remodeling, and environmental degradation . . . a social entity within which and through which people live significant segments of their lives, share their most intimate activities, and find their strongest social/emotional support for coping with the harsh realities of survival.
>
> (Schwarzweller and Clay 1992: 1–2)

In spite of the centrality of the household for human existence, the socio-logical literature mainly uses the concepts of **family** and **community** to explain human behaviour. **Household** is appended to studies of the family, often in an awkward manner. Public policies and programmes too have been fashioned around the belief that families and communities are the appro-priate targets for intervention, even though households are the common unit of enumeration for census purposes (Schwarzweller and Clay 1992).

An emphasis on the household as the basic economic unit rather than the individual is a more fruitful way to approach the work of production, reproduction and consumption. In Pahl's graphic phrase, 'Households are simply units for getting various kinds of work done' (Pahl 1984: 20). To develop this theme, he explores the division of labour in pre-industrial times, 'before the dominance of wage labour so heavily coloured our conception of work'. He concludes that:

> . . . before large-scale industrialization and the development of the factory system, the importance of the household as an economic unit could hardly be questioned. In many respects its importance continued throughout the nineteenth century, but, in a flurry of male-dominated individualistic ideology, it began to get obscured.
>
> (Pahl 1984: 139)

One-sided emphasis on employment, with the implication that this is the only significant form of work, tends to emphasize the individual earner rather than the household as the basic economic unit. Pahl's concept of the household as 'a unit for getting various kinds of work done', applies with double force in agriculture where most production is still organized by family households.

Elements of the household which distinguish it from the family as a unit of analysis are location in space (residence) and the sharing of resources (co-operation). While the role of kinship must be taken into account, it is also necessary to consider how residence and physical and material factors affect the formation of households. Unlike the kinship group, households are associated with an identifiable place, for farm households normally the farm itself. 'Regardless of cultural setting, the household serves as the locational center for an individual's field of activities – the place from which an individual reaches out to work, to participate in community, and to associate with kinsfolk' (Schwarzweller and Clay 1992: 3–4).

The concept of the farm household encompasses both the material resources of the domestic group (land, labour, buildings, machinery, livestock) and the people brought into association through the use of these resources. Material aspects of the household reflect the members' station in the community and help to determine their quality of life (Schwarzweller and Clay 1992). Relations between the members are built up in the daily and annual work routines of the farm household. As the resources are subject to change through time, so these relationships change within and between farm households (Bouquet 1985). The traditional peasant household was a seamless interweaving of family and farm and for Mendras (1970), it was the separation of these two elements which signified the demise of the peasantry.

The family cycle

One of the resources of the farm household is family labour. Because the household is organized along kinship lines, the labour it supplies is not fixed but likely to fluctuate in a predictable fashion over time, as illustrated by Bennett's study of Saskatchewan farming (see Figure 1.4).

Three distinct phases in family development were identified by Nalson (1968):

- **an early phase** in which either all the children are below 15 (school leaving age) or the farmer's wife is of childbearing age but has no family;
- **a middle phase** in which some of the children are of working age, live at home and work on or off the farm;
- **a late phase** in which either children have all left home, or the wife is past the age of childbearing and has no children.

These phases are not sociologically precise but proved useful when Nalson was examining the effects of family development on farm organization. Today the early phase would need to be redefined to take account of children's extended periods of higher and further education. The late phase does not occur in families (usually on larger farms) where one or more children remain at home until the retirement or death of their parents. The stages defined by Symes (1972) to describe farm performance in southern Ireland are finer:

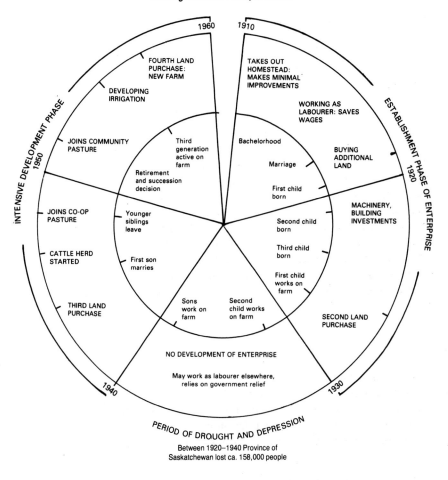

Figure 1.4. Family cycle and enterprise cycle in Jasper. Source: Bennett 1982: 141

- **inheritance and marriage** interchangeable in the time sequence;
- **expansion**, the period of family building between the birth of the first and last children;
- **stability**, between the birth of the last child and the first migration of the offspring;
- **dispersal**, with a sub-stage to take account of the death of either spouse.

Two further stages are added to allow for various forms of family failure:

- **residual household** caused by childless marriages or the failure to retain any offspring on the farm;
- **relic household** arising from failure to marry.

It is perhaps significant that Nalson describes a late phase when all the children have left the farm as part of the normal family cycle whereas Symes regards this as a form of family failure. The differences of approach reflect different inheritance practices in England and Ireland, which are discussed again in Chapter 7.

Family ideology

The household embodies the idea of shared resources. At the very least this implies a common residence and the pooling of household amenities. Since farm households combine both consumption and production activities, its members have to co-ordinate farming operations and the use of family labour as well as co-operating in matters of consumption. The suggestion that farm families do in fact pursue a 'collective household strategy', the outcome of democratic decision-making, seems rather far-fetched. Business decisions are commonly made on behalf of the household group, with adult males asserting the most influence. There must however be sufficient trust in the decision-making process to ensure that the household can continue to function. When co-operation is eroded by dissent and conflict, the household becomes unstable and cannot cope with the challenges of the outside world.

Relationships within families are popularly supposed to be based upon personal affection, care and mutual obligation, in contrast to wage labour relations which are governed by contract and rational economic behaviour. Mobilizing this ideology could give the family business a significant advantage, for example by encouraging members to work for low wages on behalf of 'the family'. The farm family business based on one or more households organized in terms of kinship obligations, marital responsibilities and emotional attachments, is likely to be more enduring than households that are formed for strictly economic reasons. 'These elements – resource pooling, a unity of production/consumption activities, family ties, and affective relationships – are present and mutually reinforcing in traditional family households' (Schwarzweller and Clay 1992). Whatmore (1991a) warns, however, that this assumes what needs to be empirically investigated; in reality the conjugal household is rarely an equitable, harmonious and utility-maximizing unit (Redclift and Whatmore 1990).

Division of labour

Families are assumed to be bound together by emotional ties but Durkheim (1933) claimed that it was the sexual division of labour, rather than the community of sentiments and beliefs, which was the main source of conjugal solidarity. He believed that attraction is based on complementarity;

'That is why we seek in our friends the qualities that we lack, since in joining with them, we participate in their nature and thus feel less incomplete' (p. 56). He argued that it was the sharing of functions, the division of labour, which creates in two or more persons a feeling of solidarity. This applied even more strongly to conjugal relations and he spoke of the 'particular solidarity which unites the members of a family in accordance with the division of domestic labour' (p. 123).

Durkheim saw the gender division of labour as having a powerful uniting force; 'Permit the sexual division of labour to recede below a certain level and conjugal society would eventually subsist in sexual relations pre-eminently ephemeral' (p. 61). Recent work portrays the gender division of labour in a far less positive light, stressing instead the unequal division of power, resources and labour relations within farm families. References to the need for a 'harmonious but not necessarily equal division of family labour' in Friedmann's earlier work have been replaced by allusions to 'the division of labour, patterns of domination and struggle' (quoted in Whatmore 1991a). Whatmore herself speaks of 'the practice and experience of women's subordination to men within the family household as a production unit' (p. 34) and refers to the 'emotional and physical violence' which is implicit in patriarchal gender relations.

Flexibility of family farms

Defining the farm family and the farm business and attempting to draw boundaries around them, is not to imply uniformity or rigidity. As this section has shown, the components of kinship, family and household show considerable variability in form and function. The family farm is extremely flexible in its response to changes in its environment:

> The extent of this pliability may lead to analytical difficulties; thus for instance it may be legitimate from a conceptual point of view, to consider both the subsistence farm of the hills of Nepal and the commercial wheat farm of the North American great plains as family farms, but one should not disregard their obvious differences.
>
> (Petit 1982: 332)

The emphasis upon structural processes and class formation in recent sociological approaches to family farming has diverted attention from the role of human agency and the reasons for the diversity of forms and processes in relations of production (Marsden *et al.* 1986b). The idea that the close affinity between the farm family and the farm business is breaking down under the influence of external forces, is widespread. Indeed, one of the themes of this book is the way in which relationships between the family and the business are transformed by capitalism. As Wilkening puts it:

> The same economic and social forces affecting the larger society have
> affected the farm family. Although there is value placed upon the
> family farm and upon traditional family patterns, both have been
> affected by processes in the larger society. The close interdependence
> of family and farm has been replaced by greater dependence of each
> upon other systems and other relationships.
>
> (Wilkening 1981a: 35)

Families are not immune to economic forces in the wider world but
neither are they wholly subject to them. Families are able to respond in a
variety of ways to changing external relations of production. No single
family form corresponds to a given economic system. Capitalist relations of
production exert a powerful influence but do not necessarily *determine*
family forms, activities or relationships. It is necessary to explore the interaction between family organization and relations of production rather than
assuming a relationship of separation or domination between them (Hutson
nd). It is important to bear in mind, too, that the capitalist economic system
is not the only type of external influence with which the farm family has to
contend. The law, the state and the church also regulate patterns of kinship
and marriage, farm inheritance and livelihood.

Farm families, then, adapt themselves in varying ways to the legislative,
political, economic, social and religious influences which impinge on their
lives. The behaviour of farm families, the way they organize work and make
decisions in the farm business, their reactions to the rapidly-changing
economic climate for agriculture, cannot therefore be predicted entirely from
a knowledge of the structural constraints. This does not mean that their
behaviour is unstructured. Understanding the context within which farm
families have to act, the limitations on their freedom, the imperatives which
drive them from outside and within the family enterprise, will go a long way
to explaining their actions, but not all the way. The external forces shaping
the farm business are referred to throughout the book and discussed in
some detail in Chapter 3, while farm household responses are the subject of
Chapter 9. We try to take both structure and agency into account in
attempting to explain the behaviour of farm families.

ISSUES ARISING FROM THE DEFINITION

The final section of this chapter focuses on the interplay of farm families and
the businesses they run. Its purpose is to draw attention to relationships
inherent in the nature of the farm family business, which will be explored
and documented more fully in later chapters. As suggested above, it is the
way the farm business and the farm family relate to one another, the
'chemistry' of the reaction between them, that gives rise to particular
features in the farm family business. These features may confer benefits or

disadvantages on the family enterprise compared with the non-family business.

Business Ownership Combined with Managerial Control

The first and most crucial criterion for defining the farm family business is that business ownership is combined with management control in the hands of a single family. The entrepreneur is therefore responsible for both day-to-day tactical management and longer-term strategic decisions. That the two functions should sometimes conflict seems inevitable, especially where the family owns the land as well as the business which it manages. For example any labour and material resources devoted to land improvement or conservation work are not available for farm production. Where, as in the majority of UK farm businesses, the farmer does manual work as well, there are consequences for the way the farmer allocates his time. Chapter 4 develops the idea of multiple and conflicting objectives for the farm operator and between family members and Chapter 5 considers the impact of multiple roles on labour performance.

Business Principals Related

The second criterion used to define a farm family business, of the principals being related by kinship or marriage, focuses attention on the identification of the family with the farm. The unity of business and family implies a single fund of capital to satisfy both investment and consumption needs. Particularly in the early stages of the business cycle, consumption may be deferred in favour of building up the enterprise. When the business is under pressure, the family's level of living is depressed; wives and children are expected to do more manual work as expenditure on regular or seasonal labour is reduced. Unity of business and family also means that fundamental decisions have to be made about the allocation of family members' time between competing activities – production and reproduction in the farm business, off-farm work and leisure (see Chapter 5). Farmers may tend to assume that the farm always has first rights over the disposition of family labour and capital. On the other hand, having the business operated by and for family members instead of on behalf of shareholders is likely to raise the salience of 'family' goals among the array of business objectives, a point developed in Chapter 4.

Family Members Provide Capital and Labour

For the farm family, farm work is as much a family matter as is sharing the same table.

(Arensberg and Kimball 1968: 49)

In the ideal type of farm family business, family members are involved in farm work. The unity of kin group and work group creates multiple roles for each member: father/farm manager/farm worker; mother/domestic worker/ child minder/accountant/personnel manager/occasional farm worker; child/ farm worker/domestic help (Friedmann 1986: 48). The combination of family roles and relationships with working roles and relationships can be stressful, as Chapter 5 will show.

In farm families tasks are customarily assigned on the basis of gender and age, not according to the skill and knowledge of the workers, with consequences for labour productivity (Chapter 5). Task allocation is not necessarily rigid or immutable, however. Technology may alter the rationale for the gender and age division of labour (see Chapters 6 and 8 for examples). Within families there is normally some room for negotiation over the allocation of tasks, even if patriarchal authority sets the limits within which this exchange takes place.

One corollary of the use of family labour in the farm business is that the labour force will vary in quality and quantity over the course of the family cycle. Where family labour is the principal input, this can create problems which the non-family farm does not have to cope with. As Abrahams (1991: 73) puts it, 'A piece of land will not move, grow or reproduce itself, and this does not bode well for its relations with a living human group'. The progression of the family cycle also imposes a pattern of growth, maturation and decline on the farm business. The concept of the family cycle may therefore be extended to 'the family-firm cycle'. Efficiency of the farm business varies over the course of the cycle (Chapter 5), unlike a company where continuity of management makes for greater efficiency.

The Family Lives on the Farm

> . . . here home and work, and all the cemented associations that these small words have come to signify, are located in the same place.
>
> (Whatmore 1991a: 3)

Since the farm is usually a place of residence as well as a workplace, the family's consumption and leisure activities are also likely to revolve around the farm, making it difficult to separate the business from the way of life. Activities usually regarded as sporting or recreational, such as shooting rabbits or simply walking the dog, can also be functional for the business. Operating a business from the family home makes it especially difficult to draw a line between **productive** and **reproductive** activities. To a degree all households with productive workers must purchase inputs of food, shelter and so on to maintain themselves in good health so that they can continue to sell their labour services. The need for subsistence in order to maintain the stock of labour is not usually considered a business cost. Instead tax law normally provides for subsistence inputs by giving individuals a fixed personal allowance against tax (Casson 1982). When the family business is run from home, the overlap between production and reproduction is considerable. By securing part of the costs of reproducing the labour force by consuming what is produced at home, the family farm is able to compete in selling its products with non-family firms which may have the benefits of larger scale (Chapters 3 and 6).

Inter-generational Transfer

The final distinguishing feature of the ideal type of farm family business is that business ownership and management control are handed down within the family. As already pointed out, this is a stringent condition; many businesses otherwise qualifying as family farms do not meet this criterion. Nevertheless the fact that a farm business has been inherited and the expectation that it will again be transferred within the family raises certain issues, to be discussed in more detail in Chapters 7 and 8. Chapter 4 assesses the impact of farm inheritance on farmers' objectives. The apparent resilience, survival and continuity of family farming is documented in Chapter 2 and considered further in Chapter 9, which concludes that survival is not consonant with unbroken continuity or the absence of change.

SUMMARY AND IMPLICATIONS

This chapter has defined the farm family business in terms of the unity of business ownership, management control and labour and the identification of the business with the household. The central concern of the book is the interplay of the farm business and the farm household, a second theme being the future of the farm family business in a world dominated by capitalism. The following chapters examine aspects of the relationship between the family and the business in more detail, using empirical studies for illustration.

The family farm can be studied from a number of angles – as a business subject to universal laws of economics, as a constellation of management practices, as an anomaly in a world dominated by capitalism, as a household exemplifying the pre-industrial mode of getting work done, as a labour process structured by gender and generation, as a repository of cultural values and practices, as the embodiment of ideology. Each perspective tends to be associated with a certain discipline whose followers adhere to a particular paradigm, defining both the distinctive types of problem they explore and the common set of analytical tools with which they conduct these explorations. Each approach can help to account for the way people behave in farm family businesses; no one discipline has a monopoly of insight. Our underlying philosophy is that a holistic approach to the study of the farm family business provides a better framework for understanding and a sounder basis for policy-making than a series of narrow, fragmented approaches.

The terms **farm family** and **family farming** are common currency but open to a wide range of interpretations. A review of the literature reveals how meanings change with the times. Requirements that the family farm should be self-supporting and employ no outside workers have been relaxed, the labour criterion becoming less relevant as the organizing principle of the family business switches from labour to capital. For present purposes the farm family business has been defined in terms of business principals being family members, the unity of business ownership, management and labour, the family living on the farm and being involved in farm work and inter-generational transfer of the business. This is to be understood as an **ideal type** rather than a working definition. Incidentally, the definition we have developed is not specific to farming. It may be relevant for family businesses in other industries. Many of the issues we have identified as arising from the definition are likely to be pertinent in other sectors.

Definitions provide a framework for collecting, ordering and analysing data but they do not imply uniformity. While kinship obligations, the farming activity and the capitalist mode of production help to shape the form and content of farm family relationships, they do not determine them entirely. Farm families respond with some flexibility to the economic, political, legislative, social and cultural pressures which bear down on them. Both structural processes and human agency need to be taken into account in explaining the activities of farming families.

The nature of farm households and family farming have a number of implications for farm production. Operating a business from home makes it difficult to draw a line between 'productive' and 'reproductive' activities and between 'work' and 'leisure'. These distinctions have to be made for accounting and taxation purposes. They reflect the modern preoccupation with wage labour but do not sit easily with the notion of the household as a unit for getting work done. Emphasis on the male 'breadwinner', the head of household responsible for one or more dependants, upon which the welfare state operates, is similarly misplaced when all household members contribute to the work of the farm. Insistence that one member of a farm household be nominated as *the* farmer/holder/operator and others as family workers does not do justice to reality since the process of transferring control of the farm business from parent to son or daughter can take up to twenty years and throughout that period either could be described as 'the farmer'.

Reliance on family labour can be a source of strength to the farm business, in that wages do not have to be paid, but a drawback in that low quality or surplus family workers cannot easily be sacked. The family cycle can also contribute to low productivity on farms heavily dependent on family labour. Entry to farming is largely determined by birth, which helps to account for low levels of formal education and training among farmers and family workers.

The farm household being a unit of production as well as consumption has a number of implications for its members. Having a common fund of capital means that farm investment decisions have repercussions for the household and vice versa. The division of labour, typically along lines of gender and age rather than qualification and skill, can be viewed from outside as a cause of friction or a source of solidarity. Farmers like other household members play multiple roles, which can lead to conflicting objectives in the business and stress in the family. Close ties between home and work can themselves be stressful and economic interdependence makes it difficult to escape inflamed relationships. Two qualifications to bear in mind are that there is usually some room for negotiation over work roles, and that as the material resources of the farm business change, so do working relationships between household members.

Finally, inter-generational transfer can impose great strains on family relationships. In crude terms a choice may have to be made between efficiency and equity – between keeping the farm business intact and treating all family members equitably. These issues have to be faced and overcome if family farming is to continue. Chapter 2 presents the evidence for the persistence of family farming and its continued importance today.

2

THE IMPORTANCE OF FARM FAMILY BUSINESSES TODAY

> Sometimes, half a dozen figures will reveal, as with a lightning-flash,
> the importance of a subject which ten thousand labored words, with
> the same purpose in view, has left at last but dim and uncertain.
>
> (Twain 1984: 209)

In this chapter we draw together information on numbers of farm family
businesses in the UK in terms of our definition. As in other market industrialized countries, the vast majority of UK farms are operated as family
businesses. Comparisons over time suggest that the farm family business
has not only survived but actually increased its numerical importance in
Britain over the last hundred years. In other developed countries where
family farming was historically predominant, it remains the largest sector.

CURRENT IMPORTANCE OF FARM FAMILY BUSINESSES

> There are no national data bases for researching the processes of
> getting into, staying in or getting out of farming, or for researching
> farm development and decline. National data sources that determine
> important farm and farm family characteristics are too limited for
> adequate analysis.
>
> (Coughenour and Wimberley 1982: 351)

This criticism of US data sources applies equally in the UK. No direct
information is collected on the numbers of farms operated as family businesses. Our understanding of the structure of the agricultural industry,
though sharpened by the periodic EC Farm Structure surveys, remains
incomplete in respect of who owns the land and who manages and controls
farm businesses. We are forced to rely on possibly unrepresentative surveys
with limited geographical coverage or official data collected for other
purposes. Inappropriate inferences may be drawn; the tendency, for
instance, to equate 'family farm' with 'small farm' means that any decrease

in numbers of small holdings may be interpreted as a decline in family farming. The remainder of this chapter gathers together the information that is available on aspects of the 'familiness' of farming but the reader should be aware that much of this material is based on the narrower view of a family-worked business.

Family Control

The farm family business is defined in terms of business principals being related by blood or marriage, ownership being combined with managerial control, inter-generational succession and the family living on the farm and possibly (but not necessarily) supplying a substantial share of the capital and labour required. On the first criterion, no less than 97.5 per cent of farms in England in 1969 were found to be genuine family businesses in the sense that all the principals were closely related by blood or marriage (Harrison 1975). Figures from the 1975 EC Farm Structure Survey showed that 94 per cent of holdings in Great Britain were run as sole proprietor-ships, partnerships or private (typically family) companies. In the United States too, 88 per cent of farm corporations in 1982 were held by families while non-family corporations accounted for only 6.5 per cent of total farm sales (Reinhardt and Barlett 1989).

The second criterion is that business ownership is combined with managerial control. Only about 7000 salaried farm managers are employed on the 180,000 main agricultural holdings in England and Wales. Managers were employed on 5 per cent of English farms in 1969, according to Harrison's study, but only on 3 per cent of farms was there a manager who devoted more than half his time to managerial activities. The importance of inter-generational transfer of the farm business is again illustrated by Harrison's survey; 76 per cent of farmers declared that a successor was required to their business interests and 64 per cent had successors identified and available to take over the farm. Over 99 per cent of successors were members of the farmer's family.

Family Provides Capital

British farmers as a whole provide most of the capital they need to run their businesses. In 1963, net worth was some 80 per cent of total assets. In the early 1970s, total assets of UK agriculture were about £10,000 million, of which £6000 million was represented by land and buildings. Bank borrowing amounted to about £550 million, other institutional borrowing to £200 million and private and trade credit were estimated to be in excess of £600 million. Liabilities were therefore little more than 10 per cent of assets (Harrison 1972). By 1980 net worth was still around 90 per cent, despite enormous increases in the amount of capital employed on UK farms; the aggregate net worth of farmers grew from some £4000 million in 1963 to £43,000 million in 1980, representing more than a doubling in real terms. Much of the increase was due to soaring land prices.

The national farm balance sheet for 1987 showed that total external liabilities were only about 18 per cent of total assets, so farmers' net worth was still over 80 per cent of those assets. High interest rates, falling real incomes and falling value of assets, especially land, are making the farming community increasingly vulnerable to risk. Nevertheless, in 1987 over three quarters (77 per cent) of farmers in England were operating on a liabilities to assets ratio of under 25 per cent, including assets of land, buildings and fixed equipment. Excluding fixed assets, the figure fell to 47 per cent. This means that even at a time of declining economic fortunes for agriculture, roughly half of all farmers are still largely independent of external sources of capital (Harrison and Tranter 1989).

Importance of Family Labour

The narrowest definition of a family farm is one where the family supplies all the regular labour. Any attempt to estimate the relative importance of family labour as a component of the aggregate input of labour to agricultural production is fraught with difficulty. Even where the statistical base is good, there are so many 'grey areas' in the definition of what constitutes farm work (see Chapter 1) that any estimates should be treated with caution. For example, even in Britain with its annual census covering eighteen different categories of labour there has been some criticism of the data available: the census only provides a head count at a particular point in time; while the farmer's spouse is now included in the census form, there is no indication of the proportion of her time devoted to farm work; because the measurement of casual labour is for a particular day in June, it is likely to be a gross under-estimate of the total amount of casual labour employed; 'flexible' workers such as contractors tend to be overlooked and so on.

Nevertheless, using this data source, Lund *et al.* (1982) estimate that 64 per cent of the total labour input to agriculture and horticulture in England and Wales in 1980 came from the farm family. (This can be compared with Blanc's (1987) parallel estimate for France of 85 per cent.) Many of the hired workers in UK agriculture are concentrated on a few very large farms and by 1986 only 28 per cent of UK holdings employed any hired workers (as against 40 per cent in 1950). Thus 72 per cent of farms were **family labour farms**. It has to be borne in mind that the labour available from a given family will vary with the stage in the family cycle and a much larger proportion of farms may move through a labour-hiring phase at some stage. More liberal definitions allow for this and require only that the family provides more than half the labour. According to Lund *et al.*, more than half

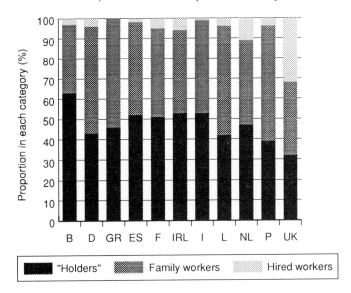

Figure 2.1. Composition of the EC's agricultural workforce, 1987. Source: 1987 EC Structure Survey (Eurostat, 1992)

of the regular labour on the *national* farm comes from farmers and their families.

Most statistical sources for most market industrialized countries suggest that family labour is of paramount importance in farming. Figure 2.1 shows that the UK is still rather exceptional in the proportion of hired workers employed on its farms, though long-term trends are bringing the UK much closer to its continental neighbours in this respect.

Some authorities define family farming in terms of the ratio of non-family to family workers while others prefer absolute measures, as Chapter 1 showed. On average there are between 1.5 and 1.75 farmers and family workers per holding in England and Wales. Following Nikolitch's approach, farms with less than 1.5 non-family workers, or 3 workers in total, can be regarded as family farms.

The 1987 EC Farm Structure Survey recorded 81 per cent of UK holdings using less than 3 Annual Work Units (AWU) of labour. In the rest of the EC, family farming is of still greater significance, with 96 per cent of all holdings using less than 3 AWU of regular labour. Overall 93 per cent of the regular labour is supplied by farmers, spouses and other family members. The UK stands out with its heavy dependence on hired labour. France, Denmark and The Netherlands with their well-developed commercial farming sectors still rely on farm family members for over 80 per cent of the regular labour input. In the rest of the Community family labour accounts for over 90 per cent (Table 2.1).

Table 2.1. Importance of family labour on EC farms in 1987.

Member State	Holdings with 3 AWU or more (per cent)	Regular labour supplied by farm family (per cent)
Belgium	2.3	95
Denmark	na	85
France	4.5	83
Germany	3.1	95
Greece	1.7	100
Ireland	3.5	92
Italy	2.8	98
Luxembourg	8.8	94
Netherlands	9.1	84
Portugal	8.6	93
Spain	3.3	95
UK	19.4	67

Source: 1987 EC Structure Survey

Family farming is predominant in the United States too. Historically the industry has been characterized by relatively small farms showing little differentiation between the ownership of capital and land, management and labour. 'Family-type' farms in Rodefeld's terms have traditionally accounted for more than three-quarters of US farms by number and half of the output sold. His 'tenant-type' farms, some of which would qualify as family businesses on our definition, numbered one sixth of the total in 1964. Larger-than-family farms and industrial farms together made up less than 5 per cent of US farms in 1964 but accounted for over a third of gross sales (Figure 2.2).

According to the official USDA definition, all farms using less than 1.5 man-years of hired labour and operated by risk-taking managers can be considered family farms. On this basis, family farms accounted for 95 per cent of all US farms in 1969 and 62 per cent of the total value of farm products sold. Including also the larger, family-owned farm businesses, families were estimated to own 98 per cent of all US farms and account for 90 per cent of total farm production (Nikolitch 1972). In short, on all the common measures, farming in the major market industrialized countries of the world is predominantly a family business.

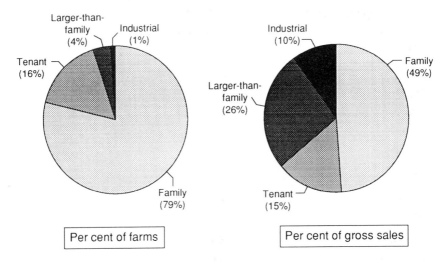

Figure 2.2. Numbers and output of US farms by type, 1964. Source: Rodefeld 1978

Variations by Farm Type and Region

There is considerable regional variation in the importance of the farm family labour input in England and Wales, illustrated in Figure 2.3. Family labour tends to predominate in areas characterized by smaller farms specializing in dairying, beef cattle and sheep production. This may reflect the greater flexibility of family labour and its ability to respond to the substantial and often daily fluctuations in labour requirements of such enterprises or the greater importance of 'psychic income' accruing to some of these enterprises, which might be unprofitable in conventional accounting terms. We return to these points in Chapters 4 and 5.

There may be smaller scope for capital:labour substitution in grazing livestock enterprises than in arable. Support for this argument is provided by Table 2.2, which shows how the importance of family farming within the EC varies between types of farming. This analysis of 1987/8 results for all holdings in FADN, the EC's Farm Accounts Data Network, defines family farms as those where unpaid labour supplies more than 95 per cent of the total labour input. Family farms account for 70 per cent of all holdings by numbers but they occupy only 56 per cent of the utilized agricultural area and produce 54 per cent of the output. They are over-represented among dairy, drystock and mixed farms and less important in horticulture, vine-growing and other permanent crops.

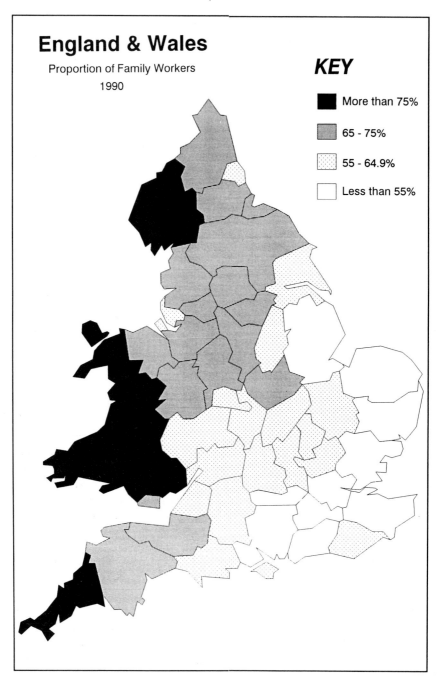

England & Wales
Proportion of Family Workers
1990

KEY

- More than 75%
- 65 - 75%
- 55 - 64.9%
- Less than 55%

Figure 2.3. Regional variations in importance of family labour in England and Wales. Source: Errington 1992b

Table 2.2. Importance of family farms in the EC by type of farming, 1986.

Type of production	Proportion accounted for by family farms (per cent)		
	Holdings	Output	Utilized agricultural area
Cereals	80	57	57
General cropping	63	39	37
Horticulture	46	16	31
Vines	42	28	30
Other permanent crops	53	31	34
Dairy	82	66	70
Drystock	84	74	66
Pigs and poultry	66	50	53
Mixed	79	62	59
All types	**70**	**54**	**56**

Source: Hill 1991, Table 1

HISTORICAL TRENDS

Empirical evidence suggests that farm family businesses as defined in this book are not only the dominant form in the agricultural structure of market industrialized countries, they may actually be accounting for a growing share of farms by number, if not their share of farm output. According to Nikolitch (1972), family farms maintained their importance as a proportion of all US farms and their share of sales between 1949 and 1969. Within the category, however, the number and share of sales by larger family farms rose rapidly while smaller family farms declined (Figure 2.4). This can be interpreted as proof of the ability of the family farm to adjust to technology and keep pace with events; family farms have to become larger in order to continue earning adequate incomes.

If however a family farm is defined as a farm business where most of the ownership, management and labour is supplied by one family, a decline relative to non-family farms is apparent. Using his more restrictive definition, Rodefeld (1982) interpreted a decline in land ownership by farm operators, a decline in farmland acquisitions by existing farmers, a decreasing share of working capital owned by farmers and an increasing reliance on hired managers, full-time and seasonal workers as evidence for a

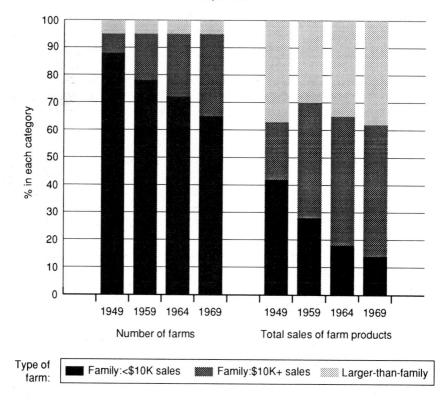

Figure 2.4. Numbers of farms and sales of farm products by type of farm, United States 1949–1969. Source: Nikolitch 1972, Table 14.1

swing away from family farming and towards corporate farming in the United States:

> Many of the conditions responsible for the past predominance of individual and family farm owners have been altered. There are reasons to expect that future farm owner-operators will have a reduced share of land and capital ownership and will provide less management and labour, resulting in a decline in family farms.
>
> (Rodefeld 1982: 329)

Historical Evidence in the UK

Contrary to the picture Rodefeld paints for the United States, the family farm in Britain appears to have gained prominence, though its rise over the past two centuries may have been somewhat over-stated as a consequence of earlier neglect. The transformation of British agriculture from the mid-eighteenth century and the emergence of the large capitalist enterprise was significant enough to capture the attention of social and economic historians of the day. The tripartite structure of agriculture with separation between the classes of landowners, tenant farmers and hired labourers, was seen by many contemporary observers as the model for other industrializing nations to follow. Features of this system, notably the theory of ground rent, engaged a number of the founding fathers of classical economics, including Ricardo and Marx. Policy-makers too were diverted from other concerns. At the end of the eighteenth century, for instance, the Board of Agriculture dismissed small farmers as having no role to play in the development of agriculture. Preoccupation with capitalist agriculture and concern with such manifestations as landlord-tenant relations or the plight of labourers, meant that little attention was paid to the farm family or family farming.

Historians have since queried the supposedly rapid decline of small landowners following the era of parliamentary enclosure from 1760 to 1830. The suggestion that they were forced to quit farming because they could not meet the cost of enclosure is now open to doubt. A high turnover of small owners could have been the result of a developing land market, fuelled by the prosperity enjoyed by farmers after 1760 (Mingay 1990).

> It is evident, then, that in spite of the changes of the eighteenth and nineteenth centuries ... the small farmers in general suffered no catastrophic decline in numbers. Anyone who is willing to believe that small farmers 'disappeared' in the eighteenth century must be prepared to explain how it was they re-appeared in such strength in the nineteenth century.
>
> (Mingay 1962: 470)

Although the nineteenth century is popularly perceived as a period dominated by the large capitalist farm, the structure of agriculture at that time was already quite diverse. Historical evidence points to continuity and renewal of family farming in Devon in the late Victorian era. Devon in 1851, in common with most counties of England, was mainly farmed in medium and small units dependent on family labour but supplemented by hired labour at certain phases in the family cycle. The ending of the Golden Age of British agriculture in the 1870s ushered in a time of transformation which did much to increase the significance of family farming. The origins of family farming in Devon can be traced to the convergence of three previously quite separate groups. First there were those erstwhile medium-scale capitalist farmers who shed labour and came to depend wholly on family labour, a change often associated with a switch from arable to livestock production. They were joined by existing small-scale family farmers, uniquely placed to take advantage of the expanding markets for milk, poultry and market garden produce at the end of the century. A third and much smaller group consisted of new entrants to farming, artisans and ambitious farm workers who took advantage of a depressed land market. Some landlords even sub-divided their estates to accommodate these new specialist producers, in advance of the creation of statutory smallholdings (Winter 1986).

At the opposite end of the country, the tripartite structure of landowner, farmer and worker was well established on Humberside by the middle of the nineteenth century. Of the three social classes, tenant farmers may have been the least secure:

> Despite the stability of the land owning structure, instability characterized the relations of production. To judge from contemporary accounts the relationship between landlord and tenant at the end of the eighteenth century was tenuous and insecure with 'many tenants being even without a written agreement' and 'want of a proper confidence between tenant and landlord'.
>
> (Symes and Marsden 1983a: 82–3)

There was little evidence, either, of stability based on generational continuity on the same farm. The nuclear farm family frequently failed to provide a line of succession and it proved altogether inadequate to meet the demands of large-scale arable farming. 'Its weakness was however buttressed by the strengths of the other components of the system – the landowning classes and the agricultural labour force, both of which were to be eroded in the following years' (Symes and Marsden 1983a: 89).

From the tripartite system which emerged in England in the late eighteenth century and reached its zenith in the mid-nineteenth, the swing has been from tenancy to owner-occupation and from hired to family labour. At the beginning of the twentieth century approximately one eighth of the farm land in England and Wales was owner-occupied, by 1930 about one third and today about two thirds. In the middle of the nineteenth century there were almost three non-family workers to every family member working on the land. By 1930 the ratio was still 2.5:1 but today there is only about one regular non-family worker to every 2.5 family workers. Since the mid-Victorian era of high farming, then, a reduction in the numbers and power of landed estates and the shedding of much hired labour has meant that the farm family has become the strongest rather than the weakest link:

> Today the farmer and his family own more of the land they cultivate and provide a much higher proportion of the labour resources. The process of accumulation and concentration of farmland has been renewed but with the farm family, and its often complex business organization as the central institution ... a group in society who have considerably more control over their own actions and the actions of others than was the case a hundred, or even fifty years ago.
>
> (Marsden 1984: 136)

International Comparisons

In the United Kingdom, trends in land ownership and hired labour have moved in the opposite direction from the United States, strengthening rather than weakening the dominant position of the farm family business. The USA has large numbers of hired workers in the farm and horticultural sector, though almost half work less than 25 days per year and many of these are illegal immigrants (Gunter and Vasavada 1988). Whitener and Munir (1990) report stabilization of the US hired farm workforce in the 1970s and 1980s in the face of continued decline in farm operators and family workers. Consequently the proportion of family workers has decreased, from 78 per cent in 1945 to 64 per cent in 1987. Canada has also seen some decline in the proportion of family labour in the agricultural sector. Britain has also moved against the trend in OECD countries, where the proportion of employed workers in agriculture increased from around 21 per cent in the mid-1960s to 26 per cent in the mid-1980s (Errington 1987). Within the EC, despite a general decline in non-family labour, the hired workforce grew to around 15 per cent in Denmark, France and The Netherlands in 1985, though results of the latest (1987) Farm Structure Survey suggest that the trend has since reversed.

Contemporary Trends in the UK

Forty years of economic security and relative stability following the Second World War have enabled British farmers to consolidate their position. Figure 2.5 illustrates how the 'social income' of agriculture was allocated in the period from 1945 to 1975. The workers' share was falling while the farmers' share grew significantly after the mid-1950s. The landowners' share rose steadily from 1949/50 for a period of twenty years and then declined (Britton 1977).

The situation for the farmer who inherited his farm or bought land on favourable terms as a sitting tenant, and who has dispensed with hired labour, appears from Figure 2.5 to be very secure. More than financial security is involved here. Writing at a time when about two-thirds of farmland was rented, Orwin believed that 'In no other industry is the *entrepreneur* dependent, to such an extent, upon another party at once for the factory equipment, so to speak, and for the raw material of his trade' (Orwin 1930: 13). A century of legislation has progressively reduced the power of veto of the landowner and increased the security of the tenant farmer, but tenants still need the landlord's permission to make certain improvements and are not free to make decisions about major capital investments. Similarly, although it can be argued that farmers as employers have exercised a large measure of control over the lives of their employees, the rights

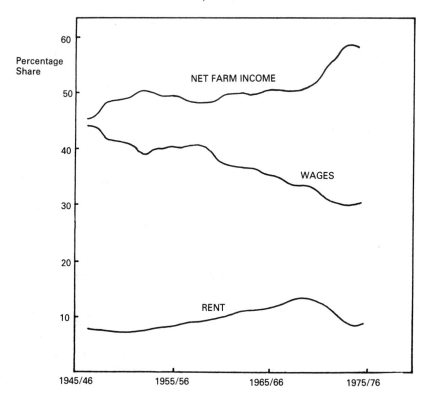

Figure 2.5. Shares of farmers, farmworkers and landowners in the income generated by UK agriculture (3-year moving averages). Source: Britton 1977

of employers have been limited and those of workers reinforced by employment legislation. The labour-employing farmer still has to consider the rights of his workers, conform with safety legislation and pay the wages. Thus contemporary owner-occupiers employing only family labour could be said to enjoy a greater measure of independence than farmers at any previous point in history.

Dependence on Borrowed Capital

What Figure 2.5 does not show is the increasing reliance of British agriculture on borrowed capital. Between 1950 and 1960, for instance, the value of the average annual increase in the area of owner-occupied land in the UK was estimated to be over £24m. By the early 1980s this figure had risen to nearly £240m per annum. The farmer who buys the freehold of his farm on mortgage or who borrows from the bank to purchase new machinery to replace a regular worker, is switching his dependence from the owners of land and labour to the owners of capital. With an increasingly capital-intensive agriculture, it has become progressively harder for farmers to obtain all the capital they need from internal savings and traditional sources of equity. It seems unlikely that family farms will be able to provide the same *proportion* of capital from savings out of income as they have in the past. Therefore farmers are turning increasingly to the use of credit, leasing, corporate finance and other sources of capital.

Historically, it is assumed, British agriculture has been largely self-financing, the main sources of capital being inherited wealth and retained profits[1]. UK farmers still enjoy a high ratio of owner equity overall but recent evidence show a rapid rise in borrowing from a low base. UK farmers' total indebtedness to banks and other long-term lenders increased by £375m during the 1950s, by about £2400m during the 1970s and by over £3500m between 1980 and 1985. During the 1960s and 1970s, heavy debts were incurred by new entrants to the industry, especially those without family backing. The value of land bought into owner-occupation represents a large but diminishing proportion of the increase in debt, being equivalent to two thirds of the total debt burden during the 1950s, only one third by the early 1980s. It was estimated that in 1969, 5 per cent of English farmers carried 65 per cent of the total burden of debt. Because of inflation and rising money incomes, the weight of servicing the debt was soon reduced. The proportion of all farmers heavily indebted remained around 5 per cent but the individuals within that group soon moved out, to be replaced by another intake of heavily indebted new entrants (Harrison and Tranter 1989).

The financial fortunes of farming deteriorated dramatically after the mid-1970s and hence the ability to service debt was undermined. Total assets declined in value in real terms while short-term borrowing increased rapidly and longer-term borrowing somewhat less so. The result was that farmers' real wealth fell by about 10 per cent in the first half of the 1980s (Harrison 1986). By the early 1990s, the interest repayments by UK farmers on all forms of debt including land exceeded 40 per cent of farming net income (MAFF 1990). While lower farm incomes make it harder to service loans, falling land values add to the farmer's problems by reducing collateral values and increasing leverage, thus adding to the risk of borrowing, and by making it harder to sell land to clear debts. The number of heavily indebted farmers has grown rapidly and is now estimated to be more than 20 per cent (Harrison and Tranter 1989).

---

[1] In fact little historical research has been carried out on the subject. It is now thought that by the time of the Napoleonic Wars, the larger farmers at least were heavily dependent on bank loans to establish their businesses (Mingay 1990).

SUMMARY AND IMPLICATIONS

On all the criteria used, farm family businesses comprise the largest single category of farms in British agriculture and they tend to be more important still in the United States and the European Community. Within the United Kingdom, family-worked farms are more prevalent in the pastoral regions of the north and west where dairying, beef cattle and sheep production predominate.

In terms of the structure of agriculture, the family-owned and family-worked farm has not declined, as nineteenth-century thinkers had predicted. The evidence is ambivalent, depending how the family farm is defined. Some American agricultural economists, taking a broad view of what constitutes family farming, see both family and larger-than-family farms successfully adapting themselves to changing economic conditions (see for instance Nikolitch 1969, 1972). Using a more restrictive definition of the wholly owned, family-worked farm, rural sociologists Rodefeld *et al.* (1978) report a decline in family- and tenant-type farms in the United States relative to larger-than-family and industrial-type farms, which they expect to continue. Yet almost in the same breath these authors cast doubt on their own interpretation of the facts:

> Almost all past studies of farm change have shown no declines in levels of land and capital ownership and of labour provision by farm managers and no decline in the status of farms with family-type characteristics. However, *numerous inferential reasons suggest declines should be occurring.*
>
> (Rodefeld *et al.* 1978: 175, emphasis added)

Historically and in recent decades, the trend in Britain has been towards rather than away from family ownership and operation of farms. The price paid for increasing owner-occupation and substituting capital for hired labour has been increased dependence on external sources of finance. The crucial question then becomes, not whether families can continue to own and operate farms within an advanced capitalist system but how far they can be said to *control* businesses which are so heavily dependent on borrowed money. Family farmers may still dominate the structure of the industry, but within that structure their power to control what happens on their farms may be seeping away. To pursue that question, we need to consider the processes of capitalist development in agriculture.

3

Family Farming, Capital and the Role of the State

Introduction

> Research is needed to clarify the meaning of 'family farming' and on
> the motivations and sources of satisfaction of family farmers. Research
> is also needed on the extent to which family farmers are losing control
> over their own farming operations.
>
> (Stockdale 1982: 323)

Previous chapters have attempted to clarify the concept of the farm family
business and indicate its significance in market industrialized countries
today while the next considers the objectives, motivations and sources of
satisfaction of family farmers. The present chapter addresses the issue of
family farmers losing control of their businesses. While the book is mainly
concerned with the internal dynamics of the farm family business – what
happens on the farm and within the farmhouse – this chapter has a different
focus. It attempts to set the farm family business within a wider context,
seeing how it is affected by the development of capitalism and intervention
by the state.

Chapter 2 has established that most farms in the world's market
industrialized countries are operated along family lines. The farm family
business has not only survived but may actually be increasing in numerical
terms in the UK, while in other developed countries it remains predominant.
Predictions of the demise of family farming under capitalism were clearly ill-
founded. Closer examination shows, however, that the family farm only
survives by adapting in some way to the demands of capitalism. Whatever
form this accommodation takes, the integrity of the relationship between
family and farm is compromised to some extent. State agricultural policies in
market industrialized countries tend to reinforce the trend towards fewer
and larger farms. Thus family farming may persist but it cannot continue
unchanged.

PAST PREDICTIONS

> We live essentially on ideas that were bequeathed us by the nineteenth
> century, and are today obviously anachronistic. It is important to revise
> these ideas and to look at the countryside with a new eye; otherwise
> we will remain blind to the great movement that is carrying the
> agrarian societies of the entire world toward a complete remodeling of
> their technology and their social equilibrium.
>
> (Mendras 1970: 5)

The belief that family farming is doomed to disappear has a long history.
Such thinking can be traced back at least as far as the Physiocrats of the
eighteenth century and it still has its adherents today. The founding fathers
of sociology dismissed the small family farm as a thing of the past. Marxist
theory confidently predicted the demise of family enterprises, which were
seen as laggardly and traditional. According to *The Communist Manifesto*:

> Capitalism arises and develops as the inexorable negation of all
> pre-existing forms of economic and social organization – penetrating all
> sectors of the economy, transforming all social relations, and
> eliminating all 'pre-capitalist' forms of production. Sweeping before it
> the organizational detritus of the past, capitalism prepares the ground
> for industrial growth and future economic development . . . capitalism
> progressively 'creates a world in its own image'.
>
> (Davis 1980: 133)

While many theorists draw from the Marxist heritage, there does not seem
to be one definitive Marxist position on the future of the family farm under
capitalism (Buttel and Newby 1980). One body of thought holds that the
family farm is inexorably destined for extinction due to the overwhelming
forces of concentration and centralization of capital. Marx and more
especially Lenin envisaged a continuing process of differentiation in agriculture, with peasants emerging as fully-fledged capitalists and absentee
landlords, or sinking into the mass of impoverished tenants and landless
labourers. Where Marx anticipated **horizontal** concentration in agriculture –
the amalgamation of many small farms into a few large units – Chayanov
foresaw **vertical** integration of farming with more powerful industrial firms,
the providers of agricultural inputs and processors of farm products
(Djurfeldt 1992). Only Kautsky among the Marxist theorists perceived that
family farms might persist in the long term, with the proletarianization
process creating worker-peasants or part-time farmers rather than
destroying non-capitalist forms of production (Marsden *et al.* 1986b). In a
different tradition, although Weber recognized that certain conditions might
favour small-scale farming within a rationalized market economy, he
expected each branch of economic activity to be characterized by an

increasing level of bureaucracy and a complex division of labour (Winter 1986).

Political economists and sociologists were not alone in predicting the end of farming on a family scale. In *The Future of Farming* published in 1930, the agricultural economist C.S. Orwin described the family farmer as 'an economic anachronism in an industrial country'. He believed family farmers could never escape the limitations imposed by the small size of holdings, lack of mechanization and shortage of capital. In his vision, the future of farming lay in the hands of large-scale operators, despite the fact that 'not one example can be found of farming on factory lines, for which all the portents should be favourable'. While admitting that some branches of farming lent themselves to a middle-scale or even a family farm system, he believed that:

> in no case and under no system can an economic gain be expected by a departure from the factory scale; the most that can be claimed is that, granted any social advantages or the chance of satisfying the desires of individuals under an organization of production by smaller units, these can be provided in certain branches of farming without much actual loss.
>
> (Orwin 1930: 116)

As the previous chapter has shown, farming continues to be organized largely along family lines; that is to say families own and manage farm businesses, which may be transferred within the family, and family members provide at least some of the labour and capital. As capital requirements of modern farming have grown, farm families have been forced to rely more and more on borrowing. To what extent can they be said to *control* their businesses when they are farming on borrowed money? How does dependence on outside sources of capital affect internal relationships in the farm family business?

PENETRATION BY CAPITAL

> ... farming is unique in that, the separation of management from the ownership of capital which has contributed so much to economic growth, especially since the introduction of public limited liability companies late last century, has, as yet, made virtually no impact on it. Currently, however, farmers are being subjected to pressures which may force them to restructure their financial and business arrangements.
>
> (Harrison 1972: 1)

The persistence of farming on a family scale within a capitalist economy has exercised the minds of political economists and rural sociologists for decades. The main points of the debate can only be sketched in briefly here, drawing heavily on the work of Davis (1980), Goodman and Redclift (1981, 1986), Winter (1984) and Marsden *et al.* (1986b).

In a nutshell, the 'logic' or objective of capitalism is to convert factors of production (land, labour, capital assets, management) into commodities with a market value and to extract a profit for the owners of capital. Capitalists are not interested in financing production which is not giving an adequate return on capital. Profit is a *functional necessity* for the capitalist firm but not for the family business. The concept of family farming within the capitalist mode of production starts from the 'ideal type' of simple commodity production. In simple commodity production, all labour requirements are met within the household. Since there is no wage labour, there is no separation between ownership and labour, and hence no need to separate profits and wages in the internal organization of the family business. This is the essential difference between family and non-family businesses. Profit is a *functional* necessity for capitalist firm but not for the family business. This does not mean that farmers who are simple commodity producers do not strive for profits and try to expand their businesses, but that it is not *functionally* necessary to do so (Djurfeldt 1992).

According to the logic of simple commodity production, there are no economic pressures for expansion. Maintenance of production at the existing level is adequate for each household. It is enough for them to subsist and to 'reproduce' their means of production – to save or buy seed, to replace breeding livestock, to repair or renew tools and the physical infrastructure of the farm and provide household members with the socially accepted level of consumption.

Where farming relies on family labour, the farm family produces a certain amount of food, fuel and so on for its own consumption, thereby securing part of its own costs of reproduction. This represents a potential gain to outside capital, since by subsidizing the cost of the labour inputs devoted to commodity production, family farmers exert a downward pressure on the prices of these commodities. Thus the commodity price can fall below the level necessary to guarantee long-run average profits to capitalist producers, who must earn the average rate of return on capital in order to remain in business. As product prices fall relative to those of inputs needed for production and consumption goods, family farmers may attempt to restore their previous position by working longer hours and intensifying the use of unpaid family labour, thereby increasing the rate of self-exploitation.

> The family-farmer, wherever he is met with, works himself and his family very hard; he pays no wages to his wife and often none to his

children; their hours of work are unlimited; the remuneration per head often falls below that of wage-labour in agriculture.

(Orwin 1930: 30)

Family farmers may therefore continue in production when non-family firms would be forced out of business. Family farms release 'surpluses' for the market even when the market price falls below the actual costs of production and imputed wages. Sacrifices may be made in order to retain independence (see also Chapter 4).

By dint of accepting a low standard of living, relying on a cheap and flexible labour force and keeping subsistence costs low by consuming home produce, farm families may be able to resist the 'penetration' or takeover by capital. More realistically, these tactics may serve to delay its inevitable incursion, for the economy of simple commodity production cannot be sustained once its conditions of reproduction become dependent on capital. This dependence may come about in one of two ways.

Direct and Indirect Penetration

The essence of capitalism is that surplus value is produced by one class of persons who sell their labour and appropriated by another class who purchase it. In Marx's analysis, in the early periods of capitalist development a surplus value may be extracted from an existing labour process developed by different and more archaic modes of production, without transforming the technical conditions of production. In other words, production continues within family businesses without using paid labour. Marx defined this as the **formal** or indirect subsumption of labour under capital. The transition to a specifically capitalist labour process occurs when capital revolutionizes the nature of the labour process as a whole. In industry this transition is typically associated with a more complex division of labour and large-scale production, since the new labour process is beyond the capacity of workers to operate as self-employed producers. An example would be a farming company renting land from an institutional investor and running the business with salaried management and hired labour. Marxists term this the **real** or direct subsumption of labour.

In agriculture, the subsumption of labour by capital is typically arrested at the first stage. The structure of production superficially remains unchanged. Orwin's description of the state of British agriculture between the wars neatly illustrates the indirect subsumption of the labour process, falling short of a direct takeover by capital.

... much has been done to mechanize many of the old manual processes, but just as the farmer has confined his utilization of the discoveries of natural science to the intensification of his established practice, so his application of engineering invention has been limited by the established size of his farm ... the organization of the farm today differs very little from that of a hundred years ago, when the unit of farm management was based upon a plentiful supply of cheap labour, when the horse was the only form of power at the farmer's command ...

(Orwin 1930: 150)

The next fifty years did not witness any striking growth in the direct control of British farms by outside capital. The Northfield Committee, set up in 1977 to examine trends in the acquisition and occupancy of agricultural land in the light of growing concern about the activities of financial institutions and overseas buyers, found that the financial institutions owned less than 2 per cent of the area of crops and grass in Great Britain. The Committee thought it very unlikely that the institutions would own more than 11 per cent of the total agricultural area of Britain by the year 2020, perhaps considerably less (Northfield 1979). In the event, farmland has become less attractive as a long-term investment, its real value falling since the mid-1980s and the institutions have been shedding agricultural land from their portfolios.

Typically, then, the direct producer in agriculture retains control of the labour process. Yet it is possible for capital to exert control over the production process without having to replace the direct producers. Within a modern capitalist economy, it is increasingly difficult to remain competitive in agriculture without becoming dependent on outside capital, and such dependence inevitably means some loss of control. Farm family businesses may resist *direct* penetration by outside capital but become vulnerable through employing labour, borrowing money or adopting improved methods.

At certain phases in the family cycle, wage labour may be needed to ensure the reproduction of the family farm. Simple commodity producers are then required to earn a profit or surplus to pay the wages. The alternative to employing non-family workers may be to buy more machinery, which in turn increases dependence on outside capital. Probably more significant is the dominance of land and fixed capital in farm businesses. Land prices rising rapidly in recent decades and increasing relative to the returns from farming the land have added to borrowing costs, especially for those starting up in farming or trying to expand their holdings. Then, as Chapter 1 showed, it is increasingly difficult to stay in farming without taking advantage of new technology, which means purchasing inputs and services from the wider economy. As the farm business becomes a more open system, it comes to rely more and more on outside capital. As soon as the farmer begins to employ new technology in his business (for instance to buy in seed rather than save part of the previous crop), he is drawn into the capitalist exchange system. He has to consider the cost of the new inputs, or hired labour or extra land, and whether using them will be likely to yield any return after covering the cost, which includes a profit for the owners of capital. Thus he is obliged to make decisions in the light of economic criteria and to give more prominence to profit in his objective function. Inevitably, farming becomes more of a business and less a way of life. Farmers sum this up neatly when they speak of 'working for the bank' instead of for themselves.

The Treadmill of Technology

Not only did the process of farm technological advance force the participants in the process onto a treadmill, but it created a condition in which the strong and aggressive farmers gobbled up the weak and inefficient ... farm technological advance has resulted in widespread cannibalism ...

(Cochrane 1979: 389-90)

Once the farmer has engaged with the capitalist exchange system, he is likely to be drawn further in. According to Cochrane (1979) the individual farmer is on a 'treadmill of technology'. The early adopters of new and improved technology benefit directly as their unit costs of production are reduced. As more and more farmers adopt the improved technology (assuming it is output-increasing) output will rise against a static demand and price will fall. A new equilibrium is reached where costs of production are covered but no producers make excess profits. The long-run gainers from farm technological advance are the consumers, who can obtain the same product at a lower price. Early adopters reap an initial gain but as the treadmill speeds up, prices fall. All adopters are then back to a situation of normal rather than supernormal profit. The average farmer therefore has to adopt the innovation merely to survive, in effect running harder stay in the same position. (By way of illustration, many of the Pembrokeshire farmers interviewed by Hutson (1987) were working as hard, and under as much financial pressure, in their fifties and sixties as they had been in their twenties). Laggards who never adopt the innovation but continue producing at the old higher level of costs, make a loss and are eventually forced out of business. Their assets are typically acquired by the more competitive farmers who were early adopters and prospered from the temporary gains.

Where state intervention puts a floor under farm product prices, the effect of the treadmill is to push up the price of land. Profits are used to purchase the scarce input, land, from laggard neighbours and are capitalized into the price of land already owned, so causing unit costs of production to rise. The **product market** treadmill is replaced by a **land market** treadmill. In the process the scale of operations for stronger, more competitive farmers is increased while many of the smaller, less efficient farms go out of business (Cochrane 1979).

Family farmers are thus drawn into capitalist relations of production by employing non-family labour and purchasing industrial inputs. Business expansion, fuelled by the technology treadmill, involves borrowing money to purchase and equip land and striving for a higher profit margin to cover rent or interest payments. While formal control of the farm business, in terms of the legal ownership of the business capital and land, remains with the farm family, their management becomes increasingly dependent upon technical and economic factors controlled by external capital. But why has agriculture largely resisted a direct takeover by outside capital? Why has capital penetration been so slow?

SLOW CAPITAL PENETRATION IN AGRICULTURE

Resilience of Simple Commodity Production

A number of explanations have been advanced to account for the slow penetration of agriculture by external sources of capital. Some commentators interpret the persistence of the family farm under capitalism as an 'empirical refutation' of Marxist theory. They put forward various reasons to account for the 'survival' of family farming, including technical efficiency and the success of government policies in maintaining it. They may emphasize the positive attributes of flexibility and resilience which allow the family business to adapt successfully to changing technological and economic conditions, or the ideological commitment which enables the farm family to accept lower returns to capital and labour than would be acceptable to competing capitalist firms.

Another argument, put forward by economists, holds that family farms are competitive by virtue of lower 'transaction costs', the costs of recruiting and employing labour. Firms normally carry transaction costs as a business cost but in agriculture they are absorbed by the farm household. Transaction costs are low in farm family businesses because economic relationships are entwined with personal ones. In the non-family farms these costs increase with farm size, number of hired workers and the social distance between manager and workers. According to this theory, family labour farms enjoy a comparative advantage when it comes to supervising workers who, because of the nature of the job, cannot be gathered together in a single location. When farm tasks can be monitored easily, family farms are often over-shadowed by larger non-family businesses. For certain tasks like hoeing root crops or riddling potatoes, hired labour can be supervised directly in work gangs. With other tasks such as fruit picking, output can be measured and paid for on a piece-work basis. But since most farm tasks are not susceptible to these forms of direct supervision, the family farm has a comparative advantage and this helps to account for its numerical dominance (Pollack 1985; Schmitt 1991).

Others seek to explain the persistence of the family farm within a Marxist perspective. They may stress ways in which the family farm may be functional for the maintenance of capitalist relations of production. Advantages may be gained if family farms undertake certain forms of production (rearing dairy heifers or breeding ewes, for example) and so provide relatively cheap imputs for the large farm sector. Or they may base their explanations on factors which slow down the development of capitalist relations of production in farming; the capitalist annihilation of the family farm has been delayed, not averted. There are a number of reasons why the capital penetration should be slower in agriculture than in other industries. Principal constraints on the capacity of capital to revolutionize the means of production in agriculture are organic nature, land and space. Here a distinction can be made between factors acting as barriers to capital penetration and factors making farming unattractive to external capital.

Barriers to Capital Penetration

Certain features of agriculture, notably the importance of land as a factor of production, make it peculiarly resistant to the incursions of capital. First, to farm on a large scale requires amalgamating a number of existing holdings. Those wishing to accumulate land are dependent on the land market. This necessarily slows down the penetration of external capital, since only a small amount of land, typically 1–2 per cent, comes on the market each year. *As long as a landowner is not indebted,* his property cannot be alienated. Second, farmers who inherited their holdings or bought them cheaply long ago, are partly insulated from the rigours of the market and can resist a takeover by outside capital. Owner-occupiers of small and middle-sized farms in Britain are found to perform less efficiently than tenants and part-owners who are spurred on by the necessity of paying the rent (Hill and Gasson 1984).

> The capital-fixing nature of land and the consequent immobility of large portions of agricultural capital can foster an entrenched pattern of agricultural production which may create in turn a strong element of inertia within the organization of farm businesses, particularly when the industry is dominated by relatively small producers.
>
> (Marsden *et al.* 1987: 300)

Unattractiveness of Agriculture as an Investment

Arguments about landed property and rent suggest barriers to capital penetration and accumulation *within* agriculture. The incentive for capitalist development comes from within as well as from outside. Indeed, the greatest threat to the existence of small farms is the expansionary tendency of larger farms, which may also be family businesses (Cochrane 1979; Marsden 1984). But other explanations relate to the unattractiveness of agriculture to outside, financial and industrial capital. For one thing, capital can only circulate slowly in agriculture because of 'organic nature', that is dependence on growing seasons, gestation periods and growth cycles and all their associated risk of disease, weather and so on. In Marxist terms, the production time is considerably longer than the labour time (Mann and Dickinson 1978). Capital is attracted to those industries and those branches of agriculture where production time can be successfully reduced, such as the pig, poultry and glasshouse sectors. It is precisely in these sectors, where turnover is rapid and the environment can be controlled, that the greatest swing from family-scale to industrial-type production has occurred. Conversely those types of enterprise where the production cycle remains long relative to labour time (cattle and sheep rearing, for example) are left, with all their associated risk, largely in the hands of small producers.

A second reason why agriculture is relatively unattractive to industrial capital, is that economies of scale are difficult to achieve. In Britain it has been demonstrated that most economies of scale can be attained by a two-man unit, at relatively low levels of capital accumulation, although diseconomies of small size appear to operate rather severely below this size (Britton and Hill 1975). Similarly in the United States, most economies of scale are achieved by the efficient two-man farm (Madden 1967). On more recent evidence, the highly-mechanized one-man farm emerges as the most efficient unit in much of Europe (Djurfeldt 1992).

Third, diseconomies of distance together with variations in soil fertility, topography and climate make it harder to manage large enterprises than in other industries. Where land ceases to be such a determining factor in production, as in the pig, poultry and glasshouse sectors, in fish farming or beef feed-lots, capital is able to penetrate and re-structure the industry, with dramatic results. In the long-run, the tendency of capitalist development in agriculture is to undermine the significance of land as a factor of production (Goodman and Redclift 1986).

Arguments about long production cycles, diseconomies of distance and the importance of land all help to account for the uneven penetration of capital in agriculture. Capital is attracted to those branches where production cycles are short, the land input is either reduced or of uniform quality and direct supervision of labour is possible. Market gardening and glasshouse crop production, pigs and poultry and other intensive forms of livestock production come into this category. Conversely family farming has a comparative advantage, or is at less of a disadvantage, in enterprises where production time is long relative to labour time, where land is of very variable quality and is used extensively and where direct supervision of tasks is impossible. Livestock rearing in the hills and uplands meets these conditions, as do lowland dairy, cattle and sheep farming to a smaller extent. Hence family farming is not evenly distributed across the British Isles but tends to predominate in the pastoral north and west while large-scale non-family farms are more in evidence in the east and south. Figure 2.3 (p. 48) shows the predominance of family-worked farms in the northern and western counties, but it must be remembered that our definition of a farm family business is wider than the family-worked farm.

It follows that in the UK, family farming predominates in regions on the periphery of the capitalist state like Wales and Ulster, which have tradi-tionally been under-developed and incompletely penetrated by outside capital. In areas of low wages and high unemployment, there is little incentive for farmers or their sons to give up farming. Ideology may also be an influence here:

> Distance from the centres of economic activity implies also distance from political and ideological processes of the central state, encouraging forms of local consciousness and ideology that buttress and are supported by petty bourgeois ideology.
>
> (Winter 1984: 125)

Indirect Control by Capital

> The so-called 'independent' commercial farmers, increasingly reliant upon external credit and other inputs, are incapable of altering the 'rules' of capital accumulation. They conform to the needs of agribusiness firms in order to remain in farming.
>
> (Lawrence 1990: 112)

Certain features of agriculture make it unattractive to a wholesale takeover by outside capital while other features slow down the rate of capital penetration. Taking a broader view, however, it appears that the family farm has not resisted capitalist development but has adapted to it. Accepting that subsumption of the labour process in agriculture is predominantly indirect, at least in the initial stages, this section considers the ways in which capital *does* manage to gain a hold within the family business, including:

- use of industrial inputs
- use of credit
- vertical integration
- contract farming.

Capitalist development has brought a series of mechanical, chemical and biological innovations, progressively taking over activities which at an earlier period were regarded as part of the farm production process;

improved seed varieties, herbicides, compound feeds, artificial insemination, embryo transplants and so on. As more and more elements of farm production become amenable to industrial reproduction they are taken over, to be re-incorporated in agriculture as industrial inputs. The trend may culminate in capital eliminating the need for farming to be a land-based activity (Goodman and Redclift 1986).

Capital penetrates the farm production process by other routes too. Farmers are becoming increasingly dependent on off-farm sources of credit to finance production. In some cases the financial institution may even insist upon sharing in farm management decisions as a condition of credit; the farmer may have to present an annual balance sheet, prepare forward budgets and accept restrictions on further investments. This means that borrowing transfers not only **value** from the farmer to the lender but entrepreneurial control as well. Again, the farmer may be drawn into relations of exploitation and control when buying or leasing machinery and other major inputs. Value is transferred from the farmer to the capitalist firm in the price of the product and the credit arrangements, both of which are established by the firm.

Since the return on capital is generally lower in farming than elsewhere, the only incentive for industrial capital to invest would be if substantial economies accrued to better co-ordination between the production process and the supply of farm inputs or the processing and marketing of products. Hence vertical integration is likely to predominate, the major impetus coming from farm-related rather than non-farm industry. Such linkages can be expected to grow so long as there are significant synergistic relations between farm businesses and upstream or downstream industries (Aines 1972).

Contract farming, production based on contracts between farmers and other firms upstream or downstream in the food production chain, removes from the farmer's control some of the resources, tasks and decisions which have traditionally been part of his role as an independent entrepreneur. The degree of control surrendered to the non-farm firm can vary from dependence only slightly closer than an open market relationship to complete ownership and operation by a corporate body. At the extreme, the farmer is reduced to the status of a sharecropper, a wage-earner on his own land, providing his own labour and tools but working under supervision to produce commodities which he does not own. The capitalist firm can use contracting to intensify the farm production process through tight scheduling, a high degree of organization and mechanization to maximize output per man-hour and rapid incorporation of new techniques to increase yields, improve product quality and make maximum use of the land and equipment provided by the farmer. Some poultry enterprises come close to this extreme with the farmer receiving day-old chicks, feed and drugs from the firm that will eventually process and sell his broilers. The farmer simply provides fixed inputs, namely housing and labour.

Control may also be exercised indirectly, through a contract price set by the contractor. The farmer is paid according to quantity, quality and sometimes timing of production. Operating under such conditions, the farmer will strive hard to increase productivity and lower his own production costs. Because farmers are seldom able to bargain on equal terms with non-farm capitalists, the contract price is seldom high enough to cover the farmer's production costs and the full value of his labour embodied in the product. Production contracts therefore function to extract surplus value for capital. How effective they are depends upon the degree to which the contractor is unilaterally able to determine the contract price and the farmer's freedom of access to alternative product markets (Davis 1980).

To sum up, surplus value may be extracted from the family farm through the purchase of industrial inputs, credit arrangements, vertical integration and contract farming. Without a complete takeover of the means of production, the family farmer loses some degree of control over the way he runs his business. Viewed pessimistically,

> Family farming may cease to be a mode of production based on the independent labour of the agricultural producer; yet, because of the ideology of family farming, agricultural producers may take little account of their growing subordination to capital. Likewise, politicians may act to subsidize the family farm, college researchers may continue to 'support' the family farm, liberal activists may oppose corporate farming to 'save' the family farm, and all the while they may scarcely notice that, even as the family farm remains, family farming as an independent mode of production is gradually ceasing to be.
>
> (Davis 1980: 147)

RIVAL PERSPECTIVES

We have touched upon various approaches to the study of the family farm under capitalism. The present section reviews and compares some of the arguments while the next offers some empirical evidence to test their relative strengths.

Sociologists differ fundamentally from economists in their explanations of the tendency for farming to become more dependent on capital. While Marxists speak of the tendency for capital to *penetrate* or *subsume* the labour process and extract a surplus for the owners of capital, neo-classical economists think in terms of **capital substitution**. For these economists, the motive force for the transformation of agriculture has been rapidly advancing technology, particularly machine technology, and a decline in the real price of capital relative to labour and land. Both tendencies encourage the substitution of capital for labour in farming. At the same time, rapid progress in technologies which substitute capital for land, forces down profit margins and requires units of production to become larger to attain acceptable levels of income (Ball and Heady 1972).

The economist's argument is based upon the rational entrepreneur free to make decisions to further his own best interest. Looked at from the farm management adviser's point of view, to farm 'well' by the accepted standards a farmer must keep up with the latest technology and expand the business, which requires additional capital. As a rational businessman, the farmer should borrow so long as the anticipated return on capital exceeds the cost of borrowing. In Marxist terms, the agricultural sector is being penetrated by financial and industrial capital, resulting in the direct and indirect subsumption of the labour process. Marxists speak of capitalism 'conducting a continuous campaign' against modes of production based on the independent producer.

> Given the nature of the capitalist labour process, it is necessary to ask why any labourer would knowingly become part of it. Marx's answer is unequivocal: the capitalist labour process is built upon coercion. Only under some form of duress would persons consent to subject themselves to a system of exploitation so clearly contrary to their best interests.
>
> (Davis 1980: 138)

Economists might question whether the family farmer's obsession with owning as well as controlling the assets of the business is functional for running a successful farm today. The divorce of ownership and management of assets is, after all, the norm in commerce and industry (Reid 1974). Sociologists on the other hand would doubt whether the farmer who no longer owned all his business assets was really free to exercise control over their use. This is a fundamental question for this book and indeed for anyone concerned with the future of the farm family business. There is no easy answer. Theorists in the Marxist tradition seem unable to agree how to categorize simple commodity producers who still possess the means of production but are indirectly dominated by capitalist relations of production:

> The distinction between small commodity producers subordinated to capital and 'concealed' or 'disguised' rural proletarians is, nevertheless, a fine one and continues to be a source of debate and dissension in the literature.
>
> (Goodman and Redclift 1981: 98)

Whether the economist's or the sociologist's type of explanation is preferred will reflect individual differences in background, education and philosophy. The malign intent attributed to capital by Davis in the above quotation does not seem to ring true in the context of British farming today, but nor is the family farmer a free agent. The position taken here is that the

Table 3.1. Key elements of the subsumption and survival positions.

	Subsumption	Survival
Key position	Family farms dominated by economic structures	Family farmers respond and adapt within context of economic structures
Mechanisms	External control of debt, inputs, technology: macro factors	Adaptation via managerial flexibility, including household relations: micro factors
Role of state	Assists external capital or facilitates capitalist processes	May help or hinder family farms
Impact of increased exposure to market forces	Difficult for family farms to survive	Easier for family farms to survive
Outcomes	More corporate farms More off-farm work More part-time farmers Fewer, larger farms More hired labour, contracts Corporate farms enter new types of production	Mostly family farms More off-farm work Part-time farming may develop Little change in farm numbers More household labour Family farms enter new areas of production

Source: Fairweather 1992, Table 27

farm family business within advanced capitalism is certainly constrained by the nature of economic forces beyond its control; it is not possible to maintain the level of income from a family farm without some form of expansion or diversification. But although the options are becoming limited, some freedom of choice is still available.

Among sociologists there are 'survivalists' and 'subsumptionists', the latter divided between those who stress the inevitability of direct subsumption and those who argue that it is in the interests of capital for subsumption to be halted at the indirect stage. The 'subsumption' argument emphasizes the penetration of agriculture by capital using such means as technological change. The 'survival' school emphasizes barriers to capital penetration and the competitiveness of family farms (Fairweather 1992). Table 3.1 contrasts the key propositions.

These theoretical perspectives, stemming from different underlying philosophies, are not mutually exclusive but they lead to different interpretations of changes in agrarian structure. That is to say, the same fact or event can be interpreted as support for rival viewpoints, making it difficult to verify one position against another. For example, numbers of family farms may be holding up but production is becoming concentrated on larger-than-family farms; subsumptionists see increasing penetration by capital while survivalists see persistence. Some of the differences in approach do however lend themselves to empirical testing. Fairweather has attempted this using New Zealand data and Marsden and colleagues have explored some aspects with their studies of English farms.

Subsumption versus Survival: The New Zealand Case

New Zealand is a particularly appropriate setting in which to test rival theories about the fate of the family farm, since primary producers there were forced to make very rapid adjustments when all state supports for agriculture were removed in 1984. A survey of structural changes in New Zealand farming between 1984 and 1990 (Fairweather 1992) showed no widespread increase in corporate farms; in fact farmland was being increasingly bought by existing farmers while purchase by corporate businesses was declining. Farm numbers dropped with some slight increase in the concentration of production. While these changes are in accordance with the subsumption view of continuous pressure on farms to enlarge, they are not inconsistent with the survival school which argues that increasing scale is a choice for family farmers as well.

Subsumptionists predict growing dependence on wage labour as family farmers are forced to become wage labourers, on farms or elsewhere. The New Zealand data show, to the contrary, that family labour had increased while employment of both regular and casual labour decreased. Examples were quoted of farmers being forced into new financial arrangements, becoming managers or tenants on what were formerly their own properties, but this trend appeared to be quite limited. Subsumption would also imply the removal of farmers from full-time commercial production and a growth in part-time working, a trend again refuted by the data since financial pressures seemed to have intensified full-time farm employment. Some farm men and women had taken off-farm work, partly as a means of farm survival and partly to maintain household expenditure but there was a suggestion that as farm finances improved again, the extent of off-farm work declined. For women, the search for off-farm work can be seen as part of the general trend towards women's greater involvement in the paid workforce. Finally, family farmers in New Zealand appeared to be more dynamic in their approach to new types of production than corporate farms.

Overall, then, the New Zealand evidence does not support the subsumptionist case. Rapid exposure to international forces and a more market-oriented economy have not destroyed the family character of New Zealand farming but if anything intensified it. Family farms in general have risen to the challenge of a new market situation and most have adapted and survived successfully. Few other studies provide such convincing proof, since most researchers adopt a particular theoretical perspective at the outset and interpret their findings in that light; hence subsumption (or survival or adaptation) becomes a foregone conclusion. A series of studies carried out by a team of British researchers does, however, give additional support to the survival approach.

The English Case

Marsden and colleagues have developed a typology of farm businesses according to the degree of subsumption of both internal and external relations. Criteria used to reflect capital controlling the *internal* relations of production are the degree to which ownership of land rights, ownership of farm business capital, business management control and labour relations are

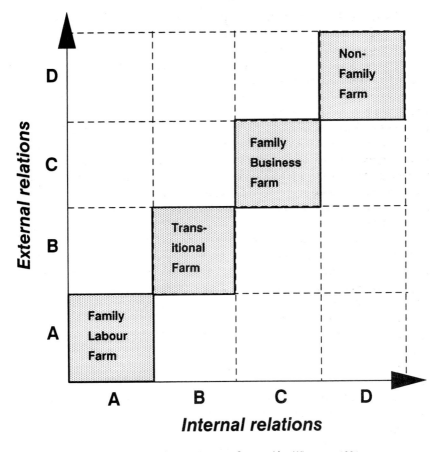

Figure 3.1. A relational typology of farm businesses. Source: After Whatmore 1991a

diffused away from a single family farm operator. At one extreme is the 'pure' type of family farm which is owned, managed and worked by the head of the farm household, at the other a farm which is a subsidiary interest of a corporation, operated by a management company using contract labour (Marsden *et al.* 1987). (The pure type of family farm is considerably narrower than the concept of a farm family business used in this book. Some researchers (Blanc and MacKinnon 1990; Djurfeldt 1992) would regard a one-man farm as a sub-family type.)

Capital can exert control over the *external* relations of production in a number of ways. Measures used in this study include technology (purchase of manufactured inputs, technical assistance and advice), credit (borrowing

Box 3.1. Ideal types of farm business. Source: Whatmore *et al.* 1987a

---

AA – Family labour farms

Marginal, closed businesses where relations of production are controlled within the nuclear family and there is little if any borrowing. A minimum of purchased inputs is used and there are no formal market linkages. These small businesses survive on the margins of commercial agriculture by limiting household consumption and/or relying on pensions or savings.

BB – Transitional farms

Transitional, dependent enterprises owned and managed by families, possibly within a formal partnership or family company and possibly employing some non-family labour, with some, limited links to external capital. Long-term survival may depend on the decision to extend their credit links in order to expand and remain viable. One alternative is to supplement household income and business capital through the development of non-farm sources of income and business interests.

CC – Family business farms

Integrated units, more complex in their internal structure owing to the development of corporate ownership and management of the farm business or links with other businesses owned by the family kin group or family-related companies. Expansion becomes a dominant influence on all business decisions. Links with external capital are extensive and actively pursued. Labour and management may be hired and contract marketing arrangements are common. Such businesses must continue to be dynamic and expansionist if they are to survive. In the process the distinctive relationship between family and farm becomes blurred.

DD – Non-family farms

Wholly subsumed enterprises where the internal structure of the business has been taken over directly by non-family capital. There is no family labour or management. Links with external capital are likely to be extensive and borrowing substantial.

Table 3.2. Distribution of farms from five study areas in England across typology matrix.

Indirect subsumption	Percentage of farms			
D	0	1.4	2.0	1.4
C	2.2	7.7	5.3	0.7
B	13.5	28.5	2.4	0.5
A	19.6	13.8	1.0	0
	A	B	C	D
	Direct subsumption			

Source: Marsden *et al.* 1992

to finance expansion, continued operation of the business) and marketing linkages (determining outlets, quality and quantity of output, returns, even management of on-farm production) (Whatmore *et al.* 1987a, 1987b). From this typology (Figure 3.1), four ideal types can be identified (Box 3.1).

Farm surveys were carried out in five contrasting farming areas. Three were in southern England: the Metropolitan Green Belt to represent the urban-rural fringe, east Bedfordshire representing large-scale arable farming and west Dorset, an area of predominantly small dairy and livestock farms. To these were added two upland areas in northern England: west Cumbria and north-east Staffordshire. Samples of farms from each area were scored according to the degree of direct and indirect subsumption and located within the matrix (Table 3.2).

Three trends can be deduced from Table 3.2. First, cases tend to cluster along the diagonal, none falling into the extreme cells AD or DA. This suggests a link between external and internal relations of production. Non-family farms are more likely to be involved in contract farming, vertical integration and so on. Second, more cases lie above the diagonal (25 per cent) than below (18 per cent), implying higher levels of indirect than direct subsumption. Third, the majority of farms (75 per cent) are located in the lower left quarter of the matrix, indicating low levels of penetration by outside capital. This was particularly marked in the upland areas. In Staffordshire only 5 per cent of farms lay outside the AB quadrant, in Cumbria 9 per cent, compared with 43 per cent for the Metropolitan Green Belt and 44 per cent for east Bedfordshire. Family labour farms made up the largest single category in Staffordshire, transitional farms in all other areas (Marsden *et al.* 1992).

The evidence suggests that while farm businesses are undoubtedly being penetrated by outside sources of capital, levels of subsumption are generally low. Large numbers of family farms are apparently managing to resist being taken over by external capital, or else they are adapting to its demands without destroying the integrity of the family business. In other words the evidence does not generally support the *direct* subsumption argument.

Evidence for Survival

The survival school of thought emphasizes barriers to the capitalist transformation of agriculture and the competitiveness of simple commodity production. Where these barriers do not operate, where land ceases to become a crucial consideration – as in production under glass, on concrete or in fish lakes – the encroachment of external capital is very apparent.

According to this argument, family farming will tend to survive longer where its comparative disadvantage is less, that is in types of farming where land is the major resource, where production cycles are long, where returns are low and uncertain and the degree of risk is high, where there are few economies of scale. Upland livestock rearing is a prime example. In the English study, lowest levels of both direct and indirect penetration by outside capital were found in Staffordshire and Cumbria, upland areas chosen to represent extensive livestock farming (Marsden *et al.* 1992). Such upland areas are, almost by definition, remote from the centres of economic activity and alternative employment. Family farming may therefore survive in peripheral areas partly by default, because agriculture does not attract outside capital and because there are few alternatives for farm household members. Remoteness may also foster a sense of local consciousness and local ideology which is in keeping with the survival of small family businesses (Winter 1984).

Adaptations to External Capital

> ... the emphasis upon structural processes and class formation, refreshing as it is in elucidating agricultural change, has, it can be argued, diverted attention from the role of human agency and the reasons for the diversity of forms and processes in productive relations.
>
> (Marsden *et al.* 1986b: 507)

Both survival and subsumptionist positions imply a rather passive stance on the part of farm families. Subsumption depicts the family farmer as powerless to act in the face of encroaching capitalism. Survival implies that family farms only remain in business by default, because of the barriers to capital penetration and the factors making farming unattractive to finance and industrial capital. The **adaptation** perspective suggests a more proactive stance, emphasizing the range of responses which farm families are able to make, though in Fairweather's scheme (Table 3.1) 'survival' seems to shade into farmer response and adaptation. Whereas earlier commentators were quick to predict the demise of the family farm, contemporary observers appear much more guarded. Almost all stress the variety of responses of the farm family to the pressures of external capital and the range of business forms likely to result. It is now believed that family relationships are sufficiently flexible to allow different strategies of family formation and organization to develop in response to the changing demands of markets and relations of production. Thus, while the form and content of relationships within the farm family are influenced by the changing forces of capitalist domination, they are not entirely determined by them (Hutson 1987). We return to this topic in Chapter 9.

FAMILY FARMING, THE SMALL FARM AND THE ROLE OF THE STATE

At one extreme, family farming is seen as an important bulwark of
democracy. At the other extreme, it is viewed as false consciousness ...
the family farm is little more than a myth used to legitimize
programmes that actually serve the interests of the largest commercial
farms and agribusiness.

(Stockdale 1982: 323)

So far we have considered the fate of the family farm under capitalism. Another powerful influence upon the functioning of the farm family business is the state. In theory the state could intervene to protect the family farm from capitalist exploitation. In practice, as Stockdale suggests, government intervention may have precisely the opposite effect. The stated objectives of policy therefore have to be distinguished from their actual effects. Confusion also arises from equating **family farm** with **small farm**.

US Support for the Family Farm

Support for the family farm has always been a conscious policy goal in the United States, where conflict over the appropriate structure of farm sizes has its roots in colonial history (Raup 1972). While settlement companies of 'gentlemen adventurers' were promised large grants of land from the British crown, Puritan colonists carved out individual clearings and insisted on a structure of small private plots, matching their convictions about the proper forms for civil and religious governance. For the squatters who pushed west, meanwhile, title to land had to be earned and defended by the hazards and sacrifices of pioneering. These conflicting attitudes towards the proper mode of settlement were distilled into the American constitution. Statesmen of the eighteenth century like Thomas Jefferson championed small farms for political and sociological reasons; freedom, independence, self-reliance, democracy, a source of employment and ability to resist oppressors. Nineteenth-century economists added the argument that an agriculture dominated by small firms guaranteed the competitive structure of the economy. Rural sociologists have suggested that the family farm and its associated infrastructure provide a higher quality of life for all rural dwellers (Heffernan 1982). Thus any threat to the structure of family farms in the US is seen as an attack on the fundamental beliefs of independence, democracy, quality of life, freedom of occupational choice and a free market, such that:

> ... any growth of concentration in agriculture, decline in family-type farms, or increasing restrictions on freedom of entry have symbolic impacts far greater than can be measured by food bills, export accounts, or fractions of the gross national product.
>
> (Raup 1972: 6)

Policy directed towards the Family

Although the idea of 'saving the family farm' continues to have popular appeal and is regularly invoked by governments and farmers' organizations, in Britain as in other market industrialized countries, state policies towards agriculture have generally been ineffective in this regard. In the first place, the failure to clarify what is meant by **family farming** means that inappropriate policies may be pursued. Family farms are generally assumed to be small but according to our definition they need not be; in fact almost all farms are run as family businesses. Policies which are intended to influence *family* relationships in farming, for instance to encourage the earlier transfer of the business from parents to children, are therefore applicable to most farms up to the very largest. As we have already shown, the greatest threat to the small family farm may not be the giant industrial-type farming corporation but the larger, more aggressive family farm. Support for family farming may therefore aid the large family farm on its expansionary path, to the detriment of its smaller neighbours.

One type of policy implicitly aimed at the family business is inheritance tax. Various concessions have enabled UK family businesses to be transferred to the next generation without a crippling level of taxation. Measures such as Capital Transfer Tax have aimed to encourage the earlier transfer of business assets to successors. Yet ironically, Capital Transfer Tax could penalize farm families who had not taken professional advice to minimize the tax burden by planning the lifetime transfer of assets (Taylor 1983). As in the United States,

The growing significance of tax policy in guiding management decisions has undoubtedly had a differentially heavy impact on businesses large enough to have significant tax obligations but too small to justify the employment of top quality professional advice in this field.

(Raup 1972: 10)

Another family policy issue which affects the farm business is the division of property at divorce. The spouse who marries into a farm family and can demonstrate having made a material contribution to the family business, may take up to half the farm property and force the sale of the farm. Ironically this legislation, designed to strengthen the rights of women, may be having precisely the opposite effect in some farming families, since parents are reluctant to take a daughter-in-law into partnership before the son's marriage has stood the test of time.

UK Policy towards the Smaller Farm

Second, the impact of any policies targetted on small, economically marginal family-run farms tends to be overshadowed by the effect of price and credit policies which encourage the trend towards fewer and larger farms. British agricultural policy-makers have rarely framed measures to assist either the family farm or the small farm as such, but one piece of legislation was specifically targeted at them. The Small Farmer Scheme, introduced in 1959, aimed to help promising small farms to develop into larger, more efficient viable units. The approach combined enhanced rates of existing capital improvement grants with differential access to the state advisory service and a strong emphasis on keeping records and accounts. The net effect was, however, to enhance the trend towards fewer and larger farms, since the majority were too small to qualify.

Within a few years, the Small Farmer Scheme was superceded by measures to hasten the amalgamation of small holdings and the retraining or early retirement of the small farmers displaced. This new approach was outlined in a 1965 White Paper *The Development of Agriculture*:

The Government believes that one of the more important problems facing agriculture is that of the small farmer trying to win a livelihood from insufficient land. As time pases, his difficulties will increase. He will find it more and more difficult to keep pace with technical advance ... to maintain a standard of living in keeping with modern times.

(Cmnd. 2738)

Grants from the UK Government towards the costs of farm amalgamation and payments to outgoers had their counterparts, when Britain became a member of the Economic Community, in EC Directives 159 (farm moderniz-ation), 160 (cessation of farming) and 161 (socioeconomic and vocational guidance). The impact of such schemes has not been impressive, as Chapter 8 will show.

British and EC agricultural support has been mainly based on product prices, favouring the larger farmer who not only produces more but may be able to achieve lower costs due to economies of size. By 1991, 80 per cent of payments under the CAP were going to 20 per cent of the farmers because of the link between price support and volume of production (Commission 1991). Capital grants, the other main support measure, have served to accelerate the trend towards fewer and larger businesses. Although mostly phased out now, the thresholds of eligibility for some capital grants discriminated against the smaller producer. Such policies have been criticized for failing to make any allowance for the special problems of the small unit. Welsh family-worked farms, for instance, were disadvantaged in a number of ways by UK agricultural policies as they existed in the early 1980s (Taylor 1983). Most damaging to the interests of smaller producers were criteria of eligibility for the generous capital improvement grants. It was estimated that about a quarter of Welsh farms failed to qualify because the business was too small or too dependent on other, often farm-based, sources of income.

Benefits of State Policy to Larger Farms

In Britain as in other market industrialized countries, the state gives considerable ideological support to the small, independent family farm while simultaneously encouraging the penetration of capital and its concentration within the agricultural sector. State intervention in the form of price support has encouraged the flow of external capital to the farm production process. The treadmill of technology has forced producers to substitute industrial capital for labour and state extension agencies have further promoted technological change on the farm. 'In this sense state policy has lubricated the relations between industrial and finance capital and individual farm businesses' (Marsden *et al.* 1986b).

Whether state policies towards agriculture which promote farm enlargement have lent more support to the larger family farm or the industrial-type non-family enterprise, is debatable. On one side, Ball and Heady argue that agricultural policy:

> ... never specifically or especially favoured small farms or mammoth units. But it has always favoured the growth of medium-large family operations. The tendency of large operator units to grow into very large family operations will, given the present generation of technology, remain as the qualitatively dominant force ...
>
> (Ball and Heady 1972: 386–7)

On the other side are those who stress the role of government in conferring benefits on large, industrial-type farms. The state of California provides probably the best illustration of farming on an industrial scale. There, artificial conditions have been created to favour large businesses through research and development priorities and access to good land, cheap irrigation water and non-competitive wage labour. American policy has also encouraged investment in agriculture as a tax shelter, conferring benefits on large multi-sector firms (Reinhardt and Barlett 1989).

The critical resource for managing farm businesses today could be information. Smaller farms are typically at a disadvantage in adjusting to the data and information revolution (Raup 1972). For one thing, the working farmer cannot easily spare the time to acquire the necessary skills. State investment in research and development, while ostensibly available to all, is in practice of most benefit to early adopters. As a result the early adopters are likely to increase their scale of operations. Where public support for agricultural research is withdrawn and replaced by private research, the information gap between large and small farms is likely to widen, making it increasingly difficult for small family farms to compete with large industrial-type units in certain high-risk and high-technology branches of agriculture (Moore and Dean 1972). The growing complexity of taxation, data collection and welfare systems, too, may have an inhibiting effect on family businesses too small to justify hiring a full-time consultant.

The Search for Alternative Policy Measures

The emergence of surpluses and the excessive cost of the Common Agricultural Policy has precipitated a crisis and encouraged the search for new support mechanisms. The MacSharry proposals (Commission 1991) combine a move towards more competitive prices for farm products with compulsory supply control measures and incentives for more extensive types of production, environmentally-friendly farming practices and early retirement of farmers. Where MacSharry breaks new ground is that payments to compensate farmers for lower prices of the main supported products (cereals, oilseeds and protein crops, milk, beef and sheepmeat) will no longer relate primarily to the volume produced. This is intended 'to maintain economic and social cohesion to the benefit of the vast majority of farmers who are less well placed to fully avail of the benefits of the Policy' (Commission 1991: 5).

One notable feature of the MacSharry proposals is the payment of direct support to the farming population, in the form of compensation, instead of indirect support via product prices. The suggestion that compensation payments should be paid in full to small producers, tapering off quite steeply above certain thresholds, was finally rejected. Although intended to aid the small family farms of continental Europe, the scheme would have discriminated severely against the majority of farm family businesses in Britain.

Direct income support to the smaller or disadvantaged farm is not an entirely novel approach. Cattle and sheep headage payments under the CAP, for instance, constitute a form of direct support to producers in the Less Favoured Areas. Direct payments have been used in Ireland to favour the smaller farm. Cattle and sheep headage payments to any one farmer were limited and targeted towards the poorest farming areas in an attempt to improve the distribution of incomes, although these subsidies amounted to less than 3 per cent of family farm income in 1977. The Small Holders' Assistance scheme, introduced in 1966, offered a means-tested weekly benefit somewhat lower than that received by the long-term unemployed. That scheme was judged to be of great benefit to the smaller farmer. It was estimated that in 1973, more than a quarter of the gross income of farms under 30 acres came from this and other direct transfer payments from the state (Hannan and Breen 1987).

Direct income payments are a possible means of assisting the most needy small-scale farmers but a more radical alternative would be direct intervention in the farmland market. The aim might be to create a desired size structure of farms, freeze an existing structure, put a ceiling on the size of individual units or prevent land being transferred out of family control. In spite of the rather envious comments of some American analysts (see for instance Raup 1972; Buttel 1982), intervention in the land markets of western Europe appears to have had a limited effect on farm size structure.

Land policies in the EC have been described as strongly nationalistic, identifying strongly with the aims and ideals of the family farm and displaying a remarkable readiness to interfere in the operation of the free market (Harrison 1982)[1]. France has made some of the most novel changes to influence the market in land towards certain ends and to facilitate inter-generational transfers of farm property. One example is the setting up of SAFER (Sociétés d'Aménagement Foncier et d'Etablissement Rural) to assist the growth of farms and the installation of new entrants to farming. The goal has been to promote a structure of owner-occupied, family-sized units (Harrison *et al.* 1982). Yet EC legislation relating to the ownership, tenure, operation and transfer of farms has been criticized for producing results often at odds with its acknowledged goals. Thus even in Denmark, where the ideals of a desirable farm structure have been most precisely specified, there were loopholes in the law aimed at maintaining a large population of small-scale, resident, owner-occupying farm operators. Urban families were able to move into farm properties under the pretext of the housewife

---

[1] This does not seem to hold in the UK. Most members of the Northfield Committee firmly rejected size limits on the ownership of farmland, action to restrict or control land prices or direct intervention to control farm rents.

declaring herself to be a main-occupation farmer (Harrison *et al.* 1982). More significantly, while national policies have generally been designed to maintain farm numbers, the funds devoted to them have been extremely modest in comparison to the sums expended on price control measures, which tend to have precisely the opposite effect.

To summarize, the predominant effect of post-war policy has been to encourage capital penetration of the industry and thus to assist the larger, more aggressive farm family business to grow at the expense of the weaker. Policies to intervene in the land market, unpopular in Britain, have been pursued elsewhere with varying degrees of success.

COUNTERVAILING POWER

If the family farm has not benefited as much as the larger non-family farm from state intervention in product markets, are there other means by which families operating farm businesses may seek to protect their own interests in the face of capitalist domination? Possibilities include forming pressure groups and associations, becoming active in democratic bodies with decision-making powers in the wider community, and co-operating with other farmers to secure some of the benefits of large-scale production.

The National Farmers' Union (NFU) is widely regarded as an outstandingly successful pressure group in defending the interests of British farmers. Inevitably there are conflicting interests within the membership – for example between cereal growers and livestock producers. Inevitably too it is felt in some quarters that the NFU is more sympathetic to the demands of larger farmers, who are more likely to hold executive positions within the organization. The NFU is very even-handed in its policy statements and it supports the continuation of the (smaller) family farm. Much of its success depends on its claim of speaking for all farmers with one voice. Thus formation of special interest groups such as the Farmers' Union of Wales or the Smallfarmers Association, which might campaign more vigorously on behalf of the small family-worked farm, is perceived by the NFU as a threat to be resisted.

Farmers and their wives/husbands can also seek to influence policies that affect their lives and livelihoods by playing an active role in local politics. They can be elected to parish, district or county councils. Newby and colleagues (1978) provide a graphic account of the place of East Anglian farmers within the local power structure, dwelling particularly on ways in which farmers and landowners influence housing and employment policy through their membership of local planning committees. Farmers can also seek to safeguard the market for their products by influencing consumers. The Women's Farming Union, whose members (whether farmers or farmers' wives) represent the interests of both producers and consumers, aims to act as a bridge between the two. The organization is very active in putting the consumer's case to the farmer, educating the consumer and trying to influence food and farming policy.

Any institutional changes that would enable small farms to reduce their costs or spread them over a larger volume of output could help to enhance their viability. Control over larger quantities of assets may be achieved by means of amalgamation, integration or co-operation. Yet while each approach might help the small business to survive, it could also undermine the relationship between the farm business and the farm family. Amalgamation means that the identity of the separate businesses is lost. With integration, whether vertical or horizontal, firms keep their identities and separate ownership but lose a measure of control. Formal co-operation, for example in the use of machinery, means commoditizing labour and machinery services and limiting the farmer's freedom to act, thus compromising what it means to be a family farmer. Restrictions of this nature may be the price for continuing to run a viable business.

Experiments in enforced collectivism have largely failed and co-operation can only work if it is entered into voluntarily. Governments in the market industrialized countries have promoted co-operation with varying degrees of enthusiasm. British farmers as a whole have never been in the forefront of co-operation in farm production, although nowadays economic expedience appears to be wearing down their resistance to machinery sharing. Co-operation over buying and selling is quite substantial in the UK. Small-scale initiatives may help to strengthen the position of family businesses in other spheres. An interesting example is the formation of local farm holiday groups among families involved in farm tourism. By joining forces they can make worthwhile economies in advertising and bulk buying, raise standards of accommodation and catering, promote recreational facilities available on other farms and avoid having to turn visitors away when one member is fully booked.

Experience of formal co-operation in some other European countries has been more positive, for example with machinery rings in Germany, relief labour co-operatives in The Netherlands, GAEC in France. On the whole small-scale farmers in Britain seem to prefer informal co-operation and mutual aid between two or three close relatives, neighbours or friends to formal, legally-binding schemes. The kind of farmer who is both economically and intellectually ready to commit himself to genuine group farming is, and may always be, in a small minority.

SUMMARY AND IMPLICATIONS

The demise of the family farm in market industrialized countries, long predicted by social scientists, is slow to manifest itself. Logic points to agriculture following the pattern of other industries in a capitalist economy, with control passing from the individual producer who owns the means of production, manages the labour process and provides the labour, to the owners of capital. The final outcome would be what Marx termed the real or direct subsumption of the labour process by capital, a separation of land, capital, business ownership, management and labour.

Two points emerging from the review of literature on the future of the family farm are that all interpretations are subjective to some degree and that 'structural' explanations do not do justice to the freedom of actors and the diversity of family responses. The weight of evidence shows that the direct takeover of family businesses by corporate, non-family capital has *not* been the dominant trend in market industrialized countries. Two sets of reasons account for the slow penetration of capital. Certain features of farming, such as its heavy reliance upon land and the fragmented nature of land ownership, make agriculture resistant to the incursion of outside capital, while other characteristics such as the high risk associated with biological processes, the slow circulation of capital and the low income elasticity of demand for food, render farming relatively unattractive to outside investors. Instead of widespread takeover of family farms by big business, the tendency is for industrial capital to permeate the production process more insidiously, by progressively transforming its inputs. The farmer retains considerable control of the labour process, co-ordinating and managing the integration of agro-industrial inputs of seeds, fertilizers, pesticides, feeds and so on with those elements like climate and soils, livestock and labour which have so far resisted the penetration of capital. (History has proved Chayanov to be more far-sighted than Marx, since vertical integration rather than horizontal concentration has been the predominant influence in western agriculture [Djurfeldt 1992].)

Even so, once the farmer begins to depend on purchased inputs, rented land or wage labour, he is drawn into the capitalist system where profit considerations become increasingly insistent in formulating objectives, setting priorities and reaching decisions. Survival of the farm family business depends on adaptation, so that present family farms only remotely resemble those of the past. Modern family farms are fewer and larger, depend more on the non-farm sector, continue to substitute capital for labour and are more likely to produce on contract under strictly specified conditions. The crux of the matter then is not whether families can continue to own and operate farms but to what extent they can be said to retain *control* of businesses which have come to rely so heavily on outside capital. (Although marketing farm products and implementing much of the technology used in production may involve fewer managerial decisions, farmers are having to buy more inputs than formerly and they need more operating capital and credit, which adds to the riskiness of their operations. While the family farmer is surrendering a measure of control over the production process on the farm, it could be argued that he is having to perform more complex managerial functions than before [Nikolitch 1969].)

Implications for the industries providing farm inputs and processing and marketing the produce are that while farms remain predominantly small, family-owned businesses, they will become increasingly dependent on those firms for technical, financial and management advice. As land becomes less significant in the production process, the prospect of direct takeover of farms by upstream and downstream firms comes closer.

Increasing dependence of modern farming on finance and industrial capital has implications for each facet of the farm family-farm business relationship. Family ownership of the means of production becomes increasingly dependent on and therefore undermined by borrowed capital. The converse of this is that by substituting capital for labour, the farm family is able to dispense with hired labour and iron out the peaks and troughs in the family labour supply over the family cycle, thereby consolidating its control over the business. Increasing capital requirements to enter farming serve to limit the number of families in the industry and reinforce the drive by successful, larger family farms to absorb the smaller. Most crucial of all, *control* of the family business is compromised as farm and family decisions must increasingly reflect the need to improve the return on capital.

Increasing capital concentration in agriculture has particular implications for inter-generational transfer, developed in Chapters 7 and 8. As capital replaces labour, the cost of entering farming at any given scale is rising but the scale necessary to provide a reasonable living is also rising. On 1980/1 figures, Furness (1982) suggested that while 74,000 UK farm businesses were capable of supporting their occupiers and generating enough income for necessary expansion, 80,000 were not. The increased size of farms and the capital investment needed to maintain them is at the root of the struggle for families to stay in full-time farming (Wilkening 1981a). The ideal of 'generational fragmentation' or establishing each child in a separate viable farm or a non-farm career has changed to one of consolidation and incorporating the next generation into an extended unit (Hutson 1987). In capitalist farming regions like north Humberside:

> ... there are now fewer opportunities for a newcomer to gain entry into the farming system. The number of small tenancies, which formerly provided the initial rungs on the farming ladder, has declined and the smaller, owner occupied farms tend to be swallowed up by the larger firms. Increasingly farming in east Yorkshire is characterized by large businesses and by the presence of several strong farming families whose influence spreads beyond the local parish.
>
> (Symes and Marsden 1983a: 100)

For policy-makers and society at large, the crucial issue is not whether we should save the family farm, but what types of farm family businesses we want to encourage and what the costs and benefits of the alternatives are. While Marxist interpretations tend to regard non-farm, industrial capital as the main threat to the family farm, agricultural economists stress the competition for land within the farming sector. We return to this theme in Chapter 9. Meanwhile, Chapters 4 to 8 examine the internal workings of the farm family business in more depth.

4

Objectives, Goals and Values in the Family Farm

Introduction

> When we begin to speak of 'the farm family' or even 'the family farm', we begin to recognize a complex personality. If any of us accept the statement that ... 'farming is not only a business but a life', we also accept the idea of complex motives and objects in economic activity.
>
> (Ashby 1953: 92)

Objectives are the mainspring of economic behaviour. The manager of a firm normally has a number of potentially conflicting objectives that he is trying to achieve through the business. Besides this, the firm typically has not one but several managers, each with their own set of preferred objectives for the business, raising again the possibility of conflict. In family businesses the managers are related, which has further implications for the way priorities are established and decisions taken.

Certain characteristics of the farm family business – the nature of the farming occupation itself, the close relationship between business and household, the combination of business ownership with management control and manual labour, the processes of inheritance and succession and the progression of the family cycle – influence the choice of objectives. This chapter draws together evidence from a number of studies to illustrate the kinds of motives that drive a farm family business, and speculates on the forces for change.

Objectives, Goals and Values

Objectives set the tone for business decisions and actions within the constraints of the resources available. A firm is inanimate and cannot have objectives, so in studying business behaviour it is the objectives of individuals that are relevant. In economic theory the relevant individual is the entrepreneur, defined as someone who specializes in taking judgemental decisions about the co-ordination of scarce resources (Casson 1982). Only individuals can take decisions; according to Casson's definition the entrepreneur is a person, not a team or committee or organization. If we accept this premise, it follows that a **family** can take decisions only through family members, who may well hold varying objectives. This raises the question of how priorities are established, conflicts resolved and decisions reached in a family business. The whole topic of decision-making in farm family businesses seems to be sparsely researched. It is a particularly difficult area to study empirically because the process is such a subtle one.

Objectives are ends or states in which the individual desires to be or things he wishes to accomplish. Typical objectives for a farm business might include maximizing profits or returns, controlling a larger business, reducing borrowing needs, having a tidy, well-kept farm or spending more time with the family. Goals are the tangible expression of objectives. Combining an objective with a target or aspiration level produces a goal. The objective of controlling a larger business, for example, might translate into the goal of doubling the acreage in twenty years.

The Theory of the Firm postulates the rational economic man who has the single objective of profit maximization and is always able to select the most appropriate means to attain this goal. Economic man is an ideal type, useful for purposes of argument but not encountered in real life. Not only do entrepreneurs pursue a number of different objectives, but the real world is so complex that the notion of perfect rationality must also be abandoned. More realistic is the principle of **bounded rationality** which visualizes the individual as 'satisficing' rather than optimizing. Instead of pursuing the unique solution which would maximize profits (or the attainment of some other single goal), he would select from among available alternatives a solution that was satisfactory with regard to his own scale of values, his perceptions and his subjective view of the situation (Simon 1957). It is possible to satisfy a number of inconsistent goals simultaneously providing the firm is satisficing rather than profit maximizing.

While objectives and goals give a sense of direction to a firm, the relationship between objectives and actions is bound to be complex. For one thing, scope for action is obviously limited by the resources available. Second, entrepreneurs may act differently because they have different perceptions of the situation arising from unequal access to information or varying interpretations of it (Casson 1982). The person's mental capacity therefore has a bearing on decision-making. Making due allowance for variations in resources and differences between entrepreneurs, it would still be naïve to expect a one-to-one relationship between goal and decision to act. Take for instance the decision to let a vacant farm cottage to summer visitors. The action might be taken in order to achieve any one of a number of objectives; to raise household income, provide an independent venture for the farmer's wife, make use of the dwelling until it is needed by the family, avoid the moral dilemma of hoarding empty property, discourage squatters ... Some of these goals are ends in themselves and others means to more distant ends such as financial security or family solidarity. Some goals, like keeping the cottage occupied, are highly specific while others, like the wife's need for an independent activity, could be pursued by different means.

Goals may change over the course of the family cycle and in response to events in the outside world. Values are a more permanent property of the individual, less likely to change with time and circumstances. Typical values are success, freedom, honesty, progress. Values are ends in themselves, pursued for their own sake. They are the criteria by which individuals select both goals and the means of attaining them. Values do not exist in isolation but are organized into hierarchies or **value orientations**. While most individuals probably subscribe to most of the dominant values of their culture for most of the time, it is how values are placed relative to one another that is the key. Knowing that certain farmers value hard work above leisure, for instance, would suggest how they might decide to act in a variety of situations.

The norms of the culture also play a role in determining individual objectives. They provide a frame of reference for both the choice of goals and the range of acceptable means for attaining them. Cultural norms can thus inhibit the pursuit of goals. In the example of the holiday cottage, the farmer might move in circles where the decision to maximize revenue from holiday lets would be applauded. On the other hand he might be put off by the thought that his diversified enterprise would be regarded as 'not proper farming'. Again, he might feel uncomfortable with the decision if he identified with, say, a church group which expressed concern about the housing needs of young people in the community.

To summarize so far, the conduct of a farm business is a function of objectives within the overall constraint of the resources available. The objectives of the firm, or rather those of the entrepreneur, can be arranged in order of priority. The rank ordering of objectives and their more tangible expression as goals and means, is a reflection of an underlying, relatively enduring value orientation. Cultural norms and intellectual capacity also influence the choice of goals and means.

OBJECTIVES OF THE FAMILY FIRM

Agriculture, as it is generally exercised in the western world, asks for a family; and its primary goal, also, is the maintenance of a family. When the family is lacking also the real goal of a farmer's life is lacking.

(Benvenuti 1961: 239)

If the objectives which steer the economic behaviour of individuals are complex, the objectives of a farm family business are likely to be more so because of the nature of the farming occupation itself and because of the characteristics of family businesses. In this section we consider how these two sets of influences might shape the objective function of the farm family business.

Objectives in the Farming Occupation

Farming is a distinctive occupation, involving as it does working outdoors in all weathers, often single-handed and in isolation, in contact with Nature and living things. Growing crops, raising animals, the seasonal variation and constant variety of the tasks, seeing the results of one's handiwork are some of the attractions of the job. The unpredictability of weather and disease make the business of farming an uncertain one. Some find the risk and gamble of farming stimulating, others a constant worry.

The unique nature of farming gives a certain flavour to the values and objectives of those pursuing the occupation which sets it apart from other types of family business. Indeed part of the uniqueness of farming does not lie in family relationships at all; employed farm managers and single farmers too exhibit a distinctive orientation to their work. As we will show, farmers as a whole tend to place a high value on aspects of the job which are intrinsic to farming itself, such as love of the land, working in the open air, variety in work, seeing things grow, taking a gamble. Instrumental rewards which follow from the work, such as financial returns, hours and working conditions, holidays and long-term prospects, are typically given a lower priority.

Other occupational groups too show distinctive value orientations related to their work. One possible explanation is that the family of origin influences the children's occupational choice and also the formation of appropriate work values, which is another way of saying that people really exercise little choice in their careers. This seems to hold true for many farmers who were born into farming families and apparently exercised little conscious choice in becoming farmers themselves. They were socialized into the role and *internalized* the values of farming (made them their own) at an early age. A second possibility is that people in a particular job will hold similar values through self-selection to that occupation. The idea of personal values steering individuals towards their chosen careers could apply to those entering farming from other backgrounds. A third explanation, not incompatible with the first two, is that a person's orientation to work develops as a result of experience on the job. Each job has its rewards and drawbacks and in order to remain satisfied, the worker will have to internalize values appropriate to the job and deny the importance of those which cannot be gratified. If farmers as a whole stress their enjoyment of the way of life and downplay the low and uncertain income, are they trying to convince others, and eventually themselves, that they have not failed in their occupation?

Objectives in a Family Business

If some objectives of farmers reflect the nature of the work itself, others are a direct result of the identification of the family with the firm. What are the implications for business objectives of ownership being combined with managerial control and handed on within the family and of family members living on the job and doing farm work?

The family lives on the business premises

In most cases the farm family lives on the farm, so objectives for the farm will almost inevitably become bound up with those of the family or household. One of the hardest tasks of the farmer is to develop an appropriate balance between the production (business) and consumption (way of life) activities of the firm (Boehlje and Eidman 1984). Increasing the family's level of living may mean deferring investment, a trade-off between current and future consumption. Some decisions do not contribute to the efficient production and may appear irrational from the business point of view, but are motivated by a desire to maximize utility from the consumption activities. Having a neat, well-kept farm, for instance, may contribute little to efficiency but be an important component in gaining acceptance and respect in the farming community. Purchasing some farm machinery could be regarded at least in part as satisfying a consumer need, in the sense that the owner derives utility directly from owning it as well as from using it. Planting an area of the farm with trees, a decision which the commercial manager would weigh up in terms of timber sales, the family farmer may justify in terms of logs for the winter and enhancing the view from the farmhouse.

Business ownership and management combined

The fact that business ownership in a family firm is combined with management control raises another set of issues. The farmer or the family is responsible for both day-to-day management and longer-term strategic decision-making. The farmer as manager may strive to increase current income while as landowner he is also concerned to maximize capital appreciation. The time horizon used in planning is longer for the family business manager and in formal terms, the implicit discount rate that he uses will be lower. He may therefore quite rationally embark on projects that the employed manager would not.

Regular labour supplied by the family

In a family business much of the labour is likely to be supplied by members of the family. Family and hired labour inputs on farms may respond to different incentives, with profit maximizing behaviour conflicting with family and leisure considerations.

One consequence of labour and management being supplied by the same family is that decisions about labour allocation have family as well as business implications. In the first place, it may be the entrepreneur's lack of skill in recruitment and selection that encourages him to use family rather than hired labour.

> The entrepreneur knows his family much better than he knows the rest
> of the labour market. Thus a man may have more confidence in
> teaming up with his own children than he would with other people.
> Again he may prefer to use his wife as secretary than to recruit outside
> help. The advantages are particularly great if the labour of other family
> members would otherwise be underutilized ...
>
> (Casson 1982: 304–5)

This is a crucial point, for so far as household income is concerned, the opportunity cost of family labour may be regarded as the wage that could be earned in other employment off the farm or, where no alternatives exist, as the value of unemployment benefit (see Chapter 5). To put it another way, the entrepreneur may attach a lower value to objectives like maximizing income or raising productivity than to keeping himself and other family members occupied.

A drawback for the business is that the range of skills available within the family may be very small. Welfare objectives such as providing useful employment for children can only be pursued so long as the business remains solvent. From the family's viewpoint, labour may be exploited. Rising expectations for wealth make it harder to reconcile the needs and objectives of the farmer and the business with those of other family members:

> As long as a farmer owns 100 per cent equity in his business he may
> set his own objectives. He can work as long and as hard as he likes for
> as little financial reward as he likes. The limiting factor is the extent to
> which other family members are willing to accept his objectives.
>
> (Reid 1974: 55)

Another problem for the farm family business is that the farmer has to provide both management and labour. Management can be regarded as the key determinant of the economic success of a business and the relative emphasis the manager places on it as against manual labour has a direct bearing on profits.

> True management as a planning and decision-making activity, does not involve physical exertion ... it involves mental effort almost entirely ... The greatest returns (economic) in farming are to be had from 'brain activity' rather than 'brawn activity'.
>
> (Heady and Jensen 1954)

Although farmers claim they are continuously involved in managing their businesses, financial management is often left to be dealt with after more 'pressing' work is done. This may reflect an older system of values associated with the Protestant Ethic where manual work comes to be seen as an end in itself. Belief in the moral virtue of hard physical work can influence the decision-making process of the farm operator. A high value is placed on achieving goals through manual labour, success is judged in terms of working hard and the farmer would always think of hard work as the method of solving problems. Taken too far, the value placed on physical work conflicts with other goals of rational economic action, resulting in lower productivity.

Inter-generational transfer

The fact that the farm business may have been inherited and the expectation that it will again be transferred within the family, raises another set of issues (see also Chapter 7). The prime objective for many family businesses is not profit maximization but succession, the desire to maintain control and to pass on a secure and sound business to the next generation. For many family firms the strategic time-scale is inter-generational, so short-term profitability might be sacrificed to longer-term growth. For the family firm, a policy which emphasizes growth as the primary objective in the short-run, in this case measured in decades, may be quite consistent with the objective of long-run profit maximization, where the long run is measured in generations. Farmers with children coming into the business may be prepared to take on heavy financial commitments (e.g. to buy more land) at a time when non-family farms might be consolidating rather than expanding.

The transfer of wealth and farm property is one of the chief incentives for building up the business and accumulating capital, affecting not just day-to-day decisions but also long-term planning (Lifran 1988). Farmers who inherited their businesses have a particular interest in keeping the farm in the family and may impose quite heavy moral pressure on one child to carry on the family tradition. Children can provide both an incentive and a means to expand the business. Not all farmers will, however, have children who are willing and able to take over the farm and to whom the skills and values associated with good farming can be handed down. Without their interest and involvement there may be little to drive an ageing couple into expansion. On the other hand, having children might also discourage an entrepreneur from taking risks. One bachelor farmer in the Pembrokeshire study, who had built up a sizeable business, admitted that he could never have taken such risks if he had had dependants to consider. In other words, family businesses can be more entrepreneurial than other firms, but equally less so when family commitments discourage them from taking risks (Hutson 1987).

The goal of inter-generational transfer can have a far-reaching effect on the conduct of the farm business. In the Corn Belt of the American Midwest, Salamon has identified contrasting farming patterns relating to ethnic differences in landholding and farm inheritance practices. A 'yeoman' pattern is associated with German immigrants and an 'entrepreneurial' style with Yankees. Each pattern embodies an over-arching goal for family and farm. A yeoman farmer desires to reproduce a viable farm and at least one farmer in each generation. To meet this goal, yeomen prefer to own the land they farm and to expand family operations only enough to accommodate children wanting to farm. Expansion is carried out conservatively, for yeomen avoid financial risks that could endanger family continuity. By contrast a Yankee regards the farm as a business that should optimize short-run financial returns. Expansion is governed more by the entrepreneur's managerial skills and capital than by family concerns. Yankees are more willing to take risks to achieve their goals. Their farms tend to be larger and more specialized, as compared with the smaller, diversified holdings of yeomen (Salamon 1985a, 1985b, 1988; Salamon and Davis-Brown 1986).

The family cycle

Reliance on family labour makes the farm family business vulnerable to fluctuations in its workforce over the course of the family cycle (Nalson 1968). Business objectives too are likely to change over the stages of the cycle, reflecting the ageing of the farm operator, variations in labour supply and the salience of family needs at the different stages.

In the early phase of the family cycle, typically with a young couple and no children beyond school-leaving age, consumption demands of the family will be high and although the parents are likely to be young and energetic, only their labour will be available for work on or off the farm. This stage typically coincides with the establishment and growth phase of the farm, making for intense competition between the consumption needs of the family and the investment objectives of the business.

High family demands in the middle phase coincide with an increase in family labour. If family labour was sufficient to run the farm in the early phase, it could be in surplus by the middle phase. This is the time when objectives of family solidarity may conflict with desires of younger members to escape from parental authority, savour their independence and increase their individual earnings. Depending on the state of the labour market and the availability of capital, family members may seek off-farm work, develop other enterprises within the framework of the farm business or merely remain at home to avoid being unemployed.

The late phase of the family cycle is likely to be marked by lower family needs coupled with declining vigour of the parents. Age alone could spell declining mental and physical energy and growing reluctance to take risks. Older farmers may be more concerned with minimizing losses than with maximizing profits. Internal capital rationing is expected to be more prevalent, the tendency to save being stronger than the urge to invest and expand. Leisure and alternative activities too may be given higher priority, farmers being motivated to reduce working hours and make life easier.

The presence or absence of a successor may have more influence upon business objectives and farm performance than the farmer's age. A farmer with a successor has a 'generational stake' in that successor which provides a constant incentive for forward planning and expansion. A farmer without a successor has none, and in old age may begin to run down the business and consume capital, if only to reduce the workload. For farmers with successors, the late phase of one family gives way to the early phase of the next. This is a time when objectives of the new generation become superimposed on the old with the potential for discord. Abrupt shifts in investment and land use could result from successors assuming control and pushing through changes. Elderly farmers without successors, on the other hand, have little incentive to expand or even maintain production (Potter and Lobley 1992).

The succession effect is expected to show up as the farmer approaches old age, but research by Potter and Lobley seems to suggest that its impact stretches much further back in the family cycle. Farmers without successors may not only behave differently in old age from those with, but could be managing businesses that have developed along different trajectories in the past. According to this model, there is constant feedback throughout the career of the farmer, with decisions made early in the family cycle with a view to the likelihood of succession acting as a constraint on decisions made later in life. The way capital is accumulated and maintained, for example, depends partly on the probability of its being passed on to a successor.

Summarizing this section, both the nature of farming and the features of a family-run enterprise have implications for farm business objectives. Farmers are expected to bring a distinctive value orientation to their work, emphasizing intrinsic aspects of the work more than instrumental rewards. The close association of household and workplace make it difficult to draw the line between production and consumption. Combining ownership with management and manual labour in the same family makes for confusion when family members have to allocate their time and energies between several roles, and conflict where roles are allocated on the basis of seniority or gender. Inheritance and succession can be a spur to business growth, the probability of succession influencing decisions from quite an early stage in the family cycle and masking any ageing effect. The next section examines the empirical evidence on farmers' objectives.

EVIDENCE ON FARMERS' OBJECTIVES

> Objectives in this context are never likely to be in the singular and are seldom likely to be simple. There will always be conflicts and compromises, and profit, important as it will always be, will have to be balanced with other requirements.
>
> (Giles and Stansfield 1990: 19)

The primary aim of many family businesses is not to maximize profits but to maintain control and pass on a secure and sound business to the next generation. Autonomy, independence, survival and succession thus mingle with the more orthodox economic objectives of maximizing profit or returns in the short or longer run. This section draws on empirical evidence to document the breadth of farmers' objectives[1] and to illustrate the way in which these objectives are shaped by the farming occupation and the interaction of family and business. Nearly all the empirical work focuses on the objectives of 'the farmer' or business principal who is usually assumed to be male. Whether other family members hold different objectives, and how conflicting interests are resolved, remains an unexplored area needing further research.

Goals and Values in the Farming Occupation

Studies of farmers' goals and values generally indicate that farmers place a high value on 'being one's own boss'. Intrinsic aspects of the job typically come higher up the list than instrumental objectives. For example, when a hundred Cambridgeshire farmers were asked to rate sixteen aspects of farming in order of importance (Gasson 1973), the top six objectives were:

- doing the work you like;

---

[1]For a discussion of techniques of assessing farm family values, see the pioneering work of Wilkening (1954). For a more comprehensive and up-to-date account of methodology, see Perkin (1992).

- independence;
- making a reasonable living in the present;
- meeting a challenge, achieving an objective;
- leading a healthy, open-air life;
- expanding the business.

In similar vein, one hundred Berkshire farmers were asked to rate thirty-six objectives in farming. 'Be my own boss' received the greatest number of 'very important' ratings. Next in importance came 'Live in the country', 'Keep my loans and mortgages below 50 per cent of my net worth' and 'Maintain my family's standard of living at its current level' (Perkin 1992). When a sample of farm managers were asked to describe what aspects of their job they liked best, 'being one's own boss' once again topped the list (Giles and Mills 1971).

Another survey questioned a large number of English farmers who had contemplated retirement about what they would miss most in farming. Over a third of respondents mentioned some intrinsic aspect of the work, far outnumbering mentions of instrumental factors, such as income, hours and working conditions. The three most popular aspects were working with animals (mentioned by 16 per cent), managing one's own business or being one's own boss (15 per cent) and being usefully occupied (14 per cent). Financial returns from farming were rarely mentioned as something respondents would miss (Errington and Tranter 1991).

Similar results have been obtained in other countries. A study of 220 small-scale farmers from Colorado, Hawaii, Montana, New Mexico and Oregon underlined the importance of intrinsic objectives. When asked why they were farming, four fifths of the farmers indicated that one of the reasons was to live on a farm and almost half regarded this as their most important goal. A quarter of them included the objective of acquiring wealth but only 2 per cent said this was their primary purpose in farming. Aspects of farm life most preferred were independence (41 per cent), farm work itself (20 per cent), a clean environment, peace and quiet (Young 1984).

It could be argued that these studies were tapping farmers' and managers' likes and dislikes rather than their goals and objectives. As suggested earlier, low scores attached to financial returns from farming might mean not that profit is not important to farmers and managers but that they do not enjoy it in large measure. (A counter-argument would be that likes and dislikes reflect underlying values, the criteria by which means and ends are selected.) In a survey in the West Midlands, Robinson (1984) expressly asked farmers about their business *objectives*. The top three proved to be:

- to make sufficient profit;
- to be good at what one does and develop personal skills;
- to have and maintain a good, contented workforce.

These represented the broad areas of financial, personal and social objectives, indicating that the farmers were trying to achieve a good balance in their working lives.

Classifying Objectives

Long lists of objectives are difficult to handle and to comprehend, so some kind of classification is called for. Objectives should be grouped together if they have the same or similar consequences for behaviour; for instance controlling a larger business and increasing net worth. Using principal components analysis, Perkin (1992) grouped the objectives of her Berkshire farmers under three headings – 'monetary', 'lifestyle' and 'independence'. Reference has been made elsewhere to **intrinsic** and **instrumental**, **social** and **personal** goals. Box 4.1 lists a number of farming objectives under these headings.

Box 4.1. Objectives in the farming occupation. Source: Gasson 1973

Instrumental
- maximizing income
- making a satisfactory income
- securing income for the future
- avoiding losses
- increasing net worth
- controlling a larger business
- providing pleasant working conditions – hours, surroundings

Intrinsic
- enjoying the work itself – individual tasks, variety etc.
- pursuing a healthy, outdoor life
- purposeful activity, value in hard work
- independence – free from supervision, free to organize time in a variety of situations

Social
- belonging to the farming community
- gaining recognition, prestige as a good farmer
- creating and maintaining good relations with workers
- continuing the family tradition
- spending more time with the family

Personal
- exercising special abilities and aptitudes
- chance to be creative and original
- gaining self-respect for doing a worthwhile job
- meeting a challenge, achieving an objective
- self-fulfilment and personal growth

Variation by Size of Business

If farmers' objectives vary in any systematic way according to personal or farm characteristics, this information could be used by those who wish to influence farmer behaviour. The salience of intrinsic as opposed to instrumental, personal or social values in farming shows some variation according to farm size. When East Anglian farmers were grouped according to size of business measured in standard man days, intrinsic aspects of farming were generally regarded as more important on smaller, family-worked farms, instrumental and personal aspects on larger farms and social attributes in the middle of the range. Looking in more detail at instrumental objectives, 'expanding the business' was the highest goal for the largest businesses while operators of smaller farms were more concerned with 'making a reasonable living' and 'making sure of income for the future'. Only the smallest firms rated stability higher than growth while the preference for growth over stability increased progressively with size (Gasson 1974b).

As we have seen, one of the most highly-valued aspects of the farming occupation is independence; 41 per cent of small farmers in the US study placed this above all other attributes. But independence means different things to different farmers. It can mean freedom from supervision, freedom from employees, freedom to make decisions, freedom to set the pace of work. Some of these freedoms reflect the fact that business ownership and management, and probably manual labour too, are vested in the same person. Other aspects of independence such as freedom to set the pace of work, are intrinsic to the work itself and are valued as highly by employed farm managers as by owner operators; 37 per cent of Giles and Mills' farm managers regarded 'being your own boss' as the best aspect of their job.

The smaller the farm, the more value tends to be placed on intrinsic aspects of farming and particularly on independence. Giles and Mills found that managers of smaller businesses were the most likely to say that being one's own boss was the most rewarding aspect of the job, whether size was measured in acres, number of employees or tenant capital. Comparing East Anglian farmers with small and larger businesses, Gasson (1973) found that 43 per cent of the smaller farm operators, but only 14 per cent of those with larger farms, regarded independence as the main attraction of farm life. More appealing to the larger farmers were personal values like achievement, creativity and pride of ownership, instrumental and social values. Why independence appeals so much to the small farmer is not clear. Operating a simple business, he may feel less trammelled by regulations than the labour-employing farmer. Another possibility is that the alternatives for the small farmer would mean employment under supervision and a loss of control, whereas the large-scale farmer might compare his present occupation with running another business or an executive position in which he would still enjoy a large measure of autonomy.

Evidence of Business–Family Relationships

Living on the job, having the family working together and transferring the farm business from father to son are potential sources of motivation. There is little evidence to show whether farmers value these aspects highly or not. Cambridgeshire farmers ranked 'working close to home and family' only tenth in a list of sixteen attributes of farming, below most of the intrinsic and personal aspects and those relating to a satisfactory and secure income. 'Following in the family tradition' came three places lower. When the sample was split according to size of business, however, 'working close to home and family' rose to fourth place for the middle-sized farmers but was ranked last of all by those with large businesses. 'Following in the family tradition' was also ranked higher by those with middle-sized farms, suggesting that this group values belonging to the immediate social group, the family. Social values which appeal more to large-scale farmers include 'belonging to the farming community' and 'earning the respect of workers'; these are values relating to the wider community (Gasson 1973, 1974b).

Objectives and Age

Earlier it was suggested that objectives could change over the course of the family cycle and a number of studies have investigated the effect of the farmer's age on objectives and values. The only consistent finding seems to be that older farmers are more risk averse than younger ones (Perkin 1992). It is debatable whether older workers emphasize security because they are nearing retirement or because they were socialized before the advent of the Welfare State when security was valued more highly than it is today. In other words age-related differences in value orientations could reflect stage in life cycle or a more fundamental change in values resulting from education and changing economic and social conditions (the so-called 'vintage effect').

There is just a suggestion that older farmers are more conscious of the values held by the community while younger ones are more motivated by income and personal aspirations. In the West Midlands study, the importance of financial objectives declined progressively with age while intrinsic and social goals played a more prominent role (Robinson 1984). Among East Anglian farmers, the overall weight given to instrumental values was about the same but while under-45s stressed the intrinsic/personal aspects of farming (enjoyable work, independence, challenge), the older farmers attached more importance to social aspects like belonging to the farming community and self-respect (Gasson 1974a).

In this section we have presented empirical evidence to illustrate the way farmers approach the business of farming. Typically they attach a high value to aspects of the job intrinsic to the work itself, such as an outdoor life and growing things, and to the autonomy of owning and running a small business. Instrumental objectives tend to rank lower, with more emphasis given to earning a reasonable living and security than to maximizing profits or growth. The importance of working with the family and belonging to the farming community appear to be valued highly by middle-scale farmers, the custodians of local farming traditions.

DEVELOPING IDEAL TYPES

The empirical approach described so far has been to identify objectives in the farm family business, to score them according to their relative importance and to look for systematic differences in scores between categories of farmers (small-scale versus large-scale, younger versus older and so on). An alternative approach is to look for common characteristics among individuals who share similar objectives. Social scientists have used the latter approach to study the orientation to work of persons in certain occupations. For example Stanworth and Curran (1981) developed a typology of small firm entrepreneurs. The prime focus of the **classical entrepreneur** is on earnings and profit, though profit maximization is by no means his only goal. The **artisan** identity focuses on intrinsic satisfactions such as autonomy at work, status and the satisfaction of producing goods or services. The **manager** identity centres on the recognition by significant others, especially those outside the firm, of his achievements. The managerial type of entrepreneur is particularly concerned with security and a major objective is to

Table 4.1. Hypothesized value relationships and functions in economic behaviour.

Function	Rational	Non-rational
Goal orientation	Emphasis on profit maximization	Occupational success defined by non-economic criteria
Cognitive or evaluative aspect	Universalistic, instrumental, scientific	Particularistic, expressive, traditional
Role definition	Emphasis on management functions, mental process	Belief in physical work as an end in itself
Social reference	Independent, individualistic, neutral	Normative, responsible, affective
Action and responsibility bearing	Risk preference	Risk aversion

Source: Hobbs *et al.* 1964: 64

Table 4.2. Contrasting farm management styles.

High profit orientation	Lower profit orientation	Source
Entrepreneur	Cautious strategist	Olsson (1988)
Accumulator	Sufficer	Pomeroy (1988)
Entrepreneur	Yeoman	Salamon and Davis-Brown (1986)
Financial manager	Individualist worker	
Productivity increaser	Lifestyler	Fairweather (1987)
Extensifier	Intensifier	van der Ploeg (1985)

Source: Fairweather and Keating 1990: 3

ensure that his children will receive the benefits of his enterprise. The entrepreneur's self-perception in terms of these three identities could help to determine the rate of growth of the firm. The artisan, the classical entrepreneur and so on are ideal types like the farm family business, designed to aid understanding but not necessarily encountered in real life. Ideal types can be developed from theory, synthesized on the basis of observation or derived more systematically using techniques like factor analysis. A theoretical approach was used by Hobbs *et al.* (1964), who related values and attitudes in farmers' economic behaviour suggested by the literature to those of the ideal type of economically rational action (Table 4.1).

A similar approach was taken by Fairweather and Keating (1990), who classified farmers' management styles (goal orientations) along this dimension. A common theme of management styles in the first column of Table 4.2 is the emphasis given to business profitability. These farmers use advanced management techniques, are flexible and responsive, spend time planning, are tuned into markets and actively participate in them, are businesslike, willing to borrow and likely to invest off the farm. Those in the second column are also motivated by profit but way-of-life considerations are also rated highly. These farmers are cautious, avoiding risk where possible. They maintain a more self-sufficient operation, seeking increases in production via the craft of husbandry.

In their own empirical study of New Zealand farmers, Fairweather and Keating used factor analysis to identify management styles. They distinguished three types, each with distinct goals, strategies and criteria of success. The **dedicated producer** thrives on farm work and achieving a high-quality product via careful planning and financial management, contributing to the farm and being the best farmer he can. In the sample these tended to be young, male and full-time farmers. The **flexible strategist** is attuned to a wider context and chooses to act in response to her environment with understanding rather than fear. She emphasizes effective marketing, pursues off-farm activities, seeks to reduce the work-load and diversify assets. Production, work and development are not the keys to success as for dedicated producers, but careful marketing combined with family and lifestyle, acknowledging the fact that decisions affect both farm and family. Compared with the first group they tend to be older and are more likely to be female. The **lifestyler** places a high value on working with Nature. Besides environmental awareness, working with the family and sustaining the lifestyle are important. This type was rather above average age and included more part-timers and more horticulturalists.

Studies using a single criterion tend to emphasize arbitrary distinctions between types; for instance entrepreneurs are seen as denying the importance of family goals which some opposing type values highly. Such a conclusion is likely to be a result of the method rather than an accurate reflection of farmers' management styles. As Fairweather and Keating pointed out, all farmers value family goals to some degree but they give meaning to them in different ways. Comparing the three types, familiar concepts have subtle differences in meaning. While all respondents would agree that the family was important to their farming, for the dedicated producer this would mean that the family should be involved on the farm, for the flexible strategist it would mean enjoying off-farm pursuits with the family and for the lifestyler it would mean the family working together to share and enjoy the lifestyle.

Similarly it would be misleading to suggest that some types are business-oriented and others are not, for these results show that there is more than one way of pursuing business goals. Farmers with family and lifestyle goals can still be top producers and vice versa. The researchers also point out that while some studies of management style have identified the type most likely to survive in the long run, their results suggest that more than one type is capable of adapting to change and that survival strategies may also vary. Besides aiding our understanding, this approach could have practical applications in extension and advisory work. The Yankee responds to commercial arguments while the yeoman farmer is swayed by considerations of security and family continuity. The dedicated producer thrives on work and the flexible strategist seeks to reduce the workload but within their frames of reference, each can pursue economically rational ends.

FARMERS' OBJECTIVES UNDER CAPITALISM

Farmers want to both modernize aspects of their farming while also clinging to some traditional values. The resultant partial embracing of capitalist relations may produce a tension in the very foundations of what it means to be a family farmer.

(Pile 1990: 177)

Values were described earlier as a relatively enduring characteristic of the individual, but it would be misleading to suggest that values never change. Certainly goals and objectives, the more immediate and tangible expression of values, are subject to change. Ways in which business objectives may change over the course of the family cycle have been discussed. Business objectives also need to change in the short run in response to market signals and developments in the wider economic and political environment. By way of illustration, one of the East Anglian surveys conducted in the early 1970s noted that younger farmers placed more emphasis on expanding the business while older farmers were more concerned with security and avoiding debt (Gasson 1974a). Yet the Berkshire farmers interviewed by Perkin in 1990 attached a low value to borrowing. 'Keep my loans and mortgages below 50 per cent of net worth' was rated third in overall importance out of 36 objectives. Two other objectives related to the avoidance of borrowing, 'Make mortgage and loan repayments on time' and 'Avoid using borrowed funds for the farm business' also appeared in the top half of the list whilst three 'growth' objectives – 'Buy more land', 'Rent more land' and 'Develop a farm business which will grow to employ more people' – were relegated to the bottom. Borrowing to expand the business, promoted as rational economic behaviour in the early 1970s, probably appears as dysfunctional for successful farming today as it did in the 1930s.

Farmers may therefore have to fine-tune their objectives in response to cyclical changes within the farm household, business cycles and fluctuations in product markets. But the underlying, long-term trend is for farming to become more business oriented, for reasons which were discussed in Chapter 3. This has important implications for the farm family:

A motivational crisis may result from the increasing separation of the idea of the farm and the idea of the family ... thus the family will be less and less a part of farming, even while the family continues to provide the labour.

(Pile 1990: 177)

One consequence of 'separating the idea of the farm and the idea of the family' may be a hardening of attitudes towards employing family members. The greater the economic pressure on the business, the greater the obligation on the family to ensure that only 'suitable' family members come into it. Succession can no longer be based on kinship alone. Criteria for judging members of the family have to embrace wider ideologies such as achievement motivation. Family relationships may limit the extent to which the farmer can rationalize his business along narrowly commercial lines but the limits are being pushed further towards the business end of the spectrum. The idea of making family workers redundant, once unthinkable, may now be seen in some circumstances as regrettable but inevitable. To borrow an example from the fishing industry, many Ulster fisherman resist the kinship obligation of giving jobs to kinsmen since the social consequences of firing a relative who proves unsuitable are far greater than the sense of offence felt by kinsmen who are not offered jobs in the first place (Byron and Dilley 1989).

The need to delegate decision-making powers can also bring family values into conflict with modern business principles. As the business grows and decision-making becomes more complex, the farmer may be obliged to delegate. Choosing the right person is much more critical in recruiting decision-makers than routine employees, so it makes sense to promote family members to decision-making posts and recruit lower quality labour from outside. The drawback with this strategy is that the pool of decision-makers is very limited and family members may not have the necessary skills. 'In this case the entrepreneur's ability to transcend the bounds of his family may be crucial to the continued success of the firm' (Casson 1982: 305).

As with families, so with individual farmers, the objectives and values which guide business behaviour are inevitably being pushed in the direction of economic rationality. Using external sources of capital, for example, is no longer a matter of morality but of expedience. As one young farmer put it, 'To my grandfather borrowing was immoral; to my father it became a necessity; to me it is normal' (Hutson 1987). Values like independence and hard work too may have become less functional for business success and survival. Levels of borrowing among Berkshire farmers were negatively correlated with the value attached to independence (Perkin 1992). A study of Indiana farmers concluded that the value of hard work had become traditionalized but was no longer necessarily associated with rational economic behaviour. High-work farmers spent longer than their neighbours on farm chores, but without any improvement in financial results; in fact their socio-economic status and the condition of their farm buildings was judged by interviewers to be lower than that of other farmers. The rational modern farmer may be one who places less emphasis on physical work. Farmers placing a lower value on work for its own sake tended to be younger, better educated and held more positions of leadership in farm organizations. As such they were in a better position to determine the future course of farming (Goldstein and Eichhorn 1961).

The Protestant Work Ethic held man to be directly responsible for his own fortunes. The Indiana farmers placing the highest value on work were more likely than others to decide for themselves when to purchase a car, what kind of machinery to buy and so on. The rational modern farmer may not feel such a strong compulsion to rely upon himself, and may make better decisions as a consequence. Sons are often better informed about machinery matters than their fathers, for instance (Hastings 1984). Sacrificing some independence in favour of group action, for example by sharing machinery, may enable the business to survive and the way of life to be sustained.

Pressures for change in the farm business can also arise from rising expectations and aspirations of family members in line with the rest of society. Wives, for instance, may desire recognition for the work they do, an independent income, responsibility either within the family business or in a separate career, a theme we take up in Chapter 6. Sons coming into the business may expect a standard of living, prospects and a measure of responsibility comparable with that of their contemporaries making their way in other occupations. Rising material expectations and desire for greater autonomy can put a strain on the economic viability of the farm at a time of generally low and falling profitability. On the other hand, efforts to contain the financial needs and demands of the family may put intolerable pressures on family loyalty.

To summarize, objectives and value orientations may be a relatively stable component of the farm family business but they are not immutable. Clinging to outmoded values and objectives in the face of changing economic, social and cultural forces in the wider world can spell the demise of the family farm.

OBJECTIVES OF OTHER FAMILY MEMBERS

The farm family business is owned and controlled by a family but almost all the studies of goals and values in farming have focused on a single actor, 'the farmer', with very little attention paid to the objectives of other family members. Decisions are taken by entrepreneurs but the family is not an entrepreneur. Therefore it needs to be asked whether family members have different objectives for the conduct of the family business. If so, how are differences resolved and priorities established?

In theory, other members of the family may well hold different objectives for the business from the principal farmer/head of household. Behavioural economists have pointed out that most firms have not one but several managers who will be unlikely to share the same objectives. Each will be likely to promote the interests of his own department within the firm over that of others (Cyert and March 1963). Where decisions must be taken, this leads to conflict unless some prior strategy has been taken to avert it. Does this also hold true where the managers are husband and wife or father and son? Little seems to be known about objectives of fathers and sons. Where farmers' wives have been questioned, discussion has usually been confined to their likes and dislikes in farming, leaving unexplored the minefield of conflicting objectives and power relations within farm families.

What wives say they like and dislike about farming, a reflection of their underlying values, seems to vary according to their role in the business relative to the husband's role. In one study, **working farmwives** who worked regularly on small farms with their husbands but as assistants rather than business principals, indicated that the most satisfying aspects of farm life were the work itself and independence. These are the aspects which male farmers also emphasize, a reflection perhaps of good teamwork among such couples. **Women farmers** who ran farms alone or jointly with their husbands, also valued farm work and independence but laid more stress than working farmwives on personal relationships – with workers or within the farming community. For **farm housewives** on larger farms who did not normally do manual work, farm life meant the pleasures of living in the countryside and enjoying the peace, quiet and privacy (Gasson 1980a). Another study found that the aspects of farm life which appealed to farm housewives most were the satisfactions of farming and living in the country, bringing up children on a farm and being involved in the husband's business. Family concerns were therefore more prominent for them than for the typical farmer (Buchanan *et al.* 1982).

Opinions on the worst aspects of farming also differed between the three groups of women. Women farmers were more likely to mention specific farm tasks (early rising, mechanical breakdowns, hoeing) and also problems in human relations (difficult workers, being let down by contractors). Working farmwives hated winter and bad weather because it meant having to work in wet and cold conditions. For women farmers bad weather meant that essential farm work was delayed, while farm housewives complained of mud in the house and being cut off in the snow. The closer the working role of the wife to that of the husband, the more likely they seem to be to share the same likes and dislikes in the farming occupation, implying a measure of agreement on objectives for the business. On the other hand, husbands being tied to the farm, working long and irregular hours was seen as a serious problem for farm housewives. For these women, most of the dislikes came down to the fact that the boundaries between home and farm, work and leisure were so blurred – whether this referred to mud and straw in the house, uncertainties over mealtimes or the difficulty of taking family holidays (Buchanan *et al.* 1982).

A more rigorous attempt to compare the business and family goals of farmers and wives was made by Wilkening (1954), a pioneer in the study of farm family relationships. When a sample of 170 Wisconsin farm operators and their wives were asked to respond to hypothetical situations involving a choice between farm and family goals, there was a high degree of consensus. On average husbands and wives agreed in two thirds of their responses. In some questions the wives favoured family goals more than husbands did; for example wives were more likely to encourage a son to attend a farm course even if it left the parents short-handed, although most husbands gave the same reply. If it came to a choice between putting new water bowls in the barn and having a bathroom in the house, more wives than husbands would put the bathroom first but again, a majority of wives agreed with husbands that the farm should come first.

In a later study, Wilkening and Bharadwaj (1966) asked a sample of nearly 500 Wisconsin farmers and their wives how they would use an unexpected windfall. Once again the extent of agreement between couples was striking. As expected, more husbands (36 per cent) than wives (29 per cent) would spend it on farm improvements and more wives (27 per cent) than husbands (17 per cent) would put it into the household. The top choice for both husbands and wives, however, was to spend the windfall for the family (holidays, education, trips). As many as 60 per cent of couples agreed upon the order of priority, with least consensus about household expenditures. In a comparative study, German farm wives placed much higher priority on household and much lower on family goals (Figure 4.1), possibly reflecting cultural differences between the two societies (Wilkening and Lupri 1965).

An interesting discovery in the Wisconsin study was that husbands who gave the family or household priority over the farm tended to have higher incomes, while the opposite was true for wives. This suggests that farmers focus on family and household needs only when farm needs are less urgent.

Use of windfall

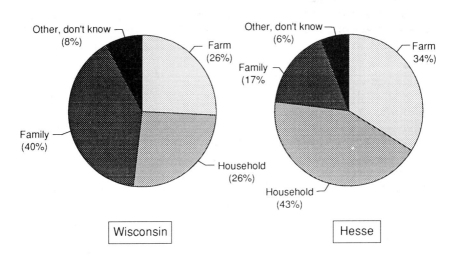

Figure 4.1. Goal priorities for American and German farm wives. Source: Wilkening and Lupri 1965

For many wives, however, extra money is seen as an opportunity to satisfy family and household needs which have been postponed.

The strength of aspirations in farm, household and family areas was measured in the Wisconsin study by asking husbands and wives separately how hard their family was trying to attain a list of goals compared with other families they knew. Husbands' aspirations tended to be stronger than wives', not only for farm and community goals but also for the household and the family. The authors suggested that the (male) head of household who has the major responsibility for its material support also feels the greatest pressure to raise its economic and social standards, and is therefore more likely to feel dissatisfied with current levels of attainment. Wives were seen as being more passive, or realistic, in accepting things the way they are rather than wanting to change them (Wilkening and Bharadwaj 1966).

The importance of wives' objectives for the farm business was under-lined in another Wisconsin study (Wilkening and Guerrero 1969). Adoption of improved farm practices was higher when both husbands and wives had high aspirations for the farm, than when only one had high aspirations. The hypothesis that adoption will be high if the husband's aspiration level is high but the wife's low, was generally not supported. For the average farm family, the wife's aspirations appear to be as crucial for the adoption of improved practices as the husband's. Although rather dated now, this is an important study in that it highlights the positive influence which farmers' wives may have on decision-making and performance of the farm business.

COPING WITH MULTIPLE OBJECTIVES

The need to find balance among multiple objectives in farming is now well established.

(Romero and Rehman 1984)

So far we have established that the farm family business is steered by not one but many objectives, which are held with varying degrees of intensity by different family members. If multiple objectives are a fact of business life, then strategies for coping with objectives, establishing priorities and resolving conflicts are an important part of the entrepreneur's role. Giles and Stansfield (1990) offer very practical advice to the farm manager on setting priorities and coping with stress but most farm management specialists are more concerned with the theoretical implications and with handling multiple objectives in decision-making models.

It is the objective of profit which is most likely to conflict with other goals. When Robinson asked his West Midlands farmers about the actual conflicts they experienced, no less than 77 per cent mentioned maximizing profitability. Maximizing profits will almost always be incompatible with other objectives but if the firm is satisficing rather than maximizing, it may be able to satisfy them all simultaneously. Some economists maintain that in principle all farmers aim at profit maximization, suggesting that many 'non-economic' goals can be redefined as economic ones. For example the goal of convenience in farming, a non-economic goal, could be expressed as a minimization of effort, the value of which could be expressed by the utility of the leisure time obtained (Petrini 1969). It might be possible to convert all non-pecuniary rewards and costs to money terms and include them, as it were, in the firm's profit and loss account. Rather than maximizing income, the entrepreneur might aim to maximize satisfaction within a given preference system. Another possibility is to impose an order of priorities on objectives and deal with one layer at a time. Some ultimate objectives, such as to continue in farming or to hand a viable business on to the successor, preclude certain alternatives from being recognized but within that restricted frame of reference, the optimum economic solution can still be sought (Petrini 1969).

Social scientists from other disciplines have developed ways of handling multiple objectives. One approach, as described earlier, is to allocate farmers to more homogeneous groups on the basis of similar objectives or value orientations and then to concentrate on the needs of each sub-group. Another is to organize objectives under a smaller, more manageable number of headings and to develop rules for assessing priorities. The first approach is potentially useful for those who have to deal with large numbers of farmers while the second is more helpful to the individual decision-maker.

Pursuing the second approach, the entrepreneur needs to identify and list all relevant objectives and then decide on priorities. Arranging objectives under headings like instrumental, intrinsic, personal and social may be one step in this direction. One way to proceed would be to arrange these larger categories in order of importance, along the lines of Maslow's hierarchy of needs. According to Maslow (1954), human needs are universal and can be represented as a pyramid with needs for survival and subsistence at the base, followed by needs for safety and security, needs for affection and belonging, needs for recognition and esteem and at the apex, needs for self-fulfilment. Maslow postulated that lower needs must be gratified, at least partially, before the individual can recognize and respond to higher needs. As a particular need is satisfied, the remaining ones are re-evaluated and greatest prominence is always given to the most basic of unfulfilled needs. Only ungratified needs can motivate. Following this line of thought, the farmer would first aim for subsistence and survival of the family and the business, then for securing future income and succession, next gaining a reputation in the farming community and finally for personal satisfaction and self-fulfilment.

SUMMARY AND IMPLICATIONS

This chapter has demonstrated that farms, like other family businesses, have multiple objectives. Two considerations are likely to colour the selection of objectives, the setting of targets and the processes of decision-making in family farm businesses. One is the desire to continue in the farming occupation with its intrinsic features of variety, contact with Nature, the outdoor life, freedom from supervision, challenge and risk. The other is the desire to hand on a viable business to the next generation. These super-objectives themselves can conflict, for instance where a farmer's enjoyment of his work makes him reluctant to let go of the reins. Whether these over-riding objectives are regarded as taking priority over others on a list, or as setting the agenda within which there is limited room for manoeuvre, the effect will be to shift the emphasis away from short-run, profit-maximizing behaviour.

Pursuit of the objectives of maintaining a valued way of life and inter-generational succession implies that farmers are cautious, aiming for a secure, stable and satisfactory level of income, taking a long-term view rather than maximizing short-term gains. It follows that they are reluctant to make changes (for example to give up an enterprise) which would put an end to enjoyable activities and chary of developments like contract farming, machinery sharing or conservation management agreements which would compromise their autonomy within the farm. In the real world the trade-off for gaining a satisfactory level of income may be some loss of independence or preferred activity (for example joining a machinery ring, selling on forward contract). The stronger the succession motive and the keener the farmer's enjoyment of the farming occupation, the more objectives, goals and behaviour will depart from the norms of rational economic action. In larger-scale businesses where the principal farmer's role is mainly managerial, securing a sound business for the successor may be foremost. On small farms where succession is not feasible or where farming is subordinate to another source of income, maintaining an enjoyable way of life may be the prime consideration. Every major decision is likely to reflect this orientation.

This chapter has provided numerous clues as to how the performance of the farm business will be influenced by objectives which stem from its being a *family* business. Added to this, the nature of the farming occupation itself imposes its stamp on the entrepreneur's objective function and hence on business performance. The argument here is not that family farms do not behave in a business oriented way but that their logic is more complex. Rational decisions are made within a framework which embraces intrinsic values in farm work, the values of autonomy and family continuity as well as maximizing profitability. Performance needs to be monitored and success judged in terms of the real objectives of the farm family business rather than imposed norms.

The 'distinct calculus of the family farm' can enable the business to persist through periods of economic adversity that drive capitalist units out of business. Family farms can more easily substitute labour for capital, accept a lower rate of return to family labour or increase off-farm employment to tide the household over a difficult period. This does not mean that family businesses fail to recognize or allow for market forces, but that they have survival strategies that are not available to other firms (Reinhardt and Barlett 1989). Economic pressures may nevertheless mean that in order to survive, farmers will have to approach ever closer to strict economic rationality in their business decisions, with some loss of job satisfaction. The alternative is to divorce farming from its economic rationale and to farm as a hobby, enjoying the lifestyle but depending on another source of livelihood.

In this chapter the emphasis has been on the objectives, goals and values of the farmer rather than those of the farm family, mainly because so little seems to be known about the motivation of other family members. This is clearly an area where further research is needed. We can however say with some conviction that the farmer's values of farming as a way of life and maintaining the farm intact for the next generation have important implications for the rest of the family. Living on the job has its own measure of pros and cons. The other side of the coin of living in the country and enjoying space and privacy is isolation, loneliness and long and tiring journeys to schools, shops and jobs. Working from home is a convenience for the farmer but a source of irritation for the wife who has to contend with mud and straw, sick animals and business callers in the house and sudden demands to drop everything to help in an emergency. Having the family working together can be a source of satisfaction for all members but the idea of patriarchal authority and tasks being allocated on the basis of age and gender seems increasingly outmoded. Inter-generational continuity, likely to be valued highly where the farm has been handed down for several generations, can become a heavy burden to the nominated successor who feels morally bound but personally uncommitted to taking over the business. We return to these themes of family labour, the spouse's contribution and inter-generational transfer in the next four chapters.

5

LABOUR USE IN THE FARM FAMILY BUSINESS

INTRODUCTION

A self-employed person may expand his business by first taking on
other members of his household, the non-resident members of his
family, then non-resident members of his extended family ... Within
the family, he may prefer to take on first those who are most
dependent upon him, for example his children, as sanctions against
them are relatively easy to enforce. The last to be taken on will be those
who because of their family status hold sanctions over him.

(Casson 1982: 198–199)

As we argued in Chapter 1, the task of any business manager is to allocate
the available resources to their most effective use in achieving pre-defined
objectives. The search for the best use of the land, labour and capital
available to the business is thus a central theme of most farm management
texts and many of the classic problems addressed by the formal discipline of
farm management have concerned the optimum allocation of these
resources between competing uses. With regard to the labour resource, the
farmer/manager must first acquire the correct amount and type of labour to
match the demands of the business, and then ensure that it is used as
productively as possible. The level of labour productivity actually achieved
will be influenced both by the manner in which tasks and responsibilities
are allocated to the different members of the workforce – the **division of
labour** – and by the use of various strategies to develop skills, increase
motivation and improve work methods.

A point too frequently neglected when considering the farm family
business is the fact that the farmer/manager himself forms part of the total
labour resource (Errington 1992a). This is the logical consequence of the fact
that ownership is combined with managerial control (see Chapter 1). At the
very least, the owner-manager is therefore contributing some of the
managerial labour input, but he often provides a substantial amount of
manual labour as well. Even on some of the largest farms in the UK, the

114

farmer/manager devotes as much as 50 per cent of his time to physical farm work (Norman, 1986).

In many farm businesses a large proportion of the remaining labour input, both manual and managerial, is provided by other members of the family. In examining the labour resource in the farm family business this chapter therefore focuses on the twin tasks of acquiring labour and improving labour productivity, taking into account managerial as well as manual labour. Our prime concern is with the use of labour in farm production activities rather than those of 'reproduction' (as defined in Chapter 1). However, it should be recognized that the welfare of the farm household will also be influenced by the efficiency of labour use in the domestic arena where parallel and related issues also arise.

If the prime concern of this chapter is with the use of labour in farm production activities, its main message is that family businesses may be particularly well-placed to meet the distinctive labour requirements of farming. Before looking at the farm family business itself, it is therefore important to consider the nature of farming.

THE DEMAND FOR LABOUR IN THE FARM BUSINESS

Fundamental Characteristics

Ever since the original hunter-gatherers settled to farm, the most important feature of the demand for labour in farming has been its seasonal variation. This results from differences in the rate of crop and grass growth in response to seasonal variations in temperature, light-interception and rainfall, all of which have knock-on effects on livestock enterprises.

It is certainly the case that the intensification of production methods witnessed in recent years has tended to reduce seasonal variation either by providing a more controlled production environment (such as glasshouses) or by requiring a progressively greater number of crop 'treatments' during the year. However, the simultaneous trend towards greater specialization has more than compensated for this so that the arable farmer now faces increasingly 'peaky' labour profiles as many of the complementary enterprises which used to fill out the various troughs in the labour profile have disappeared.

A second feature of the demand for labour in farming is the frequent necessity to work 'unsocial hours', often at very short notice. In the crop and grassland enterprise, this is typically associated with the various time-critical operations that surround hay and silage-making or harvest. For example, peas must be at the factory and frozen within hours of the appropriate 'tenderometer' reading being reached, and the feed-value of silage can drop dramatically if it is not in the clamp very soon after the optimum time. In the case of livestock enterprises, 'unsocial hours' are often associated with calving and lambing, the outbreak of disease among young-stock or indeed the break-out of the livestock themselves! As we shall see, the 'flexibility' of the family workforce has made it particularly well-suited to meeting these seasonal and *ad hoc* fluctuations in the demand for labour.

A third distinctive feature of the demand for labour in post-war farming has been the increased relative importance of the managerial as opposed to the manual labour input as a result of growing mechanization and the increased technical complexity of production methods. There are of course exceptions to this general trend and Chapter 3 has described the tight specification of contracts and provision of inputs by some some large food-processing companies. In these extreme cases of indirect subsumption the company usurps substantial areas of managerial decision-taking and control leaving the farmer in much the same position as a share-cropper in the southern USA. However, for the majority of UK farmers, the present movement towards a free and unsupported market for agricultural products as well as the drive towards diversification will accentuate the importance of managerial over manual labour.

Manual versus Managerial Labour

While the reduction in the total labour input to farming in the post-war period is well documented, the effects on the type and quality of labour required in order to meet changes in the nature of farm work have received much less attention. In some sectors such as glasshouse crops and poultry production the development of large-scale factory-like systems with a greater division of labour between different activities has probably led to a narrowing of the range of skills required by individual workers. At the same time, increasingly sophisticated mechanization and the introduction of environmental control systems may have led to a certain amount of deskilling in these same areas. But in many other sectors, the need for a shrinking workforce to deal with a much larger range of tasks will have increased the breadth of manual skills required.

Perhaps more significant than these changes in manual skill require-ments has been the increased importance of managerial skills throughout the workforce. However, there is not only a dearth of empirical evidence on this crucial issue but some uncertainty over what exactly constitutes managerial work. The ancient division between 'labourers of hand and of brain' has very little relevance to modern farming since much of the arduous labouring work has now been mechanized and few jobs rely purely on the worker's physical strength, if indeed they ever did. However, as Errington (1980) has shown, it is possible to break each job into its constituent activities and consider them separately (see Box 5.1). If this is done, the

Box 5.1. Extract from a check-list of supervisory activities. Source: Errington 1980: 74

• Teaches workers how to do specific tasks		
• Dismisses regular workers		
• Dismisses casual workers		
• Decides what work is to be done each day	(a) (b)	on the entire holding on a particular enterprise
• Decides who should do what in the day's work	(a) (b)	on the entire holding on a particular enterprise
• Decides how a particular job should be carried out (if it is not a routine task)		
• Sets standards of work (e.g. decides how much and what standard of work is expected of each person or gang)	(a) (b)	on the entire holding on a particular enterprise
• Checks work to see that it is up to standard	(a) (b)	on the entire holding on a particular enterprise
• Takes action to ensure that work is brought up to standard	(a) (b)	on the entire holding on a particular enterprise
• Sets piecework rates		
• Sets bonuses		

decision-taking component of each activity can then be ranked according to a number of criteria, such as its potential impact on the attainment of business objectives, the reversibility of the decision or the existence of clearly prescribed decision-rules. Those decisions with a higher ranking (those which have a bigger impact, are irreversible and are guided by fewer decision-rules) and *those activities involving more of these decisions* can be regarded as more 'managerial'. In this way, some broad generalizations can be made about the diffusion of managerial work throughout the farm workforce (Errington 1986b).

A good deal of decision-taking in farming has always had to be delegated by the owner-manager to others in the workforce because much of the information on which these decisions are based cannot be written down. Farming continues to rely on the accumulated experience of particular individuals – the 'stockman's eye', for example – or on the information gathered by the person who is actually on the spot and who can see how the ground 'treads', or whether the corn is 'going off'. However, a consequence of the increased technical complexity of farming is that the managerial decision-taking component of farmwork has increased relative to the manual/physical component to such an extent that a progressively greater proportion of the total managerial activity must be delegated to others. The farmer's skill in implementing the most appropriate division of **managerial** labour has thus become paramount. And the ability of the farm family business to mobilize managerial expertise has become more crucial to its success than its historic ability to mobilize manual labour to meet seasonal and *ad hoc* fluctuations in demand.

SOURCES OF LABOUR AVAILABLE TO THE FARM BUSINESS

Where traditional farm production activities are concerned, the labour input may come from a variety of different sources, not all of which are adequately measured in published statistics (Errington 1988). The characteristics of labour from each source will vary, thus affecting the scope for substitution between them. The farmer's ability to assemble and develop the appropriate mix of different types of labour input may therefore have effects on profitability and performance quite as important as his ability to manipulate aggregate capital:labour ratios.

As we have already mentioned, the farmer and his family may contribute a large proportion of the total labour input themselves. Some of this may be provided on what the official statistics regard as a full-time basis while the rest is in the form of regular part-time, seasonal or merely casual labour provided on an *ad hoc* basis. For example, the farmer's wife may spend a part of each week running her own farm enterprise alongside other work in the farmhouse (see Chapter 6) while her son might divide his time between work on the home farm and employment in some other business. Even a child still at school might help regularly with lambing or harvest each year. The farmer's parents might give a hand periodically, helping load pigs for market or moving dry cows to grazing on an outlying piece of land.

The hired farmworker provides the next source of labour and may again be formally classified as full-time, regular part-time, seasonal or casual. But while these are the main categories of hired labour distinguished in the UK agricultural statistics there are other sources of labour which may also be considered by the farmer-manager. The first of these, and a source of growing significance, is the agricultural contractor (Ball 1988) and its most recent variant, the machinery ring. The contract service may be provided by a local farmer supplementing the farm income or a full-time contracting agency employing large numbers of staff. In either case, the contractor is supplying a substantial labour input as well as specialized machinery and equipment. Indeed, there are a growing number of cases where the labour component of the contractor's work is very substantial – the specialist stockman, for example, visiting a large number of farms with a portable crush and foot-trimming equipment or the freelance shepherd with his ewe-scanner and shears. More recent anecdotal evidence in the UK even refers to the labour-only contractor such as the relief milker who brings to the farm only her energy and her skills.

The large range of so-called 'flexible' labour inputs now available from outside the family is of particular significance to the farm family business because it enables firms with only a small core workforce (of two or three people) to capture many of the economies of specialization which were previously confined to very large farms. The availability of contractors now allows the farmer to buy in the specialist expertise of the operator as well as his specialist equipment. And this phenomenon also extends to managerial skills which the farm family business can buy in from the agronomist, accountant or managerial consultant.

Finally, there are all the labour inputs provided by neighbours and kin, such as the Finnish 'holiday rings' which enable farmers to get away from the farm (Abrahams 1991). They may function on a completely informal basis without any financial transaction taking place, or they may operate more formally like the labour relief co-ops in The Netherlands.

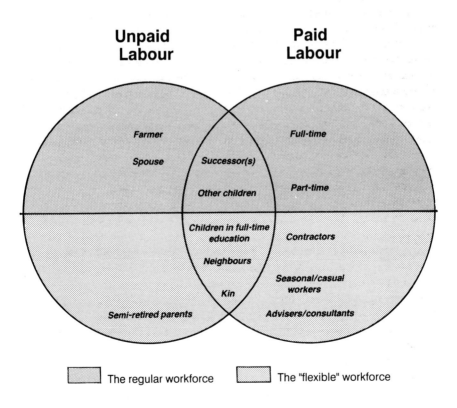

Figure 5.1. Potential sources of farm labour.

Categories of Farm Labour

Figure 5.1 summarizes the great range of potential labour sources which the farm business can tap. It highlights two important distinctions. The first is between paid and unpaid labour for in the farm family business some of the labour may be provided by family members without any overt financial transaction taking place. However, these two categories overlap since some family members may receive some direct payment for their work. Neighbours are also included in this overlapping segment to reflect traditional labour-sharing arrangements that still characterize the 'informal economy' of some farm businesses.

The second feature illustrated in this diagram is the importance of the 'flexible' workforce to which we have already referred. This can help the farmer meet the seasonal and *ad hoc* fluctuations in the demand for labour which characterize farming. The flexible workforce includes labour that can be brought into play at very short notice and might work for only very short periods of time (measured in hours or days rather than months or years). Both the paid and the unpaid segments of this flexible workforce contain groups (such as school-age children and agricultural contractors) which are not traditionally included in the industry's workforce statistics even though they may contribute a significant amount of labour to the farm. This again underlines the difficulty of measuring the net contribution of the various categories of labour to the farm family business, a fact of considerable significance when the ratio of hired to family labour is used to define the *family* farm. While there is some value in such an approach, it is important to recognize the complete range of family and non-family labour inputs when attempting to measure the family's total contribution to farm labour.

FAMILY LABOUR: DEMAND AND SUPPLY

Having looked at the demand for, and potential sources of both managerial and manual labour to the farm business, it is important to consider the factors that influence the amount of labour which the family itself will *choose* to devote to farm production activities. This is an important aspect of the labour-mix decision since the farm family business is not only a firm, which needs to decide exactly how much and what type of labour to use in order to produce its goods and services, but a labour-supplying household which must consider where best to apply the limited amount of time at its disposal (Nakajima 1986).

Traditional economic analysis of the labour hiring decision suggests that labour will be hired up to the point where its marginal cost is equal to its marginal revenue product (MRP) i.e. where the cost of an additional unit of labour is equal to the additional monetary return generated by the use of that labour. Beyond this point the returns to any additional labour would not cover its cost and the amount of labour hired would therefore tend to be reduced, while below it the returns to additional labour would be greater than its cost and the tendency would be to hire extra labour and so increase profits. But in reality, the labour-hiring decision in farming is much more complicated than this, and probably more complicated than it is in most industries.

In the first place, the effect of using extra labour is uncertain because production is based on biological systems subject to the vagaries of the weather and of disease. And where government intervenes to support agricultural prices, there may be additional uncertainty over the price the farmer will eventually receive for his crop or livestock products. The decision of how much labour to use must therefore be based on the *expected* MRP of labour which will depend on the farmer's subjective assessment of the likelihood of a range of possible outcomes.

Second, labour has traditionally been a 'lumpy' and heterogeneous resource in agriculture which has always made it difficult to match supply and demand with any precision. Once the regular whole-time worker had become the mainstay of the hired workforce and before the emergence of the 'flexible' hired workforce described above, it was not possible to employ 'half a cowman' or 'half a tractor-driver'. And even where whole cowmen or tractor drivers were hired, individuals would vary enormously in their skills and abilities.

Thirdly, the farmer, like any businessman acquiring staff, needs to take into account a whole range of different types of cost quite apart from the wages that must be paid. First, there are the 'transactions costs' involved in finding and hiring suitable staff. Next are the 'opportunity costs' of the additional time that he or another member of his staff must spend in super-vizing the additional worker(s). (If there were no such demands placed on their time, they might be used in some other productive activity, an *opportunity* which they must now forgo.) There may also be 'psychic' costs attributable to the additional stress of managing staff.

Finally, the farmer will take into account a plethora of moral, social and emotional considerations which will influence his final decision. Perhaps a particular worker has worked for the family business all his life and, hired by the present farmer's father, is kept on the payroll though surplus to immediate requirements.

Where family labour is concerned, parallel considerations will apply. Indeed, one of the attractions of using family labour is the avoidance of transactions costs by 'internalizing' the labour market (Casson 1982). However, the assessment of the marginal cost of family labour will now involve a complex computation which takes into account the wage or allowance paid to the children remaining at home as well the opportunity cost of the domestic resources (including houseroom) they absorb. But the main difference with family members concerns the opportunity cost of their time and it becomes necessary to evaluate the alternative uses to which this time might be put.

Allocating Time

> There are factors of substantial if not decisive impact on productivity that never become visible cost figures. First there is knowledge . . .
> Then there is time – business's most perishable resource.
>
> (Drucker, 1981: 63)

Time is a finite, non-renewable resource which, if applied to farm work cannot be used elsewhere. Economists such as Nakajima (1986) and Dawson (1984) have made important theoretical contributions to our understanding of this issue though some of the assumptions they employ seem especially restrictive in the light of points raised elsewhere in this book. For example, they tend to assume the farm household to be a single decision-making utility-maximizing entity, thus side-stepping the complex distributional and effort-sharing issues that arise as a result of power relationships within the household. As Nakajima graphically explains, he is assuming 'one pocket and one pain'.

Despite these assumptions, their analyses highlight a number of points that are crucial to an understanding of the amount and type of labour used in the farm family business since they switch the perspective from that of the manager hiring labour to that of the worker offering his or her labour to the business.

As the amount of labour that family members devote to farm work increases, its marginal revenue product will tend to diminish if other inputs (such as machinery, land and fertilizers) are held constant. A point will eventually be reached where the additional work adds nothing to the total output of the farm. Meanwhile, the marginal utility which accrues to the individual as a result of their work, received as monetary or 'psychic' income (e.g. job satisfaction), will also tend to diminish as the amount of work increases beyond an optimum point.

In order to decide how much time the family member should allocate to farm work, he or she needs to weigh the costs of doing that work against the monetary and psychic income expected to flow from it. Figure 5.2 indicates what these costs are. In the first place there will be the hardship or disutility of the work itself (the 'pain' to which Nakajima refers), and here the economists assume that marginal disutility increases with the amount of work done – it gets more and more painful. But there is also the opportunity cost of the time spent on farm work to be considered since the same time could have been devoted to a whole range of other activities, each with its own utility 'payoff'. In fact, there are two main types of use to which the

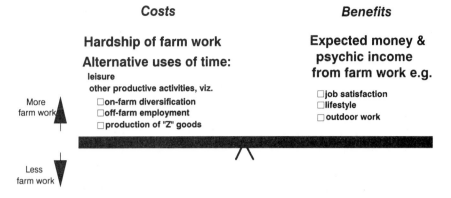

Figure 5.2. Deciding how much time to devote to farm work.

time could otherwise be devoted, namely leisure and 'other productive activities'.

These, of course, are the alternatives facing anyone (including hired workers) considering how many hours to offer to the farm business, but where the farm family is concerned the 'other productive activities' can include off-farm work, on-farm work in some activity other than agriculture (such as a 'diversification' enterprise), or the production of 'Z' goods. These latter, identified by Becker (1965) in his seminal article on the allocation of time, are particularly important to the farm family business. They involve a whole range of activities – cooking, cleaning, DIY building and decorating – that are excluded from farm (and indeed the national) accounts but are particularly significant in the farm family business where workplace and home are synonymous (see Chapters 1 and 6).

If the sum of the costs in Figure 5.2 begins to exceed the sum of the benefits, perhaps because of an increase in availability of off-farm jobs, the family member will tend to reduce the amount of time devoted to farm work. But if the benefits begin to outweigh the costs, perhaps because of a rise in agricultural product prices, the tendency will be to increase the amount of time devoted to farm work.

The Target Income

Traditional economic analyses of the issues that arise from this theoretical model tend to focus on the monetary component of the utility function and assume an upward sloping supply curve of family labour. As off-farm wage rates increase, the amount of family labour supplied to off-farm work is assumed to increase and the amount devoted to farmwork will be reduced.

Hourly wage

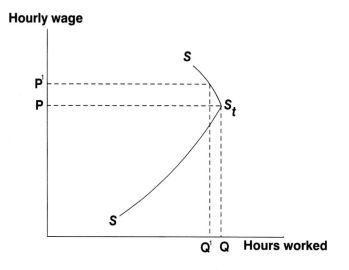

Figure 5.3. The backward-sloping labour-supply curve.

However, it may be that the non-pecuniary benefits of farm work (broadly, 'job satisfaction') are so great that off-farm work is very much the last resort, taken up only to fulfil the immediate cash requirements of the family (Streeter 1988, but see Chapter 6 for an alternative view where farmers' wives are concerned). If so, the concept of a 'target income' might have some relevance to the farm family business.

The 'target income' is conceived as the prime goal of wage labour; once the target has been reached (at point S_t in Figure 5.3, where the total income earned is the hourly wage, P, multiplied by the hours worked, Q), any subsequent wage-rate increase will lead to a reduction in the labour supplied (since the same target – P^1Q^1 – can now be achieved through less work). As a result, beyond this point the labour supply curve is backward sloping with respect to wage rates. While cultural conditioning, advertising and social norms all combine to make this an unlikely response in market industrialized countries, it may be that the 'prior charges' placed by banks on the farm family business function in a similar way and that increased indebtedness has raised the 'target income' of many farm families, shifting the entire curve SS upwards or to the right.

Whether or not this particular hypothesis is correct, it is important to recognize that money income is only one of the factors influencing the behaviour of the farm family business. The 'psychic income' derived from farming may be quite sufficient to keep the debt-free owner-occupied farm family in business in the face of falling farm incomes while the indebted farm family may be forced to leave the industry even though its business may actually be more profitable in conventional accounting terms (see Chapters 3, 4 and 9).

This theoretical description of the choices facing family workers in the use of their time is of central importance to an understanding of the behaviour of the farm family business since it transcends the artificial barrier placed between home and work in much farm business analysis. It explains why labour productivity considered in conventional accounting terms is so low on some family-worked farms and why these firms continue in business despite persistent low incomes and government inducements to quit. Moreover, since many of the items included in the analysis, such as 'psychic income' and 'Z' goods, are not traditionally ascribed any monetary value, it again emphasizes the importance of the power relationships within the family business. Insofar as that business is dominated by one decision-taker, it will be this person's subjective evaluation of these items which will determine the amount of farm work done by family members and the residue available for their other productive, reproductive and leisure activities. In this situation, there is a great deal of scope for the sub-optimal allocation of time so far as the family as a whole is concerned and individuals may be more exposed to exploitation within the privacy of their own family firm than anywhere else in the economy.

THE ADVANTAGES AND DISADVANTAGES OF FAMILY LABOUR

When the farmer seeks to match the supply of labour with the demands arising from agricultural production, the farm family business has a number of advantages and disadvantages compared with other types of farm. On the one hand, the labour supply is likely to be more flexible, more motivated and to exhibit a higher degree of commitment to the business. On the other hand, the family cycle may lead to substantial fluctuations in the amount of labour available and the use of family labour may lead to persistently low levels of labour productivity.

Flexibility of Labour Supply

As we have seen, the problem of matching a relatively fixed supply of labour with seasonally-fluctuating demand faces all farmers, and especially those concentrating on arable production. However, the farm family has traditionally provided a very important source of 'flexible' labour and it may be particularly well-suited to meeting the 'peaky' labour requirements of farming. School-age children or members of the family working away from home may help out in seasonal tasks such as harvesting and lambing. The family may also be better placed to mobilize extra labour at a moment's notice to deal with an emergency. In response to a Reading University survey, one farmer's wife said that she had to 'be prepared to do anything at any time at very short notice and regardless of what is in the oven' (Buchanan *et al.* 1982).

Level of Commitment/Self-exploitation

It is one of the strengths of the farm family business that family loyalty and commitment can produce the degree of self-exploitation necessary for survival. As Abrahams (1991) notes, 'Families are by nature highly flexible work units and they can often respond successfully to difficulties and pressures by working harder and tightening their belts'. Rees (1971) described the achievement of the typical Welsh farmer who, by drastic economizing, had managed to continue in farming throughout the depression of the 1930s 'relying on family labour, ... often by eating into precious savings'. Indeed, the position of family workers in the short term can be markedly worse than that of hired workers entitled to a minimum wage. Williams (1956) reported that in Gosforth, Cumberland in the 1950s 'farmers' sons working at home are "officially" paid wages similar to the hired workers, but in practice they rarely receive more than small amounts at irregular intervals'.

As we shall see in Chapter 7, the son's low-paid labour may simply be regarded as an advance payment for his inheritance. But conflict may still arise. In some cases the son may feel that he already has a right to his inheritance by birth; in others the discounted value of the income expected to flow from the inherited assets may be much lower than the effort expended in today's work. This latter point is particularly important in the current recession where expectations have taken a substantial knock and family members may be applying an extremely high discount rate to any future income expected to come from the farm. In these circumstances, the farmer's children may seek employment off the farm rather than face the prospect of low-paid low-productivity work at home in conditions tantamount to disguised unemployment.

But the family ties that still tend to bind the family worker to the farm family business may have assumed greater importance as the skill requirements of the agricultural workforce have increased (see above). Though many manual skills are generic and can be carried from farm to farm, this is much less true where their decision-making component is concerned. As explained earlier, many decisions in farming still require reference to accumulated knowledge, much of which is specific to a particular farm (e.g. the soil conditions of particular parts of the farm). Farmers training their own staff whether by formal or informal means therefore stand to incur substantial losses if these workers move on to other farms. Greater reliance on family members who are 'locked in' to the farm business by a web of emotional ties reduces the danger of losing these substantial investments in human capital. This provides yet another advantage in using family labour in the farm business.

Labour Productivity in the Farm Family Cycle

In course of time, a particular farm family will change in number, vigour and requirements. Frequently, the farm resources available will not change to the same extent as either the quantities and qualities of labour to exploit them, or the needs of the family. Herein lies the basic problem of family farming.

(Nalson 1968: 38)

Chapter 1 has argued that an understanding of the family cycle is funda-mental to our understanding of the behaviour of the farm family business. This is especially true where labour productivity is concerned. Typically, the family labour available for farm work will diminish dramatically as the spouse becomes involved in child rearing and it may later increase as the children grow up and begin to contribute directly to work on the farm. The amount of labour actually available will vary with the life choices and chances of each particular family, but Figure 5.4 includes a stylized repre-sentation of two cases. In the first, the couple starting the farm business shortly after they get married have two sons, one of whom leaves home while the other remains at home as a batchelor farmer. In the second, the son remaining at home marries and starts his own family in what eventually becomes a three generation family business.

This variation in labour availability over the family cycle has been recognized as one of the fundamental problems of the farm family business. With his experience of research in both Africa and Finland, Abrahams (1991) contrasts the nomadic herdsman who can increase or decrease the number of livestock to match both the labour available and the number of mouths to feed, with the settled farmer who does not have this flexibility.

There is a very large range of strategies used by farming families to overcome this problem. The family may move to a larger (or a smaller) farm at a given point in the family cycle; they may buy or sell land; they may move to a farm with better productive potential (Nalson 1968), and so on. With larger farms, periodic employment of hired labour may provide a solution (Williams 1956; Nalson 1968; Symes 1990) and as Chapter 1 pointed out, it may be a gross over-simplification to classify farms as 'family-worked' on the basis of the labour input pattern observed at one particular point in time. Alternatively, the farm may shift between more intensive and more extensive forms of production (Blanc 1987) with substantial on-farm investment coinciding with the end of the children's formal education.

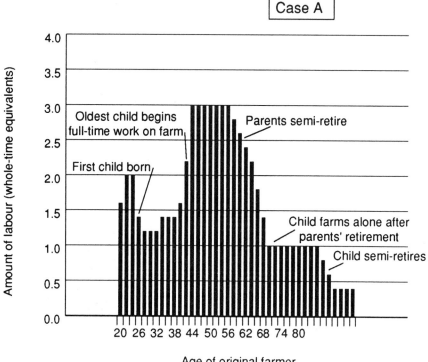

Figure 5.4. Variation in labour supply over the family cycle.

In other cases, a solution may be sought in the introduction of an alternative farm enterprise such as the establishment of an agricultural contracting business or the introduction of a farm shop. If either resources or objectives do not permit these solutions, the children may seek (temporary) employment elsewhere and indeed the *détour professionelle* is a well-established stage in the farm family cycle in many continental European countries (see Chapter 8). In short, the significant points in the family cycle may be marked by substantial changes in farm size, location or farming practice. If none of these solutions is pursued, the fluctuating labour supply will lead to considerable variation in labour productivity and the occurrence of under-employment over a substantial portion of the family cycle (see below).

Labour Productivity in the Business Development Cycle

While the supply of family labour thus varies with the family cycle, the

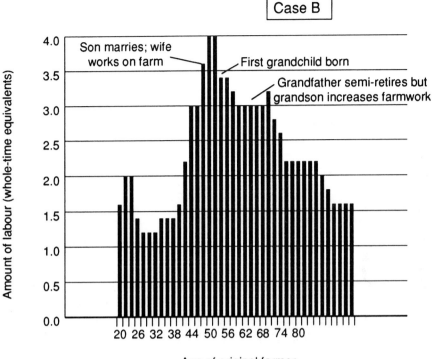

Case B

Son marries; wife works on farm

First grandchild born

Grandfather semi-retires but grandson increases farmwork

Amount of labour (whole-time equivalents)

20 26 32 38 44 50 56 62 68 74 80

Age of original farmer

development cycle of the business can also give rise to fluctuating demands for labour. Indeed, one of the greatest challenges facing the farm family business is in meshing together the constraints and opportunities of the family cycle with those of the business development cycle. Thus, labour productivity will tend to vary with each successive stage in the family cycle not only because of variation in the supply of family labour but because of investment decisions related to the development of the business itself. The business may be very efficient during the prime of the farmer's life but inefficient during the early and late stages, reflecting the availability of capital and labour as well as the changing aspirations of family members. At the early stage of the business development cycle, limited land and capital may force the farmer to operate below the optimum size. During the late phase when the operator's owner equity may be at a peak, he may be engaged in disinvestment to provide for his retirement, as well as working less hard (Harl 1972; Boehlje and Eidman 1984). Thus, on the Irish farms studied by Symes (1972), labour productivity was almost 50 per cent higher in the expansion phase than at any other time in the business development cycle.

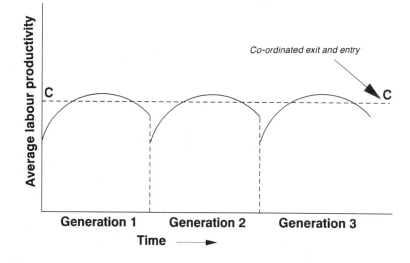

Figure 5.5. Variations in labour productivity over the course of the family cycle. Source: After Boehlje and Eidman 1984

Average labour productivity in the farm family business may be increased by co-ordinating entry and exit as illustrated in Figure 5.5, providing the business is large enough to support two households during the overlapping periods (Boehlje and Eidman 1984, and see Chapter 8). There is some evidence from the USA that incorporation is being used increasingly to aid the smooth transfer of the farm business from older to younger shareholders, since 'the corporation encourages people and their capital to move into and out of the farm business in keeping with their own life cycle but without the firm proceeding through cyclical fluctuations in efficiency each generation' (Harl 1972).

Other Causes of Low Labour Productivity

In the farm family business the farmer's choice in acquiring labour inputs might be constrained by the need to make use of family members. This may not only lead to excessive labour use and consequently lower labour productivity but also to the use of less skilled labour than would otherwise be acquired. This may be a particular problem where key managerial posts are concerned since the pool from which the management team is selected will tend to be very small and the family members chosen may not have the necessary skills. 'In this case the entrepreneur's ability to transcend the bounds of his family may be crucial to the continued success of the firm' (Casson 1982: 305).

Some Tentative Conclusions

The employment of excessive amounts of family labour is often regarded as the major constraint on average labour productivity and hence upon farm family incomes (Agriculture EDC 1973; Britton and Hill 1975). As we have seen, in the interests of business survival and long-term continuity, family members may be induced to work long hours for low returns and they may also be more flexible about how and when they work. Farmers may in effect be able to buy cheap labour with the promise of inheritance at some future date. Availability of cheap family labour may enable the farm business which owns its land and is not heavily indebted, not only to weather hard times but to continue operating almost indefinitely at a low level of productivity.

So far as the family itself is concerned, this may present no problem and if the welfare implications of low levels of labour productivity in farming are to be explored, it may be necessary to distinguish the welfare of (a) individual family members, (b) the farm family as a whole, and (c) society as a whole. For the corollary of business survival in bad times may be that in good times, labour productivity only reaches a low ceiling which satisfies a low level of needs (Chayanov 1966; Nakajima 1986). Moreover, if family labour is ascribed a low value, perhaps because the farming principal gives inadequate weight to its opportunity cost (see above), there is little incentive to raise its productivity by training or by increasing the capital:labour ratio. A more appropriate valuation of family labour may therefore be the main prerequisite for improved labour productivity on the family-worked farm.

To summarize, the family may be a more flexible source of labour, prepared and able to switch between farm production and other activities at very short notice. It may also provide a more committed and motivated workforce willing to work for very low returns in order to ensure business survival. At the same time, the family cycle makes it particularly difficult to match the supply of and demand for labour in the farm family business. This, together with the constrained choice when employing or promoting staff as well as the under-valuation of family labour by business principals may contribute to lower levels of labour productivity in the farm family business. The implications that flow from these low levels of labour productivity can only be viewed from particular perspectives, for a situation that appears sub-optimal from a national perspective might be quite acceptable to individual family members who have little incentive to change their behaviour.

EMPIRICAL STUDIES OF THE FARM FAMILY WORKFORCE

The Supply Response of Family Labour

Dawson (1984) has argued that while agricultural product price *rises* are likely to increase output on farms employing hired labour, the outcome is less certain where family labour is concerned because the increased welfare arising from the increased expected MRP of labour may be balanced by increased marginal disutility from the work itself. As a result, there will not only be a substitution effect (where leisure is exchanged for additional money income) but a 'wealth' effect which could lead to a net reduction in the family labour input.

This echoes the discussion of the 'target income' hypothesis earlier in this chapter. Indeed, the main conclusion to be drawn from the economic theory of family labour supply decisions is that even if family and hired labour were *technologically* perfect substitutes, their supply functions would be very different. Any research which seeks to predict the effect of a given economic or technological change on the agricultural workforce must therefore include separate analysis of the hired and family components.

At a time when the extent and nature of government support to farming is undergoing substantial change, the likely impact of changing product prices and input costs on farm labour assumes particular significance. Yet this topic has not been the subject of much empirical research, perhaps because the supply response of family labour is too complex to model satis-factorily. For example, Blanc (1987) concludes that:

> A realistic neoclassical model of farm family activity would have to include utility functions for each member of the family and many production functions relating to alternative farming systems.
>
> (Blanc 1987: 301)

However, one important conclusion has been drawn from analysis of changes in the US farm workforce between 1956 and 1977. Gunter and Vasavada (1988) report that while the response of hired labour to changing relative input prices was virtually instantaneous, the family/operator element took six years to adjust. As they explain, 'The slow adjustment of family/operator labour is consistent with the usual characterization of this input, reflecting in part the complexity of the utility function of farm owner/operators' (see Chapter 4).

Disguised Unemployment

The 'stickiness' of family labour highlighted by this American study probably lies behind some of the recent trends in the size and structure of

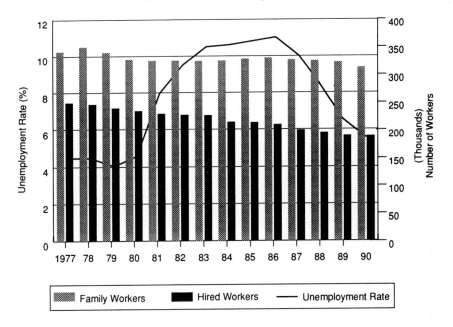

Figure 5.6. Family and hired workers in the agricultural/horticultural workforce, England and Wales 1977–1990. Source: Errington 1992a

the agricultural workforce in England and Wales where there has been a substantial increase in dependence on family labour (including farmers) in recent years (Errington 1992a). Figure 5.6 shows that this has resulted from the relative stability of the family workforce in the face of a continuing downward trend in the hired workforce. In the last decade, 1986 proved a pivotal year, marking the threshold between a period in which the number of family workers was actually rising and one in which their numbers again began to fall. Thus, between 1980 and 1986 the family workforce rose by 1.5 per cent (0.2 per cent *per annum* [p.a.]) in sharp contrast to hired workers (whose numbers decreased by 2.2 per cent p.a.). In the four years that followed, the family workforce again began to decrease, but at a rate of only 1.4 per cent p.a. compared with 2.4 per cent p.a. among the hired workers.

These trends appear to be the result of the substitution of family for hired workers, the absorption of additional family members in the face of high unemployment in the economy at large (see below), and an increase in the number of part-time farmers brought into the industry by its residential attractions (Errington 1992b).

The rate of decline among the farm family workforce appears to be associated with unemployment rates in the economy at large (see Figure 5.6). This supports the hypothesis that where the existence of a family business offers the opportunity to do so, family workers who would have

otherwise worked elsewhere in the economy may turn to the family business as an **employment refuge** when alternative jobs are no longer available.
In some cases they will be replacing hired labour (with no net effect on the
size of the aggregate agricultural workforce) but in others they may constitute a net addition to the workforce and contribute to increasing **under-
employment** or even the emergence of **disguised unemployment** in the
family business sector (Errington 1988).

Evidence from France (Blanc 1987) and the USA (Suits 1985) as well as
Germany and Italy (Fasterding 1984) similarly supports the employment
refuge hypothesis. It is also consistent with the well-established model of
rural–urban migration in which the rate of out-migration from rural areas is
related not only to the rural–urban wage differential but to the probability of
obtaining an urban job (Harris and Todaro 1970).

The disguised unemployment of farm family labour is not confined to
cases where an additional family member comes home in search of an
employment refuge. It may also overtake a farm family business where a
child (or indeed any other family member, including the farmer himself) has
been working at home for some time. Any reduction in product prices will
reduce the MRP of labour and in these circumstances disguised unemployment is particularly likely to be induced because the costs of and returns to
family labour are less likely to be assessed when that labour is already
working on the farm. The possible existence of disguised unemployment
among farm family labour is especially important at a time when agricultural
support policies are being changed, for its existence would invalidate the use
of published unemployment statistics or aggregate farm family income
measures to monitor the effects of these changes.

THE MANAGEMENT OF FAMILY LABOUR

> The farm family can no longer be regarded as an entity pursuing its
> own objectives but rather as a group whose members try to increase
> their own autonomy. Consequently, the farmer is less and less able to
> control the resources of the family labour force.
>
> (Blanc 1987: 301)

Standard farm management texts teach that 'good management' is primarily
concerned with making the best use of the available resources to achieve
predefined objectives. As we have seen, the under-employment of farm
family labour is often regarded as the main cause of low labour productivity
in farming. Improvement has been sought through a variety of schemes
promoting farm amalgamation and business growth which aim to ensure
that the available labour is fully and effectively utilized. While policy-
makers have also looked to the transfer of farm labour to other sectors of the
economy as a possible solution to the problem, more recent thinking

suggests that on-farm diversification or the combination of part-time farming with off-farm involvement in other gainful activities may provide a better alternative (Gasson 1988). But there may still be some scope for increasing labour productivity through the improved management of family members working in 'traditional' farm enterprises on an existing farm. A number of these possibilities will be explored in the remainder of this chapter.

Labour has a number of distinctive characteristics that mark it out from other resources on the farm, one of the most significant being the fact that it is an unknown quantity (though perhaps 'unknown quality' might be a more apt phrase). While the new tractor comes with a specification that promises a given level of performance and each bag of feed has its own guaranteed minimum nutrient content, members of the farm workforce bear no such label. Yet the difference in the potential performance of the best as against the worst is huge and the potential impact of good management on improved labour productivity is enormous. The farmer/manager's ability to unlock the potential of other human beings is therefore of central import-ance to good farm management. There are a variety of routes to improved labour productivity – improved work organization, improved tools and equipment, improved skills, increased motivation, and so on – but in the farm family business there is the ever-present danger that the farmer will ignore family labour in his quest for improved productivity:

> If farmers are seeking to get the best out of the labour resource they must consider how to get the best out of themselves and their families; if they are seeking to develop the skills of the workforce, they must not ignore their own training needs and those of their family; if they are seeking to motivate the workforce, they must recognize that their own motivation and that of their own family members must be considered as well as that of their employees; and if they are considering how to give their workforce a proper reward for their labour, they must consider their sons and daughters as well as the hired staff.
>
> (Errington 1992a: 103)

The remainder of this chapter considers five aspects of the management of the family workforce which have a major impact on labour productivity – the division of labour, the quality of the family workforce (in terms of its educational background, training and skill level), the 'motivation calculus', the resolution of conflict within the family, and finally, the development of management teams.

The Division of Labour

As we emphasized in Chapter 1, one of the distinguishing features of the farm family business is that the division of labour among the family workforce is on gender or generation lines rather than on the basis of inherent skills or training. Later chapters concentrate on the distinctive division of labour in the farm family business, Chapter 6 considering the division by gender and Chapters 7 and 8, the division by generation. But it is useful at this stage to highlight the importance of the division of managerial as well as manual labour. The farmer himself must divide his own time between managerial activities and physical farm work and as Chapter 4 has pointed out, there may be a tendency for him to neglect his managerial role and spend too much of his time on the tractor or with the cows. As Dexter and Barber (1961) commented in their seminal text on the farm as a business:

> Hard physical work is a great joy to many people ... (but) ... an hour or so a day spent scribbling about future farming plans is more profitable than working yourself to physical exhaustion on jobs which you would regard as a waste of time if you had time to think about them.

> (Dexter and Barber 1961: 40)

Empirical evidence in Chapter 6 highlights the role of many farmers' wives in the book-keeping aspects of management. Several surveys, in which wives have been questioned about their own involvement in the decision process, also suggest that farmers usually consult their wives over long-term 'strategic' business decisions that may involve the family, such as whether to take out a loan, buy land, or develop a new enterprise. Wives are less likely to be drawn into day-to-day 'tactical' management decisions, such as which tasks to tackle today and who does what in the day's work.

Chapter 8 suggests that the main division of labour between the generations lies in the area of managerial decision-taking (though there may be a further division of manual labour as the farming father approaches retirement). A pattern of gradually-increasing involvement in the decision process, common across a wide range of different types of farm, seems to emerge. First the successor may simply be involved in gathering information or their opinion solicited in discrete areas where they have particular knowledge or expertise. Only later are they delegated authority to take decisions, and this in progressively higher areas of management. The whole graduated process has been characterized as the ascent of a succession 'ladder'.

As the performance of the farm family business comes to rely more and more on the effective mobilization of managerial skills, the division of managerial labour among the members of the farm family becomes more crucial than the traditional division of manual labour. The farmer's ability to identify discrete areas of managerial responsibility to delegate to other family members has never been more important.

Education and Training

> That part of a holding of a farmer or landowner that pays best for
> cultivation is the small estate within the ring fence of his skull.
>
> (Dickens 1868a: 414)

Throughout this chapter we have argued that the level of skill among farmers and family workers is likely, on average, to be lower than that among employed managers and hired workers. In the first place, the farmer's choice when selecting new members of staff for employment or promotion is constrained by the need to give priority to family members for a whole range of reasons, not least the need to prepare a successor. Other things being equal, the individuals chosen are likely to be less well qualified to do the job than those selected simply on merit. Second, where family members are not paid a specific wage for their work in the business, there

Table 5.1. Educational qualifications and experience of farmers in England, 1970.

Level of education completed	(a) Farm size (acres)						
	<25	25–49	50–99	100–299	300–499	500+	All
Secondary qualifications (%)	21.6	11.4	10.4	16.4	26.6	35.7	18.1
Tertiary for Agric. qualifications (%)	10.0	6.1	6.2	8.9	16.2	24.0	10.3
	(b) Farm type						
	Dairy	Livestock	Pigs/ poultry	Cropping	Horti- culture	Mixed	All
Secondary qualifications (%)	14.5	11.3	28.4	25.6	22.2	17.8	18.1
Tertiary for Agric. qualifications (%)	9.1	5.2	13.3	14.8	12.3	10.2	10.3
	(c) Age in years						
	<26	26–34	35–44	45–54	55–64	65+	All
Secondary qualifications (%)	35.0	29.7	20.9	14.1	10.6	7.8	18.1
Tertiary for Agric. qualifications (%)	35.1	24.1	9.8	5.5	2.8	2.7	10.3

Source: Agriculture EDC 1972

will be a tendency to undervalue their labour. This not only leads to its wasteful use in tasks where the marginal product of labour may be close to zero, but it discourages investment in the development of that resource through training or education.

Evidence from the Agriculture EDC's survey of agricultural manpower in England and Wales in 1970 certainly seems to endorse this expectation. Among the farmers covered by the survey, less than 20 per cent had any secondary education qualification and only 10 per cent reported that they had or were studying for agricultural qualifications in further or higher education. As Table 5.1 shows there was a clear relationship between farm characteristics and the educational background of the farmers.

The relationship with farm size is particularly interesting, showing that the possession of educational qualifications both at secondary level and in further or higher education is greatest among farmers from the smallest as well as the largest farms. This relationship may itself be a reflection of enterprise type for the possession of educational qualifications was higher among farmers on both pig and poultry and horticultural units, which tend to be smaller in size.

However, the EDC survey also shows a relationship between the possession of educational qualifications and the age of the farmer and their report emphasizes the fact that educational provision (and particularly agricultural further education) was much more limited in the pre-war era in which many of these farmers had grown up. Yet even among those aged less than 26 at the time of the EDC survey, only 35 per cent had secondary education qualifications and a similar percentage had attended or were attending college or university.

In the light of the rapid expansion of secondary and tertiary education after the war, it is not surprising that a recent survey by the NatWest Bank (1992) reveals a much higher proportion of farmers with some educational qualification. Just over half of the sample (52 per cent) had studied 'Farming Practice' in some form or other, though in this survey short-courses provided by the Agricultural Training Board were also included as well as tertiary education. About a quarter had attended a full-time course at an agricultural college and such courses (either at college or university) seem to have become established as a standard component of the *détour professionelle* followed by many farmers' children after leaving secondary school (see Chapter 8).

The NatWest Bank survey still found some variation according to the farmer's age. Among those aged less than 35, three quarters had studied 'Farming Practice' and even among those aged 45–60 it was as high as 46 per cent. But despite the increase in the formal post-secondary education of farmers, the report still concludes that the findings show a 'low level of formal training among farmers' though it is not clear whether it is in fact lower than that among other self-employed businessmen or even the population as a whole.

Successive studies of attitudes to training among UK farmers have high-lighted the constraints on the uptake of formal training in farming – the small and scattered workforce, the reluctance to release individual workers who may constitute half the workforce, access problems where training is provided off the farm, fears that their investment will be lost as workers are 'poached' by other employers, and so on. However, the Agricultural Training Board (ATB) has not only achieved some notable success in over-coming these problems but has designed certain courses specifically for the farm family business. Some have dealt with particular family issues such as farming succession, but the most notable success has been that of short-courses on farm accounts and book-keeping developed for farmers' wives (Hastings 1987/8). The main lesson seems to be that training providers catering for the farm family business need to be proactive and not merely respond passively to the expressed demand for vocational education and training.

Motivating the Family Workforce

Motivating the family workforce is just as important a responsibility for farmers as motivating their employees. Despite the importance of the family component of the farm workforce, there is a dearth of research on the management of this part of the workforce and most farm management teaching relies on standard texts on human resource management which tend to be based on the experience of large manufacturing firms. It may be that such texts contain basic principles that are just as relevant to the management of the family workforce but such hypotheses still need to be tested.

Handy (1981) suggests that the amount of effort, energy and enthusi-asm that an individual expends in his work is the outcome of a **motivation calculus**. This calculus takes into account two factors – the likelihood of particular outcomes following particular behaviour (such as the financial reward, praise, encouragement or extra responsibility that might follow the expenditure of additional effort at work), and the relevance of these outcomes to their own individual needs. A particular outcome may be certain, but if it does not cater for an unsatisfied need, it will not motivate (Maslow 1954). Since each individual's needs are different, the manager must strike a distinctive 'psychological contract' with each person that he manages.

Handy goes on to characterize three types of psychological contract – coercive, calculative and collaborative. In the first (typified by prisons and parts of the armed services) the individual may be physically coerced into carrying out orders; in the next he is encouraged to do what is asked by the establishment of an appropriate calculative contract; in the last he does what he and the manager recognize is required because both share the same objectives for the organization, and both are thus parties to a collaborative contract.

While this analysis may be relevant to the management of the family workforce, there is little empirical evidence either on the prevalence of coercive as against calculative and collaborative contracts in the farm family business, or on the nature of the motivation calculus. Certainly, the view that regards the promise of his future inheritance as a major source of motivation for the farmer's son implies that psychological contracts in the farm family business may have a solid calculative base.

Resolving Family Differences

While there may be some inherent advantages in using family labour in terms of its commitment and flexibility (see above), the management of a workforce comprising family members is likely to be much more complex than one made up exclusively of employees since family roles and interpersonal relationships must often coexist with work roles and working relationships. Relations between the supervisor and supervised are an inherent source of tension in any organization, but these tensions are likely to be magnified when the two live together and when the supervisor regards the work requirement as open-ended, as some farm parents do (Rosenblatt and Anderson 1981). The position of sons can be very ambiguous:

> Their father teaches them their trade both in his capacity of father and in that of master of apprentices, with the result that the child never knows if a reprimand, a piece of advice, or a set of instructions belongs to everyday or professional life.
>
> (Mendras 1970: 76)

Farming fathers may expect their sons to be more conscientious than hired workers, but by the same token sons may be more independent in spirit. Their very intimacy gives an emotional dimension to the working relationship. Parents and minor children who work together do not have the option of divorcing each other. Children growing up on farms may need to find school or other interests that can keep them legitimately apart from their parents (Rosenblatt and Anderson 1981). Adult sons and daughters can leave the farm to study or work but the prospect of succession, parental expectations and filial responsibility may constrain their freedom to act.

The mismatch between the family labour supply and the farm's demand for labour is also a potential source of conflict. The seemingly insatiable demands of the farm in the early, establishment phase can be a heavy burden for a wife with young children and an imposition for the children themselves. But farms that 'needed everybody' in the early labour-intensive period of production might not require the labour of family members as a stable stage of operation is reached. This can be hard for wives who have contributed much to the success of the farm and who wish to maintain their involvement. As one American farm wife bitterly concluded, 'We are no longer a farm family' (Colman and Elbert 1984).

Behavioural theories of the firm suggest ways in which firms might resolve conflicts, both between individuals and between departments. The concept of the **coalition** was introduced by Cyert and March (1963). A coalition is defined to include everyone who has reason to expect anything from the firm – managers, employees, shareholders, customers, creditors. Most coalition members tend to take no great interest in the specific objectives of the firm provided they receive a satisfactory stream of 'side payments'. In effect managers buy off interference from outside interests by paying sufficiently high wages to employees, dividends to shareholders, producing a satisfactory product for consumers and paying off creditors in good time (Cyert and March 1963). In the same way members of the farm household who are not partners or directors may be persuaded by a satisfactory wage or comfortable living conditions, not to interfere in the setting of farm business objectives.

This still leaves the potential for conflict between managers of different departments, or in a family farm between partners. Certain managers (young or elderly partners perhaps) can be rewarded with higher salaries or greater prestige in return for agreeing not to participate in the decision-making process. Beyond this, Cyert and March suggest that intra-management bargaining will generate two sets of objectives, one qualitative and one quantitative. Qualitative objectives like 'putting the customer first' or 'producing a high quality product' sound superficially impressive. Almost any managerial objective can be justified by reference to them, inducing managers to believe that they share at least some communally-agreed objectives. This can help to defuse conflict. Quantitative goals relating to production, level of sales, market share and profit are the *real* bargaining ground where compromises have to be reached.

Management Teams

The management team is one of the most important work-groups found on UK farms today. As the technical complexity of farming has increased, the lone farmer/manager taking all the decisions on his own has become a figure of the past. Increasingly, the farmer consults and even comes to share decisions with a host of other people outside the business – his vet, his bank manager, his agronomist, and so on. As we have seen, one paradox of post-war developments in UK farming is that while the number of people involved in providing the manual labour input to the farm has decreased, the number involved either directly or indirectly in the managerial input has actually increased. In this sense, the management of farms has become more of a group activity.

Throughout this chapter we have argued that the farm family business in the UK is becoming increasingly reliant on the **managerial** labour provided by the family and this is not simply the result of technological change. As traditional markets have become less assured and farmers seek alternative opportunities for the use of their assets, the managerial competence and entrepreneurial skills of the family has assumed central importance (Hutson 1987). In the future, the strength of the farm family business may therefore rest on its ability to act as an effective management team. Abrahams (1991) certainly recognizes its potential in this respect:

> A husband and wife team which is hard-working and in which the
> spouses provide both physical and emotional support to each other in
> an atmosphere of mutual respect, is in fact a formidable workforce . . .
>
> (Abrahams 1991: 84)

Research by Meredith Belbin (1983) of the Industrial Training Research Unit throws some light on the characteristics of the successful management team. As a result of a series of experiments using middle managers attending short training courses at the Henley Staff College, Belbin and his fellow researchers came to the conclusion that the most successful teams comprise a mixture of managers with very different personalities and characteristics. The least successful team is made up of a group of people who are all brilliant, confident, outgoing and articulate. Every one of them is so busy thinking brilliant thoughts that no one has the time, still less the inclination, to put them into practice; all are speaking, and no one is listening; all are generating new ideas but no one is reviewing them critically enough to sort the good from the bad, and so on.

The best team contains a mixture of types, but not just any mixture. Box 5.2 shows the eight 'team roles' required for the effective team. Where there are fewer than eight people, some may fill a variety of roles. Of course, the key lesson of Belbin's work is that there is no one ideal type of manager (in terms of personality, outlook or intellect) and the best results always come from the interaction of a variety of different individuals in a team. In most farm family businesses at least part of the team will already be in place. The most perceptive farmer/manager (and the best team player) will first identify what roles are missing from the present team and then find ways of filling them, perhaps by involving carefully-selected 'outsiders' in some of its decision-making or even by adapting himself to fill the missing role. Thus, in the farm family business mother, father, son, feed-rep and neighbour may form the basis of an effective management team.

Box 5.2. Eight ideal types in the successful management team. Source: After Belbin 1983

Plant is bursting with new ideas like a ripe seed-pod but cannot distinguish a good idea from a bad one and is incapable of following any idea through into implementation. It is the ideas themselves that fascinate, and this team member flits from one to another like a distracted butterfly. *Monitor/evaluator* is also intelligent and this team member's analytical mind can identify the flaws in any new idea. So good is this person at seeing faults, he never generates a constructive idea of his own. Both *plant* and *monitor/evaluator* are essential members for the successful management team but they need to be balanced by others: *chairman* and *shaper*, who keep the team's attention focused on its objectives and press the team on towards achieving them; *company worker* who translates ideas into action; *resource investigator* who may not know the answer to the crucial question himself but certainly 'knows a man who does'; *completer/finisher* who is not satisfied till every 'i' is dotted and every 't' is crossed; and *team worker* whose priority is to pour oil on troubled waters and ensure that all the members of the team succeed in working together.

SUMMARY AND IMPLICATIONS

This chapter has examined the labour resource in the farm family business. It has described the distinctive characteristics of the demand for labour in farming and suggested that the farm family business may be uniquely well-placed to meet the inevitable and often unpredictable fluctuations in demand that stem from the farmer's attempt to manipulate biological systems. It has considered the supply of labour from family members and highlighted the importance of opportunity costs and psychic income in determining how much time is devoted to farm production activities. Finally, it has highlighted the fact that labour productivity tends to be low in the farm family business and discussed the ways in which the effective management of family labour can lead to its improvement.

There is clearly a good deal of scope for future research in the areas highlighted by this chapter. In the first place, we need a clearer picture of the manner in which average labour productivity in the farm family business varies as a result of interactions between the family cycle and the business development cycle. At the same time, it will be important to differentiate the welfare implications of low labour productivity for the individual family worker, the farm family, and society as a whole. Secondly, at a time of substantial change in the Common Agricultural Policy, there is a need to distinguish the response of family labour from that of hired labour in estimating the employment impact of policy changes. Finally, the insights into staff motivation and performance gained from studies of large-scale manufacturing industry need to be tested on (and if necessary adapted to) the distinctive circumstances of the farm family business.

In the final analysis the efficient use of the labour resource will depend on the correct valuation of family labour. If any segment of the workforce is undervalued, it will tend to be used inefficiently and farm family welfare will be sub-optimal. This may be a particular problem where one individual takes all the labour input decisions based on his or her subjective valuation of opportunity costs. But even where this is not the case the valuation of alternative uses for family labour may be severely constrained by lack of information on alternative opportunities. Where that information is available, the subjective valuation placed on leisure or the 'psychic' income derived from working on the farm may have a greater effect on labour allocation decisions than do prices in formal markets. One aspect of the farm family business that highlights this central issue of the valuation of family labour is the role of the farmer's spouse, and this forms the subject for our next chapter.

6

MARRIAGE AND THE ROLE OF THE FARMER'S SPOUSE

INTRODUCTION

> The success of the family farm depends a great deal upon the
> resourcefulness of the farmer's wife.
>
> (Rees 1971: 62)

To speak of a farm family is to assume a farmer and spouse living together
on the farm. Agricultural economists tend to treat 'the farmer and spouse' as
a unit; for example the Farm Business Survey (FBS) calculates Occupier's
Net Income as the return to the principal farmer and spouse for their labour
and investment in the farm business. We recognize that the farmer may be
female and the spouse male, but in this chapter we focus on the more usual
situation of a farmer and wife. We try to show how the contribution which
the woman makes to the farm family business is circumscribed by gender
and by her status as a wife. Because the wife's contribution to the family
business is taken for granted, it is easily dismissed as unimportant. In recent
years, the feminist movement has raised the profile of women's work in the
formal and informal economy. Researchers exploring the work done by farm
women have begun to question the unequal distribution of power between
husbands and wives within farm households. The main thrust has been to
underline the importance of the wife's contribution to the economic success
and survival of the farm family business.

The strains imposed on farmers' wives by the declining economic and
social status of farming together with the increasing involvement of women
in the labour market, may however be undermining accepted patterns of
roles and relationships within farming families, posing a threat to the
stability of the family and the viability of the business. This chapter aims to
demonstrate the many-sided contribution which farmers' wives make to the
family business, to suggest how it is changing and to consider what this
might mean for the business and the family. First it considers the likelihood
that the farmer will, in fact, be married.

Chapter Six

MARRIAGE AMONG FARMERS

The concept of 'the farmer and his wife' so often used in agricultural economics, is far from having universal validity.

(Ashby 1953: 97)

Between 70 and 80 per cent of UK farmers are male and married. Various post-war surveys have established that only about 10 per cent of farmers are women, some of whom are themselves married to farmers. Out of 20,000 women farmers, partners and directors on farms over 5 acres in England in 1969, Harrison (1975) suggested that 18,000 were in partnership with their husbands and only 2000 (1 per cent of all farmers) were women farming entirely in their own right. Female farmers are much more likely than male farmers to be single or widowed and to be farming on a very small scale.

The 1970 survey of the agricultural workforce in England and Wales (Agriculture EDC 1972) found that 83 per cent of male farmers were married, confirmed by Harrison's figure of 83.5 per cent for all farm business principals. The likelihood of male farmers being married is not randomly distributed, however. Marriage chances depend to some extent on the age and prospects of the farmer, the size, type and profitability of the farm, its isolation and other factors reflecting the kind of lifestyle a wife could expect. The 1970 labour force survey showed the proportion of male farmers who were married rising steadily from under 77 per cent on farms employing no regular workers to 89 per cent on farms with five or more regular employees. Farmers spending much of their time in managerial activities were more likely to be married than those doing mostly manual work. Farmers on intensive pig, poultry or horticultural holdings and those in the southern half of England stood the best chance of being married, suggesting a link with proximity to towns. At the other extreme, only 73 per cent of farmers on livestock holdings and only 72 per cent in Wales were married, recalling Beresford's (1975) description of farming in mid-Wales as 'unwomanworthy'.

The circumstances associated with farmers remaining single were investigated by Nalson (1968) in his Staffordshire study in the late 1950s. Bachelor farmers were found to be most prevalent on small full-time farms where neither parents nor children had experience of other work. Sons who worked for their parents on small farms, in the expectation of taking over the farm eventually, were tied to the farm and dependent on farming for a living. With a low income and a small farmhouse, a son might not be in a position to marry until both parents had died. By that time his chances of marriage would be low because many of his female peers would already have married or moved away. With limited social contacts, he would then be obliged to seek a bride younger than himself, in competition with younger men whose economic and social prospects were better. Whilst sons who left home to find work improved their marriage prospects, they risked losing the inheritance. Family continuity was therefore difficult to achieve on smaller farms. Sons on larger farms might be in a position to marry earlier; for instance the parents might divide the farmhouse, give the son a cottage on the farm or split the holding.

Daughters are less likely than sons to be left single on small farms after the death of parents. Daughters rarely inherit farms and are socialized at an early age towards other occupations. In remoter rural areas this usually means leaving home, which widens their 'marriage range' compared with their brothers working at home. Besides this, marriage for them is not bound up with the inheritance of the family holding or the availability of another local farm, as it is for sons who hope to marry and start farming at the same time. Daughters thus marry earlier than sons and some marry into towns.

The pattern described by Nalson for upland Staffordshire is a familiar one in areas of small farms remote from towns. One recent survey in Bavaria, for example, found that only 4 per cent of rural girls want to marry farmers and 41 per cent would not do so under any circumstances (Planck 1987). Irish agriculture has experienced a decline in family succession and in the marriage rate of successors since the Second World War, with a widening gap between large and small farms. Market conditions have improved the marriage chances of farmers with large commercial businesses while the position of small farms has worsened. By 1971, farmers between 35 and 45 with over 100 acres in the more favoured eastern region of Leinster were twice as likely as those with under 30 acres to be married. Half of all farmers in the depressed western region of Connaught in the mid-1960s were either single or had no direct heir to take over the farm, the percentage among farmers with less than 30 acres being considerably higher. By this time, almost half of all farmers on smaller acreages were not able to marry unless they combined farming with off-farm employment (Scully 1971; Hannan and Breen 1987).

This threat to the continuation of the family farm has reached such proportions that organized attempts are being made to find brides for farmers. The columns of newspapers such as *The Irish Farmers' Journal* carry numerous advertisements from intending farmers seeking wives. In Japan, boatloads of single farmers from the outlying islands are taken to the mainland in search of brides. At least one bureau in the UK specializes in making introductions between single people from farm and rural backgrounds. In Finland, the agricultural advisory association runs a computer matching programme for single farmers and farmers' offspring, contacting wishful partners at agricultural shows. Most male applicants come from farming families while a majority of the females do not. A follow-up study revealed a low success rate for the programme but suggested that female applicants had a much better chance of finding mates than the males

(Westermarck 1986). In short, while farms continue to be run by men, the chances of those men finding wives depend to some extent on the size, profitability and accessibility of the farm.

BACKGROUNDS OF FARMERS AND WIVES

Many farmers' wives grew up on farms or had some experience of farming prior to marriage but as the farming population shrinks, education and training levels both within and outside agriculture rise and personal mobility increases, growing numbers of farmers are marrying women from outside agriculture. This has implications for the farm family.

Fewer wives than farmers come from farming families and it is possible that the gap is widening. In the Staffordshire study, 81 per cent of married farmers and 69 per cent of their wives had farming fathers. Among a sample of small-scale Fen farmers, 71 per cent were farmers' sons but only 50 per cent of their wives were farmers' daughters. For small farms in Hertford-shire, a more urbanized county, the figures were 61 per cent for farmers and 30 per cent for wives (Gasson 1969).

The larger the farm and the greater the dependence on farming income, the more likely it is that both the farmer's and the wife's parents were farming. This is another way of saying that entry to farming on a large scale is made easier by gifts or inheritance of land, succession to a tenancy, farming capital or contacts acquired from farming parents or parents-in-law. In a recent study of 300 farm households in East and Mid-Devon, for example, two thirds of full-time farmers but only 15 per cent of hobby farmers had farmers on both sides of the family (Gasson et al. 1992a). (Hobby farming was defined in terms of less than 20 per cent of total household income derived from farming.) Similarly in the Staffordshire study, 71 per cent of larger-business farmers but only 45 per cent of farmers with other jobs had both parents and in-laws in farming.

It follows that younger wives and those on smaller farms will be less likely than older wives and those on larger, full-time farms, to have had experience of farming and farm work before marriage. Over time, too, the proportion of wives with previous farming experience is likely to decline. In Staffordshire in the late 1950s, for example, 55 per cent of farmers' wives had done farm work prior to marriage. In the Fens in the late 1960s the figure was 50 per cent but by the early 1980s, only 17 per cent of farmers' wives in the Reading University survey had done farm work before marriage. Younger wives will be more likely to bring the experience of the non-farm labour market to the marriage. The nature of this experience reflects the qualifications and opportunities available to women. Thus in upland Staffordshire, the majority of farmers' wives not working on farms before marriage had been employed in factories or domestic service. Wives of small farmers in the Fens and Hertfordshire had mostly worked in shops and offices while many wives of Reading University FBS co-operators had been secretaries, nurses or teachers before marriage.

To summarize, many farmers have in the past married farmers' daughters and their in-laws may have helped them to start farming. Increasingly nowadays farmers are marrying outside agriculture, which means that wives have less experience of farming but more familiarity with other occupations and with the norms, values and attitudes of the non-farming population.

THE NATURE AND EXTENT OF THE WIFE'S CONTRIBUTION

Evidence from a number of surveys, backed up with observation and common sense, suggests that the majority of wives are involved in the running of the farm business in some capacity. Most do manual work at least some of the time. Many farmers' wives undertake the greater part of the secretarial and paperwork, keep financial records and become involved in discussions about the business. Virtually all wives, if living in the main farmhouse, are expected to answer the telephone, take messages and run errands for the farm. Some wives are responsible for an activity or enterprise on the farm and increasing numbers are running separate businesses from home or taking off-farm employment. Besides this, it is taken for granted that women will be responsible for the reproductive tasks necessary to maintain the farm workforce. For those accustomed to regarding the farm as a business, it is easy to fall into the trap of focusing exclusively on the productive tasks which women undertake on the farm.

No account of the contribution which women make would be complete without mention of their supportive role. The nature of farming and the structure of the industry make the woman's social and psychological support for her partner particularly crucial. Most often this means the husband, but a woman could also be farming in partnership with a father, son or brother. In a family farm, women are also needed to support children and other family members involved in the business. Often too they provide the active links with members of the wider kin network, farm workers' families, the local community and the general public.

It is convenient to examine the work of farmers' wives under these different headings but this is an artificial distinction for in practice the various functions overlap. The very essence of the farm woman's task is to integrate the various individuals and activities concerned with the farm business. She makes appointments, takes messages, communicates, smooths out tensions within the family and with employees, fills in when regular workers are absent, provides an extra pair of hands at busy times or in emergencies, tidies up, collects essential machinery parts and generally oils the wheels of the business.

The wife's contribution tends to be greater, in absolute and relative terms, on smaller farms. Yet even on very large farms in East Anglia where their work constitutes only a small proportion of the total labour input, Newby *et al.* (1978) found that only one wife in four was not involved in the business in any capacity. It is therefore safe to assume that three out of four wives make some direct contribution to the farm family business. Assuming that between 70 and 80 per cent of UK farmers are male and married, there must be between 200,000 and 220,000 farmers' wives. Hence some 140,000 to 176,000 women must be involved in UK agriculture in their capacity as wives of farmers.

MANUAL WORK

Manual labour is the most tangible expression of the wife's contribution to the farm business. A growing body of evidence points to between 60 and 70 per cent of farmers' wives in Britain doing manual work on the farm (Ashby 1953; Agriculture EDC 1972; Buchanan *et al.* 1982; Hastings 1987/8; Whatmore 1991a). In the Arkleton Trust's survey of farm households in twelve countries of Western Europe, the figure was 76 per cent (Bell *et al.* 1990). These statistics are difficult to reconcile with FBS data suggesting that 27 per cent of spouses of farmers had done manual work in 1986/7, or with the 1990 Agricultural Census which records 77,000 spouses (28 per 100 farmers) 'doing farm work'. Involvement in manual work can vary from a full-time commitment to very occasional help and it seems likely that the Census and the FBS refer only to spouses working regularly on the farm.

Using data from the FBS, it has been estimated that farmers' wives contributed 5 per cent of the total manual hours worked by regular family and hired labour on main agricultural holdings in England and Wales in 1986/7 (Gasson 1989). When Britton and Hill (1975) analysed FMS data[1] for 1970/1 they too concluded that wives contributed 5 per cent of the manual hours on full-time farms and Sparrow (1972) reached the same figure using information from the 1970 Agriculture EDC labour force survey.

The manual labour contribution of British farm wives according to the 1986/7 FBS data is equivalent to 19,000 full-time workers, which exceeds the labour force employed on farms in East Anglia and is comparable with the total labour force on Welsh farms. Yet it is quite low by EC standards. Spouses contributed 14.5 per cent of the Annual Work Units on Irish farms in 1975 (Sheridan 1982). Wives provide about one sixth of the total labour

---

[1] The Farm Business Survey used to be known as the Farm Management Survey or FMS.

hours on Dutch farms (Bauwens and Loeffen 1983), between a fifth and a third on French farms (Berlan *et al.* 1980), about a third on Italian farms and 35–40 per cent on Greek farms (Gourdomichalis 1991).

Manual work is only part of the wife's contribution to the farm business, albeit a part which is more easily measured. From the FBS it was calculated that farm-working wives spent 14 hours a week on average doing manual work. Managerial and office work occupied wives for over 10 hours a week, according to a survey carried out by the Agricultural Training Board (Hastings 1987/8). On large farms on Humberside where wives are not usually much involved in manual work, Symes and Marsden (1983b) calculated that 39 per cent of their 'official' working time was spent out on the farm. In Devon where wives typically do much more, manual work comprised 71 per cent of the wife's weekly hours (Gasson *et al.* 1992a). Taking an average from these figures, it can be suggested that typically, half the hours which farmers' wives contribute to the farm business take the form of manual work and half of managerial, administrative and office work. It has already been shown that manual work by wives amounts to 5 per cent of the total **manual** hours worked by the regular labour force on farms in England and Wales. **Total** hours worked by all members of the labour force are unlikely to exceed total **manual** hours by a wide margin; the Agriculture EDC (1972) estimated, for instance, that 88 per cent of farmers' time and 97 per cent of workers' time was spent on manual tasks. At a rough estimate, therefore, wives may be contributing some 9–10 per cent of **total manual and managerial** hours worked by the regular labour force on British farms. Once again, it must be remembered that this excludes the time which wives devote to reproductive tasks for the business in the farm household.

The Gender Division of Labour

A basic feature of the customary organization of farm work was its division into men's work and women's work. The men were responsible for the cultivation and the general labouring work of the farm while the women undertook the dairying and the work of the farm-house and farmyard. Correspondingly it took two people to run a farm, the master and mistress, who were respectively the heads of each division of the work.

(Jenkins 1971: 75)

In the farming communities of south-west Wales at the turn of the twentieth century which Jenkins was describing, farmers and wives were supervisors of labour in their respective spheres. Today few farmers and fewer wives have any employees under them, yet on most farms there is still a clear division of labour along gender lines.

Wives tend to be allocated routine tasks which are not mechanized.

They work with animals rather than crops, in horticulture rather than arable production, in and around the farm buildings rather than in the fields. Typical tasks for women include rearing calves and lambs, feeding cattle, sheep and hens, fetching the cows, rounding up straying stock. Jobs involving high technology, like milking in a modern parlour, are regarded as men's work (though women frequently clean the milking equipment). One Irish study reported 70 per cent of farm wives regularly cleaning the milking utensils, 52 per cent cleaning out cowsheds and more than half doing field work (Sheridan 1982). In a Dutch study (Bauwens and Loeffen 1983), the kinds of tasks which farmers' wives performed most regularly were, in descending order:

- cleaning the dairy and milking equipment;
- feeding and looking after calves;
- collecting eggs;
- feeding and looking after pigs;
- cleaning sheds;
- feeding and looking after chickens;
- milking cows;
- weeding by hand;
- bringing cows in for milking;
- packing crops for sale;
- haymaking.

The kinds of tasks undertaken by British and North American farm women are illustrated in Table 6.1. Many more illustrations of the gender division of labour on farms could be produced from societies at all levels of economic development. From their study of County Clare in the 1930s, Arensberg and Kimball (1968) observed many attitudes and beliefs which surrounded this type of division of labour, confirming the view that it was largely socially determined:

> Ridicule and laughter greet suggestions that either sex busy itself with
> the work of the other, though in the case of a woman doing a man's
> work some of the praise bestowed upon surprising successes meets her
> if she does it well. There is also an entire body of popular belief and
> superstition surrounding the dichotomy in farm labor.
>
> (Arensberg and Kimball 1968: 49)

Among the reasons put forward to account for the gender division of labour on family farms in contemporary western society are: women's lack of strength and physique; family and domestic ties; a mental blockage about mechanical matters; lack of training; inadequate instruction on the job; male prejudice. On the other hand manual dexterity, patience and the maternal instinct are believed to be essentially female qualities which fit women to perform certain tasks better than men. Biological explanations are of

Table 6.1. Women's involvement in farm tasks.

	Per cent who perform this task			
	Regularly	Occasionally	Never	Total
Task				
(a) *UK farm wives*				
Rear calves or lambs	43	30	27	100
Feed poultry, collect eggs	39	16	45	100
Round up straying animals	30	59	11	100
Milk cows	12	19	69	100
Drive a tractor	11	55	34	100
N = 1215				
(b) *US farm wives*				
Take care of animals including milking cows	32	30	38	100
Harvest crops, including running trucks	18	27	55	100
Do other field work without machinery	19	24	57	100
Plough, disc, plant, cultivate	12	25	63	100
Apply fertilizers, herbicides, pesticides	4	10	86	100
N = 497				

Sources: (a) Gasson 1980b; (b) Jones and Rosenfeld 1981

doubtful validity. For many personal characteristics such as height and physical strength, male and female distributions overlap. That is to say, the average man is stronger than the average woman, but some women are stronger than the average man. By the same token, some men are more patient, gentle and dexterous than the average woman. As will be shown, the work wives do depends to a great extent on whether or not men are available to do it. Thus on the small farm with only the farmer and wife to do the work, she may have to do heavy lifting and other tasks which on the larger farm would be considered unsuitable for a woman.

Whether or not girls are born lacking a certain mechanical aptitude which is present in boys, it is a fact that most farmers' wives today grew up in a world where boys were encouraged but girls discouraged from taking an interest in mechanical matters. In a *Farmers Weekly* survey in 1980, only 2 per cent of the 1600 women responding said that they repaired machinery regularly whereas 48 per cent regularly fed calves or lambs. Milking, predominantly a female task when it was done by hand, becomes man's work when machines are introduced. This is demonstrated in Table 6.2,

Table 6.2. Division of farm work between farmer and wife.

Task	Husband only	Husband mainly	Shared equally (%)	Wife mainly	Wife only	Total
(a) *Finland*						
Machine repair and maintenance	89	8	2	0	1	100
Seeding	87	8	5	0	0	100
Forestry work	75	14	9	1	1	100
Threshing	69	13	18	0	0	100
Building repair and maintenance	33	19	40	5	3	100
Feeding livestock	8	5	58	17	12	100
Care of sick animals	6	4	66	12	12	100
Milking and milk processing	6	4	42	19	29	100
N = 776						
(b) *Wisconsin*						
Driving tractor and doing fieldwork	47	50	3	0	0	100
Feeding livestock	47	36	11	4	2	100
Milking cows	39	27	25	7	2	100
Cleaning milking equipment	19	8	6	19	48	100
Keeping chickens	13	6	12	24	45	100
N = 510						

Sources: (a) Siiskonen *et al* 1982; (b) Wilkening 1981b.

which illustrates the typical gender division of tasks on farms in Wisconsin (USA), and Finland. Milking is predominantly the wife's job on Finnish farms, but predominantly the husband's in Wisconsin where the dairy enterprise would typically be much larger and more capital intensive.

Another factor helping to account for the gender division of labour on farms is the importance of the activity to the economic success of the business. In south-west Wales at the turn of the century women used to do all the milking as well as calf rearing and dairy work. It was considered degrading for a man to milk, one explanation being that a woman's smaller hands make it 'natural' for her to be better at the job. This attitude only changed with the development of a guaranteed market for milk following the establishment of the Milk Marketing Board in 1933, when milk production became important for the economic success of the farm business (Jenkins 1971).

Sources of Variation in the Wife's Manual Contribution

Personal and family characteristics like age and number of dependent children do not have much bearing on the amount of work women are expected to do on farms (Whatmore 1991a). The wife's manual labour input does however vary systematically by size and type of farm and by region. The larger the farm business, the less likely is the wife to be involved in manual work. The Essex University survey found that on very large East Anglian farms, only 9 per cent of wives regularly worked compared with 18 per cent on a cross-section of Suffolk farms (Newby *et al.* 1978). Analysis of FBS data reveals a wide range, from 45 per cent of wives working on farms below 8 BSU[2] to 4 per cent on farms over 100 BSU. Wives are most likely to do manual work regularly on horticultural holdings and upland beef and sheep farms, least likely on cropping farms. Not only are they more likely to work, but wives typically put in longer hours and contribute a larger share of the total labour input on small farms than on larger farms (Figure 6.1).

Reflecting variations by farm size and type, the manual contribution which farmers' wives make to agriculture increases moving from east to west across the British Isles. Only 7 per cent of wives do manual work regularly in East Anglia compared with 37 per cent in the north west and

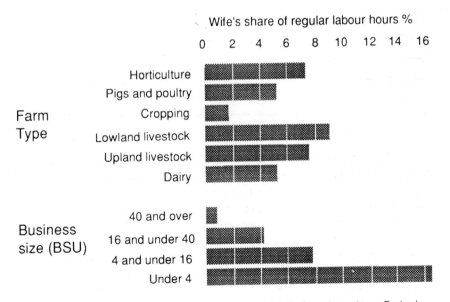

Figure 6.1. Proportion of manual hours worked by farmers' wives by farm size and type, England and Wales 1986/7. Source: Gasson 1989, derived from FBS 1986/7

[2]British Standard Units or BSU have now replaced ESU as a measure of business size: 1 BSU = 2 ESU.

over 40 per cent in Wales and the south west (Gasson 1989). The declining involvement of wives in manual work as farm size increases appears to hold in all countries and however size is measured. As farm businesses become fewer and larger, an inevitable consequence of the capitalist development of agriculture, the labour contribution of wives to the farming sector should therefore be shrinking. Opinion is however divided with some arguing that women will be displaced, others maintaining that they will continue to play an important role.

To understand the variation in farm women's activities, it is necessary to develop an analytical framework sensitive to the complex nature of capitalist development in agriculture. Shaver (1991) distinguishes two key elements in the process, one **the modernization of agriculture** and the other **the development of capitalist relations of production**. Modernization refers to the development of technology and commercialization. Signs of modernization are mechanization, specialization and consolidation of enterprises and increased dependence upon capital investment. Development of capitalist relations of production at the farm level is characterized by replacement of family with paid labour, the separation of labour and capital and the segregation of manual work and management. 'Modernization' in Shaver's terms approximates to indirect subsumption of the labour process by capital and 'the development of capitalist relations' to direct subsumption.

Shaver classified a sample of Quebec farms according to level of modernization (based on capital value of land, buildings and machinery) and capitalist relations of production (presence or absence of paid labour) and compared women's work between categories. She concluded that the contribution of women remained important despite the radical transformation of the agricultural sector in a capitalist economy. Her findings indicated that variations in the type and amount of work performed by women were largely determined by the *interaction* between the two forms of subsumption. On family-labour farms, modernization tends to maintain if not increase women's contribution to farm work whereas on farms dependent on capitalist relations of production, modernization reduces women's farm work while increasing their domestic work. Data from a 1989 *Farmers Weekly* survey of the activities of UK farmers' wives were analysed along similar lines. Wives were found to be more intimately involved in all aspects of the farm business on family-worked farms than on labour-employing farms, whatever their size (Gasson 1992). In other words, it is the separation of business ownership and control from family labour, rather than business size itself, which accounts for variations in the wife's role.

To sum up, seven out of ten farmers' wives do manual work on UK farms. On a conservative estimate they contribute 5 per cent of the regular manual labour input in British agriculture and probably a larger share of total labour inputs. On smaller, less mechanized farms and family-labour farms in the UK and elsewhere, the wife's contribution is typically larger.

ADMINISTRATION, MANAGEMENT AND DECISION-MAKING

Besides doing manual work, the majority of farmers' wives share in the office work, administration and decision-making for the farm business. Even so, manual work seems to carry a particular significance in defining the wife's contribution. As one woman on a large farm in East Anglia put it, 'I never really consider myself a "proper" farmer's wife as I don't do any manual work'. A double standard may be operating here, since the time that farmers spend in management is regarded as more valuable than their manual work. The FBS, for example, attaches a higher value to farmers' managerial hours than to manual hours.

Office Work

Activities like answering the telephone, taking messages and running errands for the business appear to be almost universal for farmers' wives, especially for wives of senior partners living in the main farmhouse. They seem to be regarded as a 'natural' part of the wife's role, an extension of her domestic duties. Table 6.3 shows how common such activities were for three samples of farmers' wives. The UK sample was drawn from *Farmers Weekly* readers who completed a questionnaire printed in the paper in 1989, the Irish sample from women responding to a similar questionnaire in *The Irish Farmers' Journal* in 1990.

Table 6.3. Wives' involvement in farm business administration.

Activity	Reading FMS	UK sample	Irish sample
	(per cent of women doing this regularly)		
Dealing with callers, telephone	88	90	87
Running errands for the business	48	72	76
Discussing the farm business	68	70	70
Work in the farm office	42	67	72
Dealing with employees	20	27	32
Number in sample	156	1091	509

Sources: Buchanan *et al* 1982; *Farmers Weekly* 1989 survey; *Irish Farmers Journal* 1990 survey

Compared with the self-selected samples of British and Irish farmers' wives, the Reading University sample appeared less likely to do the office work on a regular basis. Higher figures may however be more typical of the country as a whole. In a survey of 600 wives of agricultural training group members from all parts of Britain, nearly 70 per cent said that they undertook the greater part of the secretarial and paper work for the business, 62 per cent keeping financial records, 63 per cent sorting and filing paper work. Their role was not confined to secretarial and clerical duties, for 52 per cent said that they regularly decided when to pay bills and 27 per cent dealt with suppliers and dealers (Hastings 1987/8). Other studies suggest that between one third and two thirds of British farm wives are responsible for the farm accounts (Gasson 1980b; Whatmore 1991a). Similar figures have been reported for France (Berlan *et al.* 1980), Ireland (Sheridan 1982), The Netherlands (Bauwens and Loeffen 1983), the United States (Jones and Rosenfeld 1981) and New Zealand (Allan 1985). As a result, the women are often in closer contact with the financial side of the farm business, and more concerned about the bank balance and cash flow than the men. They are well placed to advise on the long-term future of the business and perhaps better-placed than their husbands to take advantage of training in financial management.

Decision-making

How are decisions reached in a farm family business? As we have already pointed out, empirical evidence on this topic is very sparse. Intuitively we feel it would be wrong to characterize the decision-making process in terms of a single entrepreneur making decisions in the light of his own objectives but equally wrong to visualize a group of decision-makers (the family) making decisions on the basis of several sets of possibly conflicting objectives:

> In reality, on different farms the true nature of the decision-making process will come somewhere between these two extremes, but the person who ignores the fact that many farm business decisions are in fact family decisions, as much influenced by family developments as business developments, is taking large strides away from reality.
>
> (Buchanan *et al.* 1982: 8)

Evidence from a number of surveys in which wives have been questioned suggests that farmers usually consult their wives over long-term strategic business decisions that may involve the family, such as whether to take out a loan, buy land, develop a new enterprise; for instance 95 per cent of Dutch farm wives are involved in such discussions (Bauwens and Loeffen 1983). In the *Farmers Weekly* sample, 43 per cent of wives felt they would be

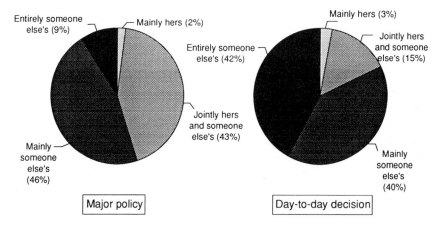

Figure 6.2. UK farm wives' involvement in decision-making. Source: Gasson 1990

jointly responsible for major decisions. Comparable surveys suggest figures of about 40 per cent for New Zealand and 50 per cent for the US (Allan 1985; Jones and Rosenfeld 1981). Wives are typically drawn less into day-to-day tactical management decisions which depend much more on the technical knowledge of the person on the spot (Figure 6.2).

Some wives in the Reading University survey drew a distinction between 'being there' to help and support when necessary and 'interfering' in the business. The very nature of decision-making in farm families makes it difficult to identify the principal actor. To determine who came up with a new idea or who took the final decision would be a complex and probably fruitless exercise when the rules of interaction are implicit and never questioned. So much depends on the nature of the relationship between the spouses. Tensions between the generations add to the complexity. For instance one young farmer's wife and partner in the *Farmers Weekly* survey complained 'I would like more consultation but father-in-law is still the only one consulted even though he has in most respects handed over the reins'. Another woman was more philosophical: 'I have not been married long, so feel I should not impose influence too quickly. Being involved in business decisions is sometimes a subtle process . . .'

Enterprise Management

Wives may be excluded from some areas of decision-making but fully involved or even solely responsible for others. Some 38 per cent of women in the UK sample and 59 per cent of the Irish wives said they were personally responsible for some enterprise or activity on the farm. Typical activities are calf rearing, keeping dairy records, running a flock of sheep, organizing a Pick Your Own enterprise, hiring casual labour for fruit-picking. A number of Irish women taking part in the survey were responsible for the dairy herd, the main enterprise on over half the Irish farms studied. UK farm wives are more likely to run a marginal, diversified enterprise such as making cheese or keeping geese or bees.

Legal Status

One sign of the wife's involvement in the business is her legal status and typically around half of all farmers' wives are partners or directors in the family enterprise (Whatmore 1991a; Gasson 1992). A partnership is a tax-efficient form for the medium-sized farm business, which raises the question of whether wives are made partners for tax reasons only. At an Agricultural Economics Society conference, one speaker queried results of a survey showing what proportion of wives work on the farm:

> ... I think it would be very misleading to apply them [the figures] more widely. To what extent, for instance, are the figures influenced by the fact that if a farmer's wife does farm work, or even secretarial work for her husband, she can claim an earned income allowance in Income Tax?

> (Ashby 1953: discussion)

Since that comment was made, the introduction of Capital Transfer Tax provided a much stronger incentive to give wives partnership status. One respondent in the *Farmers Weekly* survey complained 'I was made a partner on the advice of a solicitor early on but most of the decisions about the farm have been taken by my husband'. Notwithstanding such examples, survey evidence suggests that wives who are in partnership are generally more active than other wives in decision-making. In the *Farmers Weekly* survey, wives who were partners were three times more likely than wives without legal status to have an equal say in major policy decisions.

Variations in the Wife's Managerial Role

Size of farm, a potent influence on women's manual work, seems to have little bearing on the frequency with which wives will deal with callers, answer the telephone, run errands and do office work. These appear to be universal activities for farm wives. On smaller family-worked farms, however, wives have a greater share in making decisions. The 1980 *Farmers Weekly* survey shows the proportion of wives who are legal partners and who have joint responsibility for major decisions declining as farm size increases. On larger farms the wife may not even be consulted about major policy matters (Table 6.4).

Table 6.4. UK farm wives' involvement in major decisions by farm size (per cent).

Farm size (ha)	Responsibility for major decisions		
	Wife is legal partner	Shared equally	Wife not consulted
Under 20	65	52	8
20–39	58	49	5
40–99	56	34	10
100–199	53	25	17
200 and over	41	21	29

Source: Gasson 1980b

Table 6.5. Decision-making and reliance on farm income among farm households in East and Mid Devon.

Decisions	Household reliance on farming income			
	0–20	21–50	51–100	All households
	(per cent of households)			
Major financial				
Farmer alone	37	50	36	38
Farmer and spouse	52	35	30	35
Farmer and family	7	13	33	25
Other	4	2	1	2
Total	100	100	100	100
Day-to-day				
Farmer alone	45	63	42	45
Farmer and spouse	43	23	22	27
Farmer and family	8	12	31	24
Other	4	2	5	4
Total	100	100	100	100
Numbers	61	29	210	300

Source: Gasson *et al* 1992a

This variation is partly a reflection of the wife's involvement in manual work, those women who are more familiar with the everyday work of the farm having a greater say in matters which closely concern them. It may also reflect the presence or absence of other family members or business partners. A farmer usually needs someone to act as a sounding-board for ideas. On a small farm the wife may be the only person available but in a larger business the farmer may discuss the business with his parents, brothers or sons. Decision-making may require highly technical knowledge and these other family members may be better informed than wives. The Devon survey showed that the greater the household's level of dependence on farming income (and by implication the larger the business), the greater the involvement of other family members in decision-making (Gasson *et al.* 1992a). The role of wives was greatest on farms providing less than one fifth of total household income (Table 6.5).

This section has portrayed the typical farmer's wife as involved in the management side of the business without having major responsibility for it. As with manual work, the woman's contribution tends to be greater on smaller farms, although survey data cannot really do justice to the complexity of the decision-making process.

HOURS OF WORK

It is difficult to quantify the amount of work which wives contribute to the farm business. Their hours of work are not specified, may vary from day to day and from season to season and overlap with domestic and other duties.

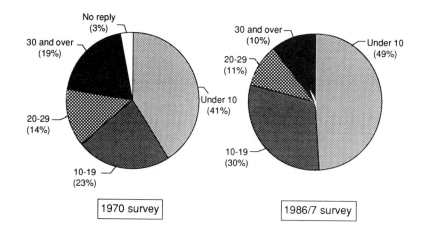

Figure 6.3. Distribution of wives by hours of manual work per week. Sources: Agriculture EDC 1972; Gasson 1989

Nevertheless fairly consistent figures seem to emerge. Wives in the FBS sample who were recorded as doing any manual work averaged 14.2 hours per week in 1986/7, while in the 1970 Agriculture EDC study, farm-working wives averaged 17 hours. In both cases the distribution was skewed, the majority probably averaging about one hour a day but a substantial minority putting in over 30 hours (Figure 6.3).

Respondents in the *Farmers Weekly* and Irish surveys were asked to estimate how many hours a week, on average, they spent in manual, secretarial, administrative and managerial work for the farm business. As one respondent from a large farm observed:

> The number of hours actually 'working' each week is very small, but I am constantly on 'standby duty', waiting for calls, or waiting to give messages, or waiting to meet someone etc. Just like a receptionist, I suppose. But I feel I cannot include those hours as work as it is impossible to calculate them.

Even so, nine out of ten respondents in both samples did manage to answer the question. The mean was 28 hours a week for the UK sample, 38 hours for the Irish women. Over a quarter of the UK wives and more than a third of the Irish averaged over 40 hours. Although wives on larger farms are generally less involved in manual work, they do not necessarily put in fewer hours in total for the farm business, devoting their time instead to office

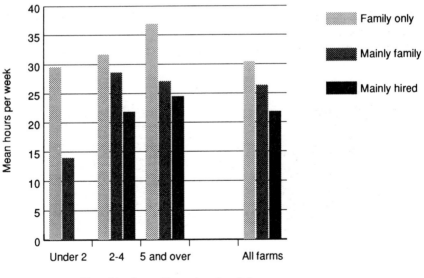

Figure 6.4. Mean weekly hours worked by farmers' wives by size of business and type of labour force, UK 1989. Source: Gasson 1992

work, administration and a share in management. Where there is more reliance on hired labour, however, the wife's involvement is clearly curtailed (Figure 6.4). Once again it appears that the development of capitalist relations of production, rather than size of business, that is associated with the smaller contribution of wives on large farms.

OTHER CONTRIBUTIONS TO THE FARM BUSINESS

Besides doing manual and managerial work for the family business, some wives bring land or capital to the farm at marriage and some use their earnings to help finance business expansion or even survival. Wives may also bring their 'personal capital' of knowledge and skills, which does not only mean farming skills. UK farmers' wives from a farming background are understandably more likely than those from non-farm backgrounds to have brought land and also capital to the marriage and more inclined to believe that they contributed useful skills. Wives from other backgrounds, and younger women, appear somewhat more likely to have contributed income. It is noticeable that older women tend to be the ones bringing a dowry of land or capital to the marriage (Table 6.6).

Farm Diversification

Downward pressure on farm incomes is forcing many farm families to seek additional sources of income. The thrust of Government policy in recent years has been to encourage farm diversification, that is to say alternative uses of the farm's resources of land, buildings or other assets. This covers the provision of tourist accommodation, sport and recreational enterprises,

Table 6.6. UK farmers' wives' financial and other contributions to the farm business by age and background.

| Type of contribution | Wife's background | | Age range | | |
| | Farm | Non-farm | Under 40 | 40+ | Total |
		(per cent contributing)			
Land	21	4	8	15	12
Capital	55	44	44	53	49
Private income	20	23	23	20	22
Knowledge, skills	70	57	64	63	64

Source: Gasson 1990

processing and retailing of farm products, producing and selling craft goods and speciality products and a wide range of other possibilities. Many farmers' wives provide farmhouse bed-and-breakfast and other forms of tourist accommodation like caravans and campsites. Riding schools and other horse-based enterprises, food processing, farm shops, Pick Your Own and educational enterprises are also frequently run by farmers' wives. Among respondents in the *Farmers Weekly* sample, 27 per cent ran a diversified enterprise on the farm. Several commented that the viability of the whole farm business depended upon the market outlet or the income contributed by the wife's enterprise.

Although it is often assumed that farm diversification is a response to low farm incomes, no association was found in the *Farmers Weekly* survey between size of business and the likelihood of the wife's running a diversified enterprise. An in-depth study of farmers' wives taking in summer visitors in the Devon parish of Hartland suggests a more complex set of motives (Bouquet 1985). Many Hartland farms specialize in milk production, an activity which has become increasingly capital-intensive and has been largely transferred from the female to the male domain during the twentieth century. Self-employment is one means for the woman who is marginalized from the larger farm business to regain status, recognition and a personal sense of achievement as well as helping to finance farm modernization or reduce the overdraft. Hartland's location on the north coast of Devon and its isolation from large towns with more diverse employment opportunities for women made taking in visitors an obvious choice of enterprise for farmers' wives. Prominent participation in 'good causes' was another way in which the Hartland women competed for status.

Off-farm Employment

Growing numbers of farmers' wives are taking off-farm employment and this is especially important in more urbanized parts of the country. Among the *Farmers Weekly* sample, 18 per cent of the women and 15 per cent of their husbands had off-farm jobs. To a growing extent it is the women who, with better qualifications, wider job experience and more marketable skills than their husbands, are finding off-farm employment (Symes 1991). Younger wives and those from non-farm backgrounds are more likely to work off the farm, suggesting a rising trend. In the *Farmers Weekly* sample, for instance, 24 per cent of the under-40s but only 15 per cent of wives over 40 had off-farm jobs. Already the tendency has been noted in France and other parts of Western Europe for pluriactivity of the farm family and notably of the spouse to expand while pluriactivity of the farm operator is declining (Fuller and Brun 1988). In Denmark the proportion of farmers' wives working off the farm nearly trebled between 1960 and 1968, a trend which may have made it less necessary for farmers themselves to find other work (Morkeberg 1978).

Off-farm employment of farmers tends to decline with increasing farm size while the employment of wives shows only a weak association, if any, with business size (Gasson 1988). On small farms, off-farm work for one or both spouses is often a financial necessity. On larger farms which are capable of generating an adequate income for a family, off-farm work for the wife might be rather an expression of personal choice. As one woman put it, 'A farmer's wife with no agricultural qualifications or aptitude often finds herself trapped in a domestic role. I wish I had continued my own career.' The assumption that they will always be available if required to help on the farm may prevent wives seeking outside employment. Their *presence* on the farm may be judged essential even if their skills remain seriously under-employed (Symes 1991).

To conclude, besides contributing directly to the productive activities of the farm business, increasing numbers of wives are running diversified enterprises at home or seeking off-farm employment. Having another job can spell independence, status and self-confidence for the woman as well as more disposable income.

THE WIFE'S ROLE IN REPRODUCTION OF THE FARM HOUSEHOLD

Capital cannot operate without subsistence production since the goods and labour power it appropriates are based on previous expenditure of labour which takes place within the household.

(Long 1984: 8–9)

The work that women must do to 'reproduce' the labour force, to maintain other members of the household in good health so that they can continue working, ought to be included as part of their 'economic participation' in the farm family business (Fassinger and Schwarzweller 1984). The wife's role in reproduction does quite literally include producing and rearing the farmers of the future. Bringing up children can thrust all other tasks into the background. On the smaller farm where the wife's labour is essential, it can be hard to satisfy the demands of children and the farm. Women are often restricted to jobs they can do with a child in tow. Part of the wife's role is to socialize children towards careers. This may entail preparing one child, nearly always a son, to take over the farm eventually and others to look elsewhere. In today's harsh economic climate there is anecdotal evidence of parents discouraging children from aspiring to farm, or at least from starting to farm with no other job qualifications or useful skills. Mothers who have experience of non-farming occupations can provide alternative role models for their children.

While most wives, and indeed most women, are responsible for house-work, shopping and cooking, the domestic burden on a farmer's wife may be heavier than that of the average housewife, for a number of reasons. Husbands and possibly other family members or employees on the farm may require a hot midday meal. Farm work is hard on clothes, necessitating much washing and mending. Farmhouses are likely to be large and old, demanding more upkeep and repair than the average family home. The garden may be large too, and farm women typically produce, process and preserve more food than the average housewife (see for instance Morkeberg 1978; Guillou 1991; Sachs 1991). Rural living adds to the time spent shopping, transporting children, transacting business and running errands.

Survey evidence from the United States suggests that farmers' wives receive less help in the home from husbands than the average city wife; 70 per cent of farm wives but only 39 per cent of city wives handled more than half of a list of tasks themselves. The list included lawn mowing, a task always undertaken by 44 per cent of farmers but 66 per cent of city husbands. Similarly 55 per cent of farmers but 73 per cent of city husbands did all the home repairs. A possible explanation is that the farmer's constant involvement in his work makes him relatively unavailable for household tasks whereas the city husband's separation from his place of work makes him highly available, and morally defenceless, when there are tasks to be done at home (Blood and Wolfe 1960).

While farm wives may receive less help from their husbands in the home, they are more involved in their husband's work than the average wife. Coping with competing demands is part of the wife's lot. As the woman in the Reading University survey observed, the farmer's wife 'has to be prepared to do anything at any time at very short notice and regardless of what is in the oven'. This is not a new situation, as this extract from the diary of an eighteenth century farmer's wife indicates:

> We not to church yester eve, John and me and Sarah bein bussie at
> cuvvering the hay stackes, now that they be sunk well and wethered.
> We at it all day between the milking and feeding of pigges and calves;
> so no tyme to cook, at which John not verrie pleased.
>
> (Hughes 1980: 37)

A number of observers have commented on the role of the farmer's wife as mediator in disputes between father and son (Buchanan *et al.* 1982; Hastings 1984; Hutson 1987; see also Chapter 8). Women have traditionally been seen as the managers of kinship links. As the trend has been for family farms to expand to incorporate children rather than setting them up in independent units, kinship ties become focused within the family business rather than linking one farm to another. The wife's role as a mediator could therefore become increasingly important.

A study in Wisconsin shed some light on how conflicts are settled when

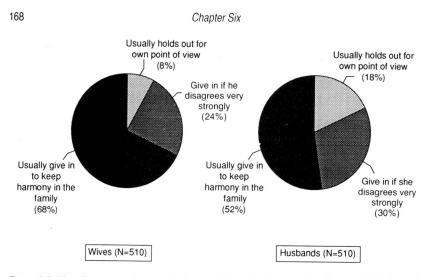

Figure 6.5. How disagreements are settled among Wisconsin farm couples. Source: Wilkening and Bharadwaj 1966

farm husbands and wives disagree (Figure 6.5). More husbands than wives said that they 'usually hold out for their own point of view' while more wives than husbands 'usually give in to keep harmony in the family'. Comparing couples' responses, it emerged that in 38 per cent of families, both would give in to keep harmony in the family, in 33 per cent husbands tended to dominate, in 18 per cent wives tended to dominate. In the remaining families there was potential for conflict as both would hold out for their own point of view, or only give in if the other argued very strongly (Wilkening and Bharadwaj 1966).

Physical and Moral Support

No account of the contribution which farmers' wives make to the business would be complete without mention of their supportive role. The Reading University researchers summed up the wife's role as 'backbone, backstop and background'. Wives form a **backbone** to the business in the sense of supporting their husbands, being ready and willing to listen to new ideas and plans and sympathizing when plans go awry. They must always be on hand as a **backstop**, ready to provide the extra pair of hands (or wheels) in an emergency. The nature of farming adds immeasurably to the significance of having a second person available on the spot to deal with emergencies. As one woman put it, 'There is not much time involved actually helping, but you have to *be there* to provide bottles for lambs, hold the lantern in the dark ...' Most of the time, though, the farmer's wife will be in the **background** so far as the farm business is concerned.

Part of the wife's role is to listen sympathetically to her husband's complaints. At the present time the farming industry is under great pressure to adapt to a new market situation, the future is uncertain and real incomes are falling. If this were not enough, farmers are feeling increasingly isolated, blamed by the general public for rising food prices, over-production, cruelty to livestock and damage to the environment. The high suicide rate among farmers, first publicized by Jollans (1983), is a continuing cause for concern. With a shrinking workforce, many farmers have only their wives to share their anxieties about the business.

Public Relations

Another way in which farmers' wives can contribute to the reproduction of the farm family business is by trying to influence public opinion. Farm wives as consumers, parents, members of voluntary organizations and increasingly as employees, are in a position to explain the farming case to other groups in society. The Women's Farming Union has taken on the role of bridge building between the British farmer and the consumer. In less formal ways, for instance as members of the Women's Institute, the Parish Council, the Parent Teachers' Association or conservation bodies, farmers' wives can seek to inform and influence public opinion on issues which are crucial to the survival of the family farm. By inviting the general public on to the farm as customers for farm shops or farmhouse bed-and-breakfast, or by accepting school visits, farm women can demonstrate the value of their products and so help to defend and maintain the position of the farm family business.

IDEAL ROLE TYPES

Farmers' wives form a very heterogeneous group but certain patterns seem to be emerging, for example the greater involvement of women on family-worked farms in all aspects of the business. By dividing the population into more homogeneous sub-groups, differences in roles and relationships are brought into sharper focus, which can prove helpful in explaining differences in behaviour and predicting future trends.

Various attempts have been made to identify ideal role types among farmers' wives. One of the first was Pearson's (1979) classification of farm women's roles in Colorado:

- **independent producers** who manage farms or ranches largely by themselves;
- **agricultural partners** who share all aspects of work, responsibility and decision-making with their husbands;

- **agricultural helpers** who only participate in farm work at busy times when extra help is needed;
- **farm homemakers** who contribute to farm production indirectly by preparing meals and running errands.

Building on Pearson's work, Craig (no date) distinguished five major roles of women on farms in Australia:

- **independent operators** who may have come into control of the farm due to the death or incapacity of the male farmer, who may farm independently because the husband works elsewhere or who may have taken up a farming career after inheriting the family farm;
- **active partners** who participate fully in the business, sharing tasks with husbands on a complementary or joint basis;
- **helpers** called into service at times of peak labour demand, not involved in deciding but in doing;
- **homemakers** who have little direct involvement either in decision-making or in the physical work of the farm but who contribute indirectly by preparing food and running errands but whose major fulfilment lies in the domestic sphere;
- **matriarchs** who contribute little labour to the farm but who make important management decisions, by virtue of their superior education or the capital or land they brought to the marriage, or because they are widows continuing to manage the farm until a son is capable of taking full control.

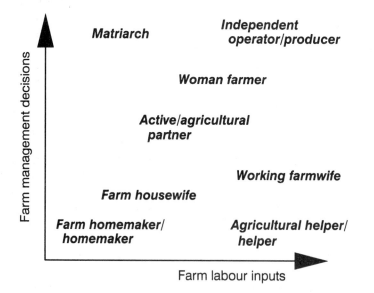

Figure 6.6. Ideal role types of farm women. Source: after Craig nd.

From a study of farm women in southern England, Gasson (1980a) identified three dominant role types – the woman farmer, the working farmwife and the farm housewife. Following Craig, the basic criteria were the woman's involvement in manual work and management. These groups bear a strong resemblance to Pearson's and Craig's ideal types but do not mirror them exactly. Figure 6.6 shows the relationship between the various ideal types.

Women farmers may be farming actively in partnership with their husbands, fathers, children or siblings, or farming alone because they are single, widowed or married to non-farmers. Women farmers work regularly on the farm, possibly spending more time outdoors than in. Typically they enjoy farm work and dislike many of the tasks assigned to women such as cooking and housekeeping. If business partners they are fully involved in management, sharing equally with their husbands in long-term policy decisions. Husbands and wives may share tasks jointly, either spouse doing much the same kind of work and sharing equally in decisions, or they may have a complementary working relationship, each specializing in tasks and decisions within their own spheres. Further, these activities need not be those regarded as 'suitable' for a woman.

Working farmwives spend part of every day working manually on the farm, possibly longer than they spend on housework. The working farmwife and her husband make a good team, working together for much of the time but with a clear division of labour. Typically she feeds calves and cleans dairy equipment while he milks cows and drives the tractor. The wife's place is to assist her husband but not to challenge his authority. She is rarely in charge of an enterprise unless it is closely linked with home consumption, like keeping chickens. Control rests with the man who makes day-to-day decisions affecting them both. The wife may however be a legal partner in the farm and will share in making major decisions in the absence of other family partners. If she has some office experience she is likely to be responsible for the farm accounts.

The **farm housewife** is a home-centred person. Domestic and family tasks absorb most of her time and are regarded as her main and probably most enjoyable function. Division of labour and interests between husband and wife is marked. The wife does not work regularly on the farm and is not responsible for any farm enterprise, although she is expected to be available in emergencies and lend a hand at busy times. Rounding up straying livestock, bottle-feeding lambs and watching the grain dryer are typical duties of a farm housewife. Being somewhat remote from day-to-day happenings on the farm, the farm housewife has little control over short-term management decisions, although she is likely to be consulted or at any rate kept informed on major policy matters. Farm housewives are expected to answer the telephone, see callers and run errands for the farm business. Whether they are also responsible for the farm accounts and other paperwork may depend on the husband's enthusiasm for these tasks or the employment of a professional farm secretary. Any surplus energy is likely to be directed away from the farm, into paid work or into the local community, welfare work or women's organizations.

Farm size, or rather the development of capitalist relations of production, goes a long way to explaining the role differences between working farmwives and farm housewives. Working farmwives are typically found on small, family-labour farms where they may be the husband's only helper and confidante. Farm housewives are typical of larger farm family businesses where full-time labour is employed and other family partners are available to discuss the business. The wife is more likely to have a role in decisions if she keeps the accounts and if she contributed land or capital to the farm but where she is excluded, she may seek fulfilment in her children or outside the farm.

The husband's position at marriage can also influence the wife's role. Women who marry established farmers, accustomed to running the farm and making decisions without a wife's help, tend to be cast in the role of farm housewives. Especially where the husband is farming in partnership with his parents or brothers, the new wife has to tread warily and has little influence in the business, at least initially. On small farms, sons may not be in a position to start farming until the father retires or both parents die. By this time the son could be married, so the couple embark on farming together and the wife is as much involved in the venture as the husband. Wives who play the role of independent producer or active partner, on the other hand, may have decided on a farming career before marriage. Some inherit the parental farm in the absence of sons and a few manage to build up a business by buying or renting land. Then the husband may marry into the farm and become a partner, with the wife retaining more control, or he may pursue another career. To suggest this is a reversal of the normal pattern would be an over-simplification. Research suggests that the non-farming husbands of farmers tend to assume responsibility for well-defined areas of work, such as book-keeping or maintenance of machinery, but not the combination of productive and reproductive roles which is expected of wives (Gasson *et al.* 1992a).

Symes (1991) has added the role of **working wife** to that of working farmwife and farm housewife. He argues that when the farmer's wife enters regular non-farm employment she moves away from a farm-centred life into a different universe dominated by the regional economy, though he concedes that in practice she may have to alternate between the two roles. A counter-argument is that the move towards pluriactivity is not confined to one type of wife.

Examples can be found of women farmers, farm housewives and working farmwives each adding other gainful activities without destroying the distinctive pattern of their farming and conjugal relationships. The women of Hartland, marginalized from the farm enterprise and taking in summer visitors, illustrate one typical response of farm housewives (Bouquet 1985). Where more employment is available farm housewives may resume their previous careers, typically in teaching, nursing or secretarial work. Women farmers and working farmwives are more tied to the farm, which restricts their choice of jobs. Either they have to take any work that is available locally (e.g. care assistant, domestic help) or they set up their own enterprises at home.

These ideal role types have implications for the socialization of children and the grooming of successors. Working farmwives are perhaps the most likely to encourage sons to come back to the family farm, in order to relieve the burden of physical work on the parents. Opposing tendencies may be the inadequate size of the business, too small to support two families if the son marries and too small to guarantee a livelihood in future. Working farmwives may present a less attractive role model to daughters, who may be understandably reluctant to follow their mothers into a life of hard work for relatively meagre returns. Farm housewives may also encourage sons to come into the family business, especially where the inheritance is substantial and family ties are strong. Here it is more likely that a son or sons will be taken into partnership, which enables the son to marry and start farming at a younger age but raises the issue of integrating the daughter-in-law into the family enterprise. The daughters of farm housewives will very likely be educated away from the farm, their mothers' experience of other occupations helping to widen their horizons. Women farmers provide role models for their daughters but may be reluctant to surrender their own role in the farm to their sons and retreat to the farmhouse.

REWARDS, REMUNERATION AND RECOGNITION

Most farmers' wives are involved in the business in some capacity. In aggregate it is estimated that they contribute 5 per cent of the regular manual labour and 9–10 per cent of the the total labour input on UK farms. For this work, two out of three respondents in the *Farmers Weekly* sample said they received some form of payment. Most common was a share of the profits, the appropriate reward for a partner or director. Hardly anyone was paid a commercial wage. A few wives received a fee or a fixed sum and slightly more were paid in kind, for example in free petrol for the car or keep for a horse. One wife in three was not paid and these women worked longer, on average, than those paid in cash or kind. In practice the 39 per cent credited with a share of the profits might be little better off than the 32 per cent receiving no payment for their work; the Reading University study combined these two categories. Even when the farm shows a profit the wife's share is likely to be reinvested in the business. (Here we should

Table 6.7. Methods of payment for wives' work by region and size of farm business.

EC region	Profits	Wages, fee	Perks, payments in kind (per cent of wives)	None	Total
North/Scotland	36	14	19	31	100
East	32	22	13	33	100
West	49	12	12	27	100
Wales	37	4	11	48	100
Ireland	11	2	10	77	100
Size of business in AWU[3]					
Up to 2	38	10	15	37	100
2 and under 5	39	15	14	32	100
5 and over	40	28	13	19	100
All wives	39	15	14	32	100

Source: Gasson 1990; *Irish Farmers' Journal* 1990 survey

remember that most male farmers are in the same position of not drawing a regular wage from the business. Sons and daughters working at home may be paid in the early years but if they are made partners, they too may see their share of any profits reinvested in the business.)

The way wives are paid varies according to the region and size of the farm (Table 6.7). Nearly half the respondents in Wales and 77 per cent in Ireland were not paid. This is partly explained by farm size variations in methods of payment, with twice as many wives on small as on large farms not being paid at all. Wives on large farms were the most likely to receive a commercial wage or a fixed amount in cash and a third of wives on the predominantly large farms in the Reading University sample were paid this way. Only 57 per cent of the farm wives in Whatmore's sample received any form of payment for their work. She suggests that it is the level of commoditization of the relations of production on the farm, rather than size itself, which is crucial in interpreting variations in the payment of wives (Whatmore 1991a). As Chapter 3 has shown, the family-worked farm does not need to make a distinction between wages and profits in its internal accounting, and can subsidize its costs of production by exploiting family

---

[3] AWU or Annual Work Units, a measure of size of farm business where 1 AWU represents a year's work for one adult.

labour. While this may enable family farms to survive and pursue a valued lifestyle, it may lead to a misallocation of resources in economic terms. This helps to explain why labour inputs may be higher on small family farms than in larger firms.

Some farmers' wives might regret the passing of the old system under which the wife derived her housekeeping money from the sale of milk, butter, eggs, poultry and other domestic products. In Montgomeryshire before the Second World War, Rees (1971) observed that 'the wife's budget is thus largely independent of that of her husband, and she is usually rather secretive about it'. With so few farm wives actually paid in cash for the work they do, the attractions of a paid job and the discretionary income that goes with it, can be readily appreciated. This is not the only reward attached to a paid job, however. Recognition for doing a 'proper' job can also be significant for farmers' wives, because all too often the work they do in the family business is not recognized.

Western society makes a sharp distinction between work performed at home and work performed elsewhere. Employment of both women and men outside the home is recognized as **work** and given a monetary value. Besides financial rewards and welfare benefits, a certain status attaches to a paid occupation. Higher status jobs carry prestige and open doors to membership of élite groups and organizations. A person's occupation is recognized in official documents such as the Population Census and passports. A job title becomes part of a person's identity. Now that half of all British women of working age are in paid work, those without a recognized occupation appear deviant. There can be no doubt that recognition for doing a 'proper' and worthwhile job is important to a woman's self-confidence.

Society assumes that work performed inside the home by women is done 'for love'. It is not given a monetary value. Domestic work for one's own family is not regarded as 'real' work, although the same work done for another family would be. Despite the many skills involved, little status attaches to the occupation **housewife**. Women share this evaluation when they dismiss themselves as 'just housewives'. Women working in family businesses run from home are in an anomalous position. Because they work at home, their contribution tends to be dismissed as domestic and therefore not 'real' work. It is ironic that working long hours on the farm may prevent a wife from seeking another job and thus gaining recognition as a productive worker. It is ironic too that husbands running businesses from home enjoy a recognized status (farmer, grower, etc.) while wives assisting in the business do not. The most frequently-voiced complaint from the British and Irish farm wives studied was that their contribution to the family business was taken for granted, overlooked and under-valued.

Signs of this dismissive attitude can be seen at all levels. For example in the Agricultural Census the category of 'farmers/partners/directors' excludes wives/husbands of farmers. The recently-introduced category of 'spouses doing farm work' seems intended only for those doing manual work on a regular basis, ignoring the many other kinds of contributions (managerial, secretarial, administrative, domestic, supportive) which wives make and without which the family farm could not function. In the Irish Farm Management Survey the labour input of a woman is only counted as two thirds of a male worker, even where she runs the farm. In other words, agricultural work tends to be defined in censuses and statistics as the work that men do.

At the interpersonal level, many farmers' wives complain of the dismissive treatment they receive in dealings with banks, businesses, advisers, contractors and so on. Within the family, conflict often arises because a woman marrying into a farming family feels that she is excluded by her parents-in-law from making a full contribution to the family business. She may have professional or commercial experience which could benefit the farm but the husband's parents perceive her as a threat to the business which they have built up over a lifetime.

Women as well as men argue that it is 'natural' or 'traditional' for women to work for nothing on behalf of the family, just as it is 'natural' for men to be farmers and women helpers (Sachs 1983). A series of ideological mechanisms effectively conceal the basic processes of capitalist exploitation, the ideology of familial affection being one example (Long 1984). Many participants in the British and Irish surveys subscribed to such an ideology, stressing the rewards they gained from helping their husbands, working together as a close family and contributing to the children's inheritance.

TRENDS IN THE WIFE'S CONTRIBUTION

Forces for change in the role and contribution of the farmer's wife can be considered under two headings; external pressures for farm structural change and internal pressures on family relationships. Under the first heading, the process of capital accumulation seems set to continue. Among full-time farms the trend towards farm enlargement will continue, with businesses becoming increasingly dependent on external sources of capital. Production will become increasingly concentrated on larger farms, which does not rule out the possibility of diversification if a profitable opportunity arises. At the other end of the scale, increasing numbers of farms will become subsidiary to the family's main employment, making only a minor contribution to current income while representing an investment, an alternative to unemployment or early retirement, providing a spacious home and lifestyle. Farms in between may come under increasing pressure to move one way or the other.

How will the woman's role reflect these forces for change?

> Probably the wisest answer is to suggest that there will be no profound
> change to the overall location and status of women in farming ... If it
> were left solely to the changing nature of agriculture to mediate
> women's roles, the changes would be slight indeed. It would probably
> involve little more than an exploitation of the labour value of farm
> women.
>
> (Symes 1991: 89)

A number of writers associate capitalist development of agriculture with masculinization, contending that women will withdraw progressively from agriculture and be deprived of their productive roles in the family business (see for instance Young 1978; Bouquet 1985). Others see signs of feminization in the gradual replacement of hired male by family labour (Gasson 1992) and, in the former Communist bloc in Eastern Europe, in the move towards collectivization (Cernea 1978; First-Dilic 1978). As Shaver has demonstrated, the contribution of women remains important in spite of the radical transformation of the agricultural sector. Modernization only appears to displace women from farm work when accompanied by a change to capitalist relations of production.

The effects of farm structural change on women can be considered in relation to the ideal role types. Reflecting on the apparent inconsistency of wives' views on their changing role, the Reading University researchers distinguished two divergent paths rather than a single uniform trend. On the one hand, changing attitudes and opportunities will take **farm housewives** living on the larger farms further away from direct involvement in the business. On the other hand, smaller farms which can no longer afford to employ labour will become increasingly dependent on the manual labour which the **working farmwife** can provide (Buchanan *et al.* 1982). A note of caution is needed, though. Much of the evidence for the separation of wives from the world of the larger farm relates to their direct involvement in manual work. In this chapter we suggest that the *total* labour input of wives on large farms, including secretarial, administrative and managerial work, is not necessarily less than on smaller farms. Moreover, it could be argued that the kinds of tasks usually allocated to wives, such as keeping records and accounts, are becoming more rather than less crucial for the survival of the family business. Besides this, women may have more opportunities than men to improve the public image of farming and at a time when farming seems to be a favourite target for attack, the public relations role of wives may become still more important.

The second main type of influence upon the wife's role stems from pressures outside agriculture which challenge the pattern of family relationships:

> The preoccupation with the impact of commoditization on the future of
> family farming overlooks the potential significance of challenges from

within by women, particularly younger women, for whom the gender regime of family farming is becoming increasingly archaic and insupportable in the light of developments on the wider social canvas of gender relations.

(Whatmore 1991b: 75)

These are likely to be the more potent forces for change according to Hannan and Katsiaouni (1977), who concluded from their study of couples on small farms in the west of Ireland that:

> ... wives' farm task roles are not related to the size or degree of innovativeness or modernization of farms, or even to total output. But such variation is highly correlated with the level of education, migration experience, standard of living, mass media participation and values of wives.

(Hannan and Katsiaouni 1977: 183)

The type of change being considered here includes the woman's right to a career of her own separate from that of housewife and mother, with the associated discretionary income, status and sense of self-worth. The main options for the farmer's wife are to pursue an independent career off the farm and unconnected with it, to run her own business from home or to become an active partner in the farm or even an independent operator.

Whether or not farm diversification increases the financial independence, status and power of wives within the family business is open to question (Gasson and Winter 1992). Symes (1991) believes that 'Greater hope for improvement in the status of farm women must come from increased participation in the wider labour market and from work roles which are totally dissociated from the farm business, no matter whether they take place on or off the farm'. Another possibility is for wives to become equal or dominant partners in the farm, or to farm independently while husbands work elsewhere. In Norway, a 1974 amendment to the act regulating rights to farm succession upon the death of the owner, gives the right to the eldest child irrespective of gender. Previously the senior male heir had the right to take over the farm intact by buying out the shares of other siblings. The Norwegian Government, conscious of the need to retain young women in rural areas, started a campaign in 1987 to raise awareness and encourage farmers' daughters to exercise their right of succession. If farming can offer women equal opportunities with men, and if the industry can compete with other industries in terms of working conditions and prospects, the masculinization of Norwegian agriculture could be reversed (Almas and Haugen 1991).

The theme of this book is the inter-relationship between the farm family and the farm business. It is perhaps too easy to dwell on the threats to the farm family business without reflecting on its strengths. Farms do provide opportunities for families to work together, which can be a source of satisfaction as well as conflict. The more varied talents which wives can bring from outside may indeed help to ensure the survival of the family business. There are, however, limits to which this interdependence can be pushed. Beyond a certain point family discord may destroy the enterprise and vice versa. Falling farm incomes, uncertainty about the future with the possible removal of farm support and low evaluation of the farming occu-pation all threaten the well-being of farm families and can lead to stress, mental illness or family breakdown. Dissatisfaction with farm life, conflict between a newly-married farmer's wife and her in-laws, desire for autonomy and an independent income, can threaten the stability of farm marriages. Divorce can be especially traumatic if it entails dividing the assets of the farm business and a forced sale of the property which may have been held by one family for generations.

To conclude, family farming has traditionally been organized along patriarchal lines, a point graphically illustrated by Arensberg and Kimball's study of Irish farm life in the 1930s:

> On the normal farm there is an adult male farmer who is husband,
> father, and owner of the farm. Within the group he has the controlling
> role, subject to conventional restrictions of his authority. In farm work
> ... he directs the activity of the family as it works in concert ... He
> may order as he sees fit ...
>
> (Arensberg and Kimball 1968: 46)

A shift in the power base of farm families towards greater equality between spouses and between generations may be necessary for survival. Any change produces friction but the farm population demonstrates a sturdy capacity to adopt new practices and adapt to changing circumstances. So with gender roles, there are encouraging signs of farm wives becoming more involved in the planning and management of the farm business and of husbands taking a bigger share in the running of the household.

SUMMARY AND IMPLICATIONS

This chapter has shown that most farmers' wives are involved in the farm business in some capacity. Depending on the size and type of farm and especially on the availability of other labour, the wife may do manual work on a regular or occasional basis, possibly with responsibility for a particular activity or enterprise. Many wives keep the farm records and accounts and most are expected to take messages, deal with callers, run errands and help in emergencies. Most wives are drawn into business discussions where their role may be active, as an equal partner in any decisions taken, or more passive as a sounding board for the husband's ideas. Putting these contributions together, it is estimated that wives contribute 5 per cent of the regular manual labour input on UK farms and 9–10 per cent of the total labour expended on farm production, besides being mainly if not wholly responsible for the reproductive work of the household.

The fact that most farmers' wives contribute to the farm business in some productive capacity, as well as servicing the labour force through reproductive activities, has implications for the farm business. If wives withdrew from farm work, there would be a shortfall of some 9–10 per cent in the regular labour input on UK farms. This would be felt most acutely in smaller businesses. Women's many-sided contributions to the farm business has implications for training agencies like the Agricultural Training Board, which has begun to tailor courses to the needs of farmers' wives. Farmers' wives, like other farm family workers, are rarely paid in cash for the work they do. As in other family businesses, the partners are credited with a share of the profits but do not necessarily take that money out of the business. It is the ability of family businesses not to pay family members for their labour which helps them to survive in hard times and to compete with larger firms. Putting a more realistic value on the wife's labour would reveal the economics of the family farm in a less favourable light. With increasing numbers of farm women rejoining the labour force, a realistic wage for the wife's work in the business might be her opportunity cost in terms of earnings forgone in another job. For farmers' wives to take better-paid off-farm employment represents a more efficient allocation of resources.

The rights of spouses assisting in family businesses might in time be brought within the framework of the law, with far-reaching consequences for industries like agriculture which rely heavily on unpaid family labour. The EC is committed to providing equal opportunities for men and women and to increasing women's participation in economic, social and political life. In 1986 it adopted Directive 86/613, the *Self-employed Directive*, on the application of the principle of equal treatment for men and women engaged in self-employed activities including agriculture. This Directive also covered spouses of the self-employed who were not themselves partners or employees, who habitually participated in the activities of the self-employed work. Despite apparent progress towards women's rights, a great many spouses working with their husbands in family businesses, particularly on farms, in small shops and catering firms, are not benefiting from the provisions of the Self-employed Directive because their contribution to the business is not legally recognized as work. The absence of a recognized professional status for wives in family businesses has serious consequences for their rights in taxation, rights to remuneration and social security, access to training facilities and rights to vote or to stand for election in certain professional organizations. As regards rights to welfare benefits, the *Farmers Weekly* survey revealed that few farm businesses were making private provision for wives and that many women were not aware of their entitlement under state schemes.

One possible solution would be to grant assisting spouses in family businesses the status of employees. This suggestion is not generally acceptable to farmers' wives, who feel that it demeans their contribution to the business. In this chapter we suggest that over half the wives on UK farms have the legal status of partner or director and a small number are employees of the business. Some of those with no formal status in the farm have other employment. The professional status of UK farm wives may therefore be less problematic than in other Member States. The idea of paying wives a regular wage, too, meets with much resistance, the general feeling being that many family farms simply could not survive if the wife expected to be paid. In a nutshell, farmers' wives assisting in the family business may be vulnerable in respect of their legal, financial and welfare rights, yet legislation to strengthen their position could have the effect of undermining the family business on which they depend.

Legislation on marital property is another two-edged sword. As the law now stands, a wife who can demonstrate that she has made a significant contribution to the family business, through work, savings and so on, is entitled to a share of the business assets in the event of marital breakdown. This a great improvement on the previous situation where a wife could lose all that she had put into a family business. One effect of the change, however, has been to deter farm families from taking daughters-in-law into partnership, for fear of putting the business in jeopardy. This can be a source of conflict where a young wife feels excluded from the family business and her parents-in-law question her motives for wanting to be included.

In this chapter we have tried to show that the contribution of farmers' wives is habitually under-estimated and deserves greater recognition. Legislation to give wives a recognized legal and financial status is not necessarily the most effective solution. Other changes in attitudes and practices are also needed. At 'official' level, for example, **farmer's wife** could be included as an occupational title in the Population Census. The Agricultural Census could add a category for the spouses of farmers, partners and directors who are themselves partners or directors. Both the Census and the Farm Business Survey could seek information on the administrative and managerial hours, as well as the manual labour which wives put into the business. Many complaints from wives concern the attitudes of banks, advisers, sales representatives and others who seek to do business with the farm. While there is evidence of a more enlightened approach gaining ground, many still cling to the idea of a 'normal' farm being headed by an adult male who is husband, father, owner and controller of the farm and 'who may order as he sees fit'.

7

PATTERNS OF SUCCESSION AND INHERITANCE

INTRODUCTION

> The introduction of succeeding generations into the farming business is but one manifestation of what is probably the most significant feature of UK agriculture, that is, the close and often inseparable relationship between the farm family and the farm business.
>
> (Harrison 1981: 14)

In his admirable thesis on farming succession, Hastings (1984) includes a memorable vignette in which the chief executive of a joint stock company, approaching retirement, sits at the boardroom table. He is surrounded by a crowd of eager, ambitious and highly-trained executives who have, by virtue of merit and competence, risen near the top of the organization. Which should he choose to be his successor? In sharp contrast, we then see the breakfast table on the family farm where father casts a weary and despairing eye over his three children, trying to decide which would make the least incompetent successor when he retires. Sandford (1976) is more circumspect but makes the same point:

> While continuity of ownership and management for generations has the advantage for new entrants that they can draw on pooled financial resources and need not borrow heavily when they assume control of the business, there seems little reason to believe that inheritance as a method of selecting farming's business proprietors is necessarily best for the country as a whole.
>
> (Quoted in Harrison 1981: 111)

There are clearly some major differences between family businesses and public companies where matters of succession and inheritance are concerned. These give rise to a number of questions which are addressed in this and the following chapter: why should farmers want successors, particularly successors from their own family? to what extent do farms remain in the hands of the same family for generation after generation?

how do successors acquire managerial control of the business? do farmers ever retire? and so on. While the present chapter concentrates on the **patterns** of inheritance and succession observed in market industrialized countries, Chapter 8 considers the **processes** of succession and retirement.

DEFINING TERMS

If, as we argued in Chapter 1, the combination of ownership and managerial control is the defining characteristic of the family business, then the transfer of that ownership and control to the next generation is of central importance since it is the mechanism by which the family business reproduces itself. The three terms 'inheritance', 'succession' and 'retirement' all appear in discussions of this phenomenon but they are sometimes used interchangeably, giving rise to considerable confusion. In fact the three concepts are quite distinct. **Inheritance** denotes the legal transfer of ownership of the business assets (including land); **succession** refers to the transfer of managerial control over the use of these assets, while **retirement** marks the withdrawal of the present manager from active managerial control and/or involvement in manual work on the farm. But while conceptually distinct, the three are obviously related. Retirement is the mirror image of succession – as the new generation succeeds, the old generation retires – and since ownership confers the right to take decisions over the disposition of assets, inheritance automatically reassigns ultimate managerial control.

The term **transfer** (or, more frequently, the French *transmission*) combines the sense of both succession and inheritance but is best avoided because of its implication that the two processes are simultaneous, which often they are not. But the French term *installation*, referring to the 'setting up' of the next generation in farming, is useful because it emphasizes the proactive role of the outgoing generation. As we shall see, responsibility for initiating the transfer process, whether it be succession or inheritance, usually lies with this generation.

Having distinguished the three concepts of succession, inheritance and retirement, it is important to remember that each word describes a process rather than an event taking place at a single point in time. The process forms the transition between two states, in the first of which a farming father is owner and in the second of which ownership may be in the hands of his daughter; in the first of which father has absolute managerial control and in the second of which this control is in the hands of his son, and so on. Indeed, Rosenblatt and Anderson's (1981) description of retirement – 'not an individual act but a series of extended transitions' – may be just as applicable to succession and even inheritance.

The exact nature of these three processes varies from one location to another and from one time period to another but what impresses most is the enormous variation even within a given legal or cultural framework. In order to understand the salient features of particular situations, it is helpful to describe a limited number of ideal types, or patterns of retirement, succession and inheritance while recognizing that the variation in reality is infinitely greater. But before looking more closely at these patterns and processes, we should first answer the fundamental question, why do farmers want successors?

THE NEED FOR A SUCCESSOR

'The house will once again, Mrs. Dombey,' said Mr. Dombey, 'be not only in name but in fact Dombey and Son; Dom-bey and son!'.

(Dickens 1868b: 1)

There are several possible reasons why the owner-manager of any family business will seek a successor, but where that business is an owner-occupied farm, the situation is complicated by the fact of land ownership. As we shall see later in this chapter, there is an important distinction to be made between having a successor who will carry on in the occupation of farming and having one who will continue to farm a particular piece of land (Harrison 1981; Laband and Lentz 1983; Blanc 1987). While there may be strong continuity in the occupation of farming in England, with 80 per cent of current full-time farmers themselves being farmers' children, Harrison (1981) suggests that there has nevertheless been considerable change in the ownership of particular parcels of land and only 50 per cent of current farmers are farming the same land as their fathers. The recent Scottish ancestry of so many farmers in southern and eastern England graphically illustrates the fact that family continuity in farming does not necessarily imply geographic immobility.

Why then this search for continuity? In the first place there are sound economic reasons. For example, the farm business may offer a livelihood to one or more children. Depending on the relative prosperity of farming and the employment opportunities available elsewhere, this may be particularly important for the children with few alternative opportunities or those in greatest need of continuing parental protection. But continuity of the business might also guarantee a secure home and potential source of income to the present farmer and his wife once they retire. Provided it continues to be farmed by the next generation, the farm itself is a retirement 'nest-egg', providing 'a reasonably comfortable passage through the final years' (Abrahams 1991).

Social norms are also important. In Illinois, for example, the religious and cultural identity of certain groups is strongly associated with farming as a way of life and with the occupation of a particular area of land, as Chapter 4 has shown:

Yeoman goals, often held by groups of German origin, define
agricultural success as intergenerational continuity of the family farm
... Yeomen possess a strong commitment to farming as a way of life;
this agrarian ethic sometimes also serves as the means to an end such
as preserving religious or ethnic identity or rural values.

(Salamon and Davis-Brown 1988: 196)

Other explanations of the desire to have a farming successor concern
the individual's search for immortality. The business becomes so tied up
with personal identity, that its maintenance into future generations
preserves that identity and provides a means for the present generation to
influence the lives of generations as yet unborn. Perhaps the most graphic
illustrations of this point are to be found in literature such as Dickens'
Dombey and Son and Mann's *Buddenbrooks*.

In some cases the sense of identity is associated not so much with the
family business but with the land it occupies. In south-west France, both
farms and the individuals living on them are designated by a family name
and place name associated with the land on which the farm is based:
'Individual, family and farm identity are thus inextricably tied to each other
and permanently fixed in space' (Voyce 1989). This is similar to the tradition
among German Americans where the 'homeplace' (the plot originally settled
by their immigrant ancestors) is sacred and its loss would be disastrous. In
some parts of the world such as Kenya or Jamaica the tradition may be reinforced by ensuring that family burials all take place on the family farm.

In late twentieth-century Britain, some of these explanations may seem
far-fetched or rather quaint, but even here the desire to maintain 'the name
on the land' can be deeply-rooted and the resulting emotional bonds very
strong. Certainly several authors speak in these terms when explaining the
strong desire of existing English or Welsh farmers to pass their farms to the
next generation. In a similar vein, Commins (1973) attributes the reluctance
of farmers in western Ireland to take up EC early retirement schemes to
their 'sentimental feeling about land', though he does not make clear
whether these feelings relate to a particular piece of land or to the occupation of farming in general.

Not all commentators accept the assumption that most farmers want
their children to succeed them in the farm family business. Quoting
evidence from Continental Europe, Fennell (1981) argues that: 'The literature suggests that there is clear evidence that many farmers do not want any
of the family to succeed them', often because they do not want their
children to have the same struggle as themselves on small marginal farms
where the standard of living is falling behind that of the rest of society.
Others argue that there have been changes in social norms and that
continuity may have ceased to be a prime goal now that the extended family
has been replaced by the nuclear family in which individual desires are
emphasized over family tradition. The ambivalence of the literature is

almost certainly reflected in the ambivalence of the farmers themselves, with many recommending that their children seek an easier way of life and yet unconsciously socializing at least one to take over the family farm. Indeed, many farmers state that, given their own lives over again, they would still go farming in spite of the hardships.

HOW MANY FARMERS HAVE SUCCESSORS?

Policy-makers have always regarded this as a very important question. In the first place, it gives some indication of the likely structural changes in the farming sector by highlighting the number of holdings potentially available for amalgamation. Secondly, as Chapter 4 has already indicated, farmers with successors tend to behave differently from those without. They will be more likely to acquire additional land (Hine and Houston 1973; Harrison 1981; Hutson 1987), to increase borrowings in order to finance on-farm investment (Marsden *et al.* 1989), to purchase milk quota (Burrell 1989) and to develop their business (Hine and Houston 1973; Hutson 1987; NatWest Bank 1992). Those without successors may be more conservation-minded and willing to take up extensification schemes (Potter and Lobley 1992).

The various studies in this area have in fact addressed three rather different questions – whether a successor is expected (or required) to take over the farm; whether a successor has already been identified; and whether a successor is already working on the farm. Three out of four respondents to Harrison's (1975) survey of farmers in England asserted that a successor was required for their business. In contrast, Commins and Kelleher (1973) estimated that in the twelve western counties of Ireland, half the farms with farmers over 50 years old would have no successor.

Two thirds of Harrison's respondents already had a successor – almost invariably from within their own family – 'positively identified, ready and available' at the time of the survey. This proportion is somewhat higher than the 50 per cent found by Gasson in 1984 and Errington and Tranter (1991) and Natwest Bank (1992) at the beginning of the 1990s. The size of farms in the respective samples could be an influence here, though the main bias in the latter surveys was towards larger farms and the available evidence suggests that such farms are *more* likely to have identified a successor. This relationship with farm size is reported by both Gasson (1984) and Errington and Tranter (1991), who found that on farms in their sample of 50 acres or less, only 35 per cent of respondents had identified a successor while the proportion rose to 62 per cent among those farming 500 acres or more. As Symes (1990) concludes '(economic) pressures will perhaps be most severe on the smaller farms where the younger generation may resist a lifetime of self-exploitation and reject farming as a career'. Indeed, the difference in the proportion of English farmers with an identified successor observed by Harrison in the early 1970s and Errington and Tranter in the early 1990s might itself be attributable to the deepening agricultural recession in the latter period.

As these findings suggest, the presence or absence of an identified successor depends on the framework of constraints and opportunities within which the farm family business operates. Three main factors are relevant – the characteristics of the family, the characteristics of the farm and the economic health of farming and of the economy at large. Where family characteristics are concerned, the number and sex of the farmer's children are certainly important. A tradition of late marriage can leave many farmers without a successor simply because they do not have any children (Nalson 1968; Commins and Kelleher 1973). Alternatively, the only children in the family may be female. Errington and Tranter (1991) found that only 19 per cent of respondents without children had identified a potential successor, and the proportion barely rose when there were only daughters in the family. Where there were only sons the proportion rose to 60 per cent, almost identical to the proportion (61 per cent) where there were both sons and daughters. Clearly, the most significant factor in determining whether a successor has been identified on these farms was the arrival of one or more sons in the farming family. The authors conclude that their survey 'provides clear evidence of the continuing tradition in England of farming succession through the male line'.

Next, there are the characteristics of the farm business, particularly its size, which might make it impossible to provide an adequate standard of living for both generations at the same time, particularly in the light of rising aspirations and falling farm incomes. This might explain the finding from a survey of Devon and Grampian farms that only about a quarter of farmers 'were certain that a member of the family would take on the farm' and that 'a surprisingly large number were certain that no one in the family would succeed them' (Shucksmith *et al.* 1989). Surprisingly, there appear to be no differences between tenanted and owner-occupied farms (at least in the UK). For any given size category, both tenanted and owner-occupied farms seem equally likely to have identified a successor (Errington and Tranter 1991). This probably reflects the substantial increase in security of tenure afforded by the 1976 legislation, despite its subsequent modification.

A national survey of farm families with other sources of income found a highly significant association between the level of household dependence on farm income and the likelihood of succession. In Class I farm households, where farming was the main source of income, 52 per cent of farmers expected to hand the farm business on within the family. Among 'hobby' farm households only 30 per cent expected succession. 'Hobby' farmers were twice as likely as Class I part-time farmers to be certain succession would *not* happen (Gasson 1988). Data from the Devon study area of the Arkleton Trust project on farm household pluriactivity revealed a similar

Table 7.1. Likelihood of succession perceived by farmers over 55 and dependence on farming income (per cent).

| Family succession | Level of household dependence on farming income | | | |
	90% and over "Full-time"	50–89% "Class I"	10–49% "Class II"	Under 10% "Hobby"
Certain	56	45	13	8
Hopeful, not sure	24	20	7	16
Certain not to happen	20	35	80	76
All farmers over 55	100	100	100	100
Numbers	48	30	31	22

Source: Gasson *et al.* 1992b

pattern. Among farmers aged 55 and over, 56 per cent of full-timers were certain of family succession while 76 per cent of 'hobby' farmers were certain it would not happen (Table 7.1). Farmers' goals were patterned in the same way; 42 per cent of full-time farmers but only 4 per cent of 'hobby' farmers agreed that family continuity in farming was very important.

Finally, there is the health of the economy at large to consider, and the availability of alternative jobs for the erstwhile successor. As Fennell (1981) concludes:

> The likelihood of being a successor is affected not only by the ability of the farm to yield an adequate and rising income in the foreseeable future but also by the young person's ability to earn a satisfactory living outside farming.
>
> (Fennell 1981: 34–5)

If the standard of living and the lifestyle associated with it is not sufficiently attractive, the potential successor may not want to remain in the family business.

Since many potential successors will work away from the home farm for a time after leaving school or college, it is perhaps not surprising that only a relatively small proportion of farmers have successors actually working alongside them. Fennell (1981) estimates the proportion in the EC as a whole to be between a third and a quarter though it is naturally lower on small farms where there is less opportunity to support two generations simultaneously and more sons have to earn a living elsewhere before eventually taking over the farm (see below). Farm size might explain why Errington and Tranter (1991) found a somewhat larger proportion (36 per cent) of successors working alongside their fathers in England. Not only do

English farms tend to be larger than their continental counterparts but the sample itself was somewhat biased towards larger farms.

PATTERNS OF INHERITANCE

Family relationships governing farm entrance involve three major themes: whether or not there is a principle of equality between successors; whether or not a norm of keeping the holding as one unit is observed; (and) the nature of intergeneration relationships ranging from authoritarianism to independence.

(Blanc and Perrier-Cornet 1992: 11)

An Overview

The painstaking work of anthropologists, ethnographers, sociologists, geographers and historians has identified two main systems by which farming continuity is achieved from one generation to the next, each of which has fundamentally different consequences for families and for the structure of farms. In some peasant communities, the land is a constant to which family organization has to be adjusted according to the logic of 'keeping the name on the land'. To achieve this end, one son is chosen to inherit the family farm and the rest are obliged to 'travel', to seek a living elsewhere. In the absence of a suitable son, a nephew might be nominated as the heir. This strategy ensures a rough equilibrium between the number of farm families and a given area of land. It provides a stable environment within which social relations are maintained. The stability of the farming community in County Clare in the 1930s, as depicted by Arensberg and Kimball (1968) derived largely from this deep and unswerving attachment to family land (Williams 1963, 1973).

Contrasting with this static system is the state of dynamic equilibrium between families and farms uncovered by William's study of Ashworthy. Here a deep attachment to the family holding was generally absent. 'A farmhouse may have a certain sentimental association, but the land that goes with it is, as it were, a means to an end, to be sold or transformed according to circumstances' (Williams 1963: 80). Ashworthy farmers moved freely between farms and bought or sold pieces of land, apparently as a matter of course. This behaviour is reminiscent of the more entrepreneurial Yankee farmers of the American Midwest described by Salamon (1988). In north-east France, where partible inheritance prevails and family identity is not tied to any particular piece of land, 'successive generations never farm or own identical holdings, and in the long run land in the community is shuffled among families' (Voyce 1989). Yet there is a need for continuity of some kind if a family farming system is to be maintained.

In this constantly changing situation continuity is achieved, ideally, by each farmer attempting to set up *all his sons* as farmers in their own right. One son inherits the home farm and the others are found holdings of their own elsewhere ...

(Williams 1973: 131)

Without a deep attachment to family land, it is not necessary to bring in members of the extended family to ensure inheritance in cases of 'biological failure' where there are childless marriages or the farmer is unmarried. Some farms therefore become available for children who do not inherit the home farm. This system is inconsistent with 'keeping the name on the land', for if land remains in the hands of the same family from generation to generation, farms rarely become available for non-inheriting children.

Both systems, described here as simplified models, were probably ideals rather than common practice. The norms of inheritance are usually explained in terms of culture and tradition but other factors such as the availability of land, the profitability of farming and the potential for capital accumulation, family size and access to other employment, would be likely to play an intervening role. Besides this, the conjugal family is an imperfect device for ensuring farming succession and small-scale farming is a precarious means of supporting a family. In County Clare it was not unusual for land to pass out of the control of the elementary family. In Ashworthy, the ideal of finding a farm for every son may have grown up with the decrease in family size, for it would have been difficult to achieve when families were larger (Williams 1963).

The ideal of finding a farm for all sons wishing to farm was known to apply in Wales (Rees 1971), Cumberland (Williams 1956) and North Yorkshire (Symes and Appleton 1986). The strategies of Staffordshire farmers in attempting to match land resources to family labour likewise involved a considerable degree of mobility between farms (Nalson 1968). 'Keeping the name on the land', on the other hand, was the ideal in Ireland (Arensberg and Kimball 1968), Finland (Abrahams 1991) and many other parts of Europe.

The Fundamental Dilemmas

Being fair is not always being equal, and equal is not always the best way to go.

(Mennonite farmer, Illinois, mid-1980s)

Setting on one side the question of whether or not it continues to occupy the same piece of land, a major objective of the farm family will be to secure the future prosperity of its business. Inheritance arrangements will therefore seek to 'accommodate reallocation of property ownership in the firm without reducing or changing the size or asset composition of the firm' (Boehlje and Eisgruber 1972). The older generation must take two basic decisions – who should inherit the business and when the transfer should take place. Both decisions present their own dilemma. In the interests of fairness, parents might want each child to receive an equal share of the business but this may lead to fragmentation of the asset base with the resulting loss of economic viability so that the very survival of the business may be placed in jeopardy. Alternatively, the quest for fairness may leave the eventual farming successor not only with the farm but with substantial financial obligations either to other family members or to the bank. These may place such a millstone round his neck that the future survival of the farm is again threatened. As Salamon and Davis-Brown (1988) point out: 'Farm families planning intergenerational farm transfers confront a dilemma: how to treat all members equitably without destroying the farm in the process.'

The timing of the transfer presents another dilemma. If the farm is to be their main source of income throughout the remainder of their lives, the parents may want to secure their own future by retaining ownership of the business until their death. Yet this may inhibit innovation and cause so much frustration to build up among the succeeding generation that they abandon the family business for an alternative career.

Dimensions of Inheritance Patterns

We have already stressed the immense variety in inheritance patterns between different localities and different time-periods. These patterns change and evolve in response to a whole number of factors, economic and cultural as well as legal and fiscal, but they all have two main dimensions – partibility and timing. Each individual pattern may therefore be located at some point on the two-dimensional grid in Figure 7.1. **Partibility** refers to the extent to which business assets[1] are divided between successors. The **timing** of transfer may occur either during the owner's lifetime (as *inter vivos* gifts at the time of the beneficiary's marriage, for example) or *causa mortis*, after the owner's death. In the latter case, the transfers may either be in accordance with the provisions of a will, or if the owners dies intestate, in accordance with the prevailing legal provision for intestacy. Thus, referring to Figure 7.1, the inheritance pattern in a particular locality at a particular point in time might call for the transfer of all the property to one individual

---

[1]Where farming inheritance is concerned there may be important differences in the treatment of real estate as against other business assets. For example, well-to-do farmers in an active land market may maintain strict impartibility of the home farm while setting another child up on a new farm with some machinery and animals from the home farm.

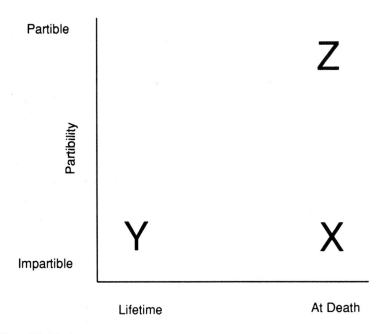

Figure 7.1. Inheritance patterns.

at the death of the present owner, and point 'X' would characterize this
pattern. However, changes in the capital tax legislation might subsequently
encourage *inter vivos* transfers and the pattern would move to 'Y', or social
norms might dictate more equal treatment of all one's children and the
pattern move closer to 'Z'.

The Timing of Inheritance

Much of the available evidence suggests that ownership of the farm family
business is usually transferred late in the life of the existing owner(s).
Noting the common practice of late inheritance in western Ireland,
Commins and Kelleher (1973) suggested that less than half the farmers in
that area transferred ownership before they were 70 years old. Their survey
findings also suggest that transfers were taking place later and later. In the
1940s, 44 per cent of the farmers were over 70 when they finally transferred
the farm while the proportion had risen to 62 per cent by the late 1960s.
Nevertheless, few successors interviewed by Commins and Kelleher
expressed dissatisfaction with such late transfer and the authors concluded
that it is the commentators rather than the farming community itself that
see late transfer as a problem. Indeed, the literature is singularly silent on
the advantages of the earlier transfer of *ownership* (as opposed to that of

managerial control) though Gamble *et al.* (1992) do point to a greater incidence of intra-family stress and the reluctance of an uncertain heir to invest money in a farm that he may not inherit.

Why should the parental generation want to hang on to ownership? Most of the explanations provided in the literature concern either financial security, daughters-in-law or both. Thus both Ruane (1973), referring to Ireland, and Voyce (1989), referring to Australia, explain that where fathers favour the postponement of transfer till after their death, it is usually because of anxieties over their own or their wife's financial security, particularly where the farm is to be their main source of retirement income. As one 68-year-old respondent to Errington and Tranter's (1991) survey explained:

> I have made the farm over to my two sons equally, retaining a quarter for my own safety. One must not get undressed until it is time to go to bed!

The point is further underlined by the written agreements found by Abrahams (1991) on some Finnish farms. In one case the agreement to transfer the farming assets was made conditional upon the beneficiary's promise to provide his parents with subsistence for the remainder of their lives, a dwelling with lighting and heating, house cleaning when the parents could no longer manage to do it themselves, and a decent funeral on their death.

Another fear is that the son's marriage will not last and that the daughter-in-law will acquire part of the family farm as part of a divorce settlement. The parents want to be assured of the stability of their son's marriage and the whole transfer process may therefore be slowed down until the marriage has passed a 'stability test'. The delay may add to the tension which already exists between in-laws working in the same business and perhaps resident in the same house. As Abrahams comments, choosing his words very carefully:

> Whereas the intrinsic tensions between parent and child are to some
> degree alleviated by the other pole of their ambivalent relationship,
> there is no such mitigating element of love intrinsic to the interaction
> between daughter-in-law and husband's parents.
>
> (Abrahams 1991: 127)

Nevertheless, in looking at the factors associated with the timing of farm transfer, Ruane (1973) found that earlier transfers are usually associated with son-related factors such as his marriage or his father having built up confidence in him whereas late transfers are usually associated with father-related factors such as his poor health or desire to qualify for an Old Age Pension.

Partibility Patterns

The literature gives some indication of the rich variety of inheritance patterns found in market industrialized countries but it is very difficult to quantify the prevalence of the different patterns. In some cases this is because of the lack of data on land ownership and in others it is because there is so much variation within the countries themselves. Though in reality there may be very few cases at the extremes of the partibility scale, it is useful to consider these extremes because the partibility question is of such significance where the family engaged in farming owns the land. Strict impartibility, where all assets and particularly the land are bequeathed to one individual, is most closely associated with *primogeniture*, where the oldest son is sole beneficiary. Partible inheritance, involving division of the assets, is most closely associated with the *Code Napoléon*, which was originally designed to ensure the breakup of the large aristocratic estates in post-revolutionary France. Indeed the Code's original provision (that the widow receive a quarter of the estate and the remainder be divided equally between the surviving children) was expected to have such a dramatic effect on the structure of French land ownership that it was referred to as the *'machine à hacher le sol'*.

Primogeniture

The normal UK practice is for landowners to leave the majority of their wealth and all their land to the eldest son 'in accordance with English tradition and the Common Law rule of primogeniture' (Harrison 1981). This practice is exemplified by the intentions of one large landowner covered in Errington and Tranter's (1991) survey:

> In order that the Estate, of which the farm forms part, should remain as an entity (more or less as it has done for 250 years) it and the farm go to the eldest boy. If he does not survive, the second boy. Failing that, the eldest daughter.

There are thus three distinct elements in the concept of primogeniture – ownership is transferred to *one* person, that person is *male* and he is the *first-born* son. It is difficult to establish the extent to which primogeniture in this strict sense is still the norm in the UK since there is no register of agricultural landownership. Nevertheless, the position of the landowner in English law is clear: he possesses the freehold interest in the land. Freehold is effectively absolute ownership and the land is held as 'fee simple'. The term 'fee' denotes that it is an estate and can pass by inheritance while 'simple' denotes that it can do so without any condition, limitation or restriction as to heirs. The holder may leave his interest by will to whomsoever he wishes (provided that the will proves valid under the Wills Act of 1837). If he dies intestate, it is held for the benefit of his spouse and heirs, and if there are none it goes to the state.

Within the EC, impartible inheritance is not confined to the UK. The Partial Federal Law for entailed estates in Germany allows farms over a certain minimum size in Hamburg, Lower Saxony, North Rheine-Westphalia and Schleswig-Holstein to pass to only one heir, though rules are set out for the compensation of excluded heirs. The heir can even be someone from outside the family provided they are commercially capable of operating the farm. Likewise the 1969 legislation in Luxembourg favoured a single heir, though again providing compensation for excluded heirs (Harrison *et al.* 1982). Indeed, there are many instances where the practice of handing down the farm to one child is combined with continuing obligations to both surviving parents and siblings. Even under the traditional conditions of primogeniture in the UK it was usual to make some provision for other children, perhaps in the form of a dowry for daughters or the provision of an education for younger sons in order to establish them in a career.

There is considerable anecdotal evidence to suggest that daughters rarely inherit UK farms though Symes' (1990) comment that 'It is manifestly clear that women suffer extreme prejudice in matters of farm succession and inheritance', has never been investigated systematically. However, Gasson (1987) did provide some evidence in a small study of the careers of farmers' daughters and Errington and Tranter's (1991) survey of English farmers showed that their views on inheritance were certainly not gender-neutral. On farms where there were only two children, and these were both sons, only 26 per cent of respondents favoured transfer of the farm intact to a single heir while on farms where the two children were son and daughter, the proportion rose to 54 per cent.

One illuminating but rather dated piece of empirical evidence on inheritance practice comes from Tarver's (1952) analysis of 636 Wisconsin farms that by 1948 had been owned by the same family for at least 100 years. In all, he analysed 1458 transfers of ownership taking place during this period. The vast majority (75 per cent) were to sons, as compared with 15 per cent to daughters and smaller numbers to brothers, nephews and other relatives. He shows that in 81 per cent of cases where there were both sons and daughters in the family, it was a son that inherited the land. He concludes, however, that 'the main reason for the more frequent transfer of farms to sons than to daughters seems to reside in the labor requirements of the farming enterprise and not in any favouritism toward sons'. Since sons tended to do farm work while daughters concentrated on housekeeping activities 'a farmer usually finds it more appropriate to transfer his farm to a son, who may have farmed with him for several years, than to a daughter and son-in-law'. While Voyce (1989) does point out that farm inheritances 'are not merely gratuitous gifts but are ... reciprocal exchanges of cheap labour in return for a promise of inheritance', Tarver's conclusion again highlights the tendency to discount the value of 'reproductive' as against 'productive' work in the farm family business.

But inheritance patterns do change over time. According to an analysis of 60 probated Ohio wills (Engler-Bowles and Kart, 1983) there were substantial changes around 1900, after which time daughters began to receive dispositions more in line with their brothers and there was no longer a distinction according to the birth-order of the sons. Another example is the recent change in Norwegian law which now gives the right of succession to the eldest child, irrespective of gender, as noted in Chapter 6.

Sibling order was not significantly related to succession among Tarver's Wisconsin farms and he concludes:

> It seems plausible that matters such as occupational interests of the different sons, their ages, health and farm management abilities, and ability to get along with their parents, may be as important as the order of birth in explaining why a certain farm was passed to a particular son.
>
> (Tarver 1952: 266)

There is certainly some evidence from this side of the Atlantic supporting the view that it is still usually the oldest son who inherits. According to Commins and Kelleher (1973), 55 per cent of the transfers of farms covered by their survey were to the oldest son. However, on small farms in Denmark, western Ireland and France it is often the *youngest* son who is selected (*ultimogeniture*) since this will minimize the length of time over which the farm will have to support two whole generations simultaneously.

Code Napoléon

The English tradition of impartible inheritance appears to stand in stark contrast to that of most other EC Member States. Thus Dutch law is essentially Napoleonic, guaranteeing equal division between children (and a child can even insist on a share in the *real* property, that is land) while in Italy, the national law also provides for sub-division between all legitimate heirs. However, closer scrutiny reveals considerable variation in actual practice. For example, in the eastern part of The Netherlands the tradition of 'stayers right' is still maintained – a single heir may take over the farm in return for undertaking welfare responsibilities for the family as a whole. In Italy, primogeniture is still followed in the autonomous Tyrol province of Alto Adige while in South Germany the tradition of impartible inheritance persists, though the succeeding child still retains financial obligations both to his siblings and to his parents (in the form of *altenteil*).

Despite the operation of the Code Napoléon in much of Continental Europe, large farms do survive. This is because the framework requiring equality of treatment between heirs has been adapted to ensure that the family farm can survive as a viable unit.

In the first place, the successor may be helped to buy the farm from his parents (who use the resulting funds to finance their retirement) or he may 'pay out' sibling shares (*soultes*). Thus it has been common practice in Denmark for one son to buy the farm from his parents, though his father will often make over 10–15 per cent of its value as a gift at the time of purchase and the State will provide a capital grant and low interest loan to help finance the transaction. One significant by-product of this approach is the high level of indebtedness among young farmers in countries such as Denmark (Perrier-Cornet *et al.* 1991). The Dutch 'Maatschap' or two-generation partnership seeks to overcome this problem by allowing the successor to build up his own share in the business gradually over a period of years in a way that may mirror the transfer of managerial control (see Chapter 8). In other cases, the amount paid for the education of non-succeeding children as well as the wages forgone (the *salaire différé*) by the child who has worked alr .gside his father up to the point of transfer may be taken into account when he buys the land.

A second strategy involves the so-called 'family advantage', an under-valuation of farmland when determining the value of assets to be divided. In some countries such as Germany, Switzerland, The Netherlands and Luxembourg farmland is valued at its 'economic', 'farming', or 'capitalized income' value which may be half or less of the market price. In Spain, the use of a *Valeur de convenance familiale* has a similar effect.

A third strategy is to divide the ownership of the farm equally between the various beneficiaries but to allow one *successeur professionel* to lease the farm from his co-inheritors. Thus, in France, from 1980 the successor has been able to take a long-term lease from the siblings who can form them-selves into a company, a *Groupement Foncier Agricole* (GFA).

Finally, the farmer may build up a fund of off-farm investments during his working lifetime, perhaps in the form of a life assurance policy, and this will eventually provide a separate estate from which the non-succeeding children can receive their inheritance. This can 'reduce the costs of asset liquidation and asset splitting and, in some cases, eliminate conflicts of interest that might arise because of co-ownership of property' (Boehlje and Eisgruber 1972).

PARTIBILITY OR IMPARTIBILITY: THE KEY DETERMINANTS

> Systems of transmission between generations ... are not eternal, but always fragile compromises between contradictory tendencies.
>
> (Augustins 1989: 143)

The enormous variation in inheritance patterns among farm family businesses across different localities and time-periods results from the interplay of a number of different factors, such as the legal and fiscal framework, prevailing social norms, and the current economic situation[2]. While each of these will have its own independent effect, the factors are closely inter-related. For example, the fiscal framework is embodied in the legal system and this in itself reflects present or past social norms as well as the current economic and political context. The remainder of this section deals with each factor in turn, using examples to illustrate the manner in which each can influence patterns of partibility and timing.

The Legal and Fiscal Framework

The law can have a major impact on inheritance patterns, securing the rights of particular individuals – the surviving parents as well as their children. There is often different legal provision for cases where there is a proven will as compared with those where the farmer dies intestate, where the law of the land will determine the share of the property passing to each legitimate heir. Thus, the 1965 Irish Succession Act abolished distinctions between inheritance rights of males and females, giving the surviving spouse a legal right to one third of the estate if there were children or one half if there were none. However, it should be remembered that our own perception of the will as 'a clear recognition of the rights of individuals to hold property for themselves and distribute it as they wish' is the product of twentieth century individualism. As Abrahams (1991) explains, freedom of testation in Finnish law was historically limited to movables and 'earned' as opposed to inherited fixed property. The general principle was that the current owner had a duty to maintain inherited land and to pass it on to her own rightful heir(s). This was embodied in 'kin redemption rights' which gave any family member, up to and including first cousins, the right to object and subsequently exercise a first option to buy land offered for sale outside the family.

The capital taxation system may have a major impact on property transfer. As Harrison writes in his report on land-ownership and inheritance patterns in the UK:

---

[2]This said, we must not ignore the role of individual 'actors' and do take de Haan's point that 'External forces cannot be interpreted in a straightforward way. They are always mediated by individuals and local social structure' (de Haan 1992: 10).

The correctness of the decision about when, to whom and how to transfer a farm business is not something to be settled according to resource use criteria but is properly, and almost entirely, to be reached on the grounds of fiscal advantage.

(Harrison 1981: 228)

However, it should be remembered that he was writing soon after the introduction of Capital Transfer Tax which offered a substantial advantage to those who planned ahead, while posing the threat of farm fragmentation to those who did not.

Tax law varies considerably over time and between countries. In the UK, for example, tax is levied on the dispersal of assets while in most other EC countries it is levied on their receipt. Despite these differences, most countries do tend to reduce the total tax 'take' where:

- transfers are made in the direct consanguine line;
- transfers are made during the owner's lifetime rather than after his death; and
- the property transferred consists of agricultural land farmed by the owner.

Thus transfers made a minimum number of years (say, five or seven) before the owner's death may be exempt from capital tax; lifetime transfers might attract a significantly lower rate; 'agricultural' rather than market values may be used in assessing tax liability; and the transfer may attract 'working farmer' relief.

Capital taxation is, of course, only one of the instruments available to governments wishing to influence the continuity of the farm family business or modify the structure of the industry. In order to understand inheritance practices in a particular country, it is therefore important to look not only at its tax law but at the various retirement or 'settlement' aids, both grants and subsidized loans, which may be available to the outgoing or incoming generation of farmers. As we have seen, some aids are designed to enable children to buy the family farm from their parents or to 'pay out' siblings. They may also be used to influence the timing of transfers, as in the case of French settlement aids which are confined to successors under 35 years old. However, a recent report (Perrier-Cornet *et al.* 1991) suggests that, with exception of France, such aids have only a modest impact within the EC at present.

It may be thought that the legal and fiscal framework will be the prime determinant of inheritance patterns, but this is not the case since in many countries the law gives the owner considerable freedom over the disposal of his property provided he makes a clear statement in a proven will. More-over, considerable ingenuity may be employed to avoid or evade the prescription of the law. This will be the case particularly where the law appears to conflict with long-established social norms or economic self-interest. In these circumstances, the intentions of the law may be thwarted where there is insufficient political will to ensure that loopholes are closed and that it is enforced to the letter.

The fact that inheritance matters are often handled by civil rather than criminal proceedings may also be significant since social norms may place a greater constraint on the actions of private individuals than they do on public functionaries. Rogers explains the continuing influence of the Aveyronnais *ostal* system which conflicts with the French Civil Code:

> Very few have judged the economic gain forthcoming from a disputed inheritance to be worth the social costs likely to be levied by family and community for transgressing the commonly held sense of the morally appropriate.

> (Rogers 1991: 96)

Governments may be particularly reluctant to intervene where inherited property is concerned. In a major EC report on the factors influencing the ownership, tenancy, mobility and use of farmland in the Member States of the European Community, Harrison concludes:

> At the end of a detailed examination of practice and legislation relating to inheritance, it is the unwillingness of governments to apply rules aimed at improving farm structure as strictly to inherited property as they do to purchased property ... that impresses.

> (Harrison *et al.* 1982: 92)

Social Norms

> Farm succession and inheritance are always mediated by specific family and kinship values, and ... it is very unlikely that these will change under the influence of economic conditions.

> (de Haan 1992: 5)

In different areas and different eras, social norms may favour consolidation or partibility whatever the stance taken by the national law. Thus, Voyce (1989) comments on the 'moral weight of the local ideology' in south-west France which maintains the tradition of single-heir inheritance in spite of a legal framework encouraging equality of treatment between the owner's children. In countries where impartible inheritance prevails, social norms may protect the rights of those children who do not inherit the farm. In Ireland, for example, one son will often be identified as the farmer-successor and if his siblings have received an education and are settled in employment, they will receive little of the property. But if they are still young the inheriting son will usually finance their education and maintain them until they become independent. The pressure for him to behave in this way is not enshrined in law but is no less powerful as a result.

In other cases, social norms will encourage non-heirs to quit the family farm without pressing any financial claim against it for, as Abrahams (1991) explains, the only way for the family name to remain on the land is for the farm business to 'slough off' some members of each generation: 'the idea of a family farm persisting as a unit over several generations depends heavily upon the shedding of at least some family members as the generations pass'. In some cases, non-heirs are encouraged to move away from the locality and possibly emigrate; if they do not, their only alternative may be to remain on the family farm, often unmarried, as landless workers.

But social norms may also encourage partibility. In the USA there is reported to be an 'emergent societal ideal for providing each child with equal resources and an equal opportunity in the world' (Salamon and Davis-Brown 1988). Changing customs among Midwest farmers have now resulted in farm daughters inheriting equally with sons. However, this does not always lead to fragmentation for the daughters inheriting portions of the family farm are under very strong social pressure to rent it to their brothers or to give them first option to buy it.

There is thus a relationship between social norms and inheritance patterns, but the causal link may run in both directions. In some areas of southern France where strict partibility is the tradition, there is some evidence to suggest that farming families deliberately have smaller numbers of children in order to avoid farm fragmentation (Lifran 1989).

The Economic Context

Drawing on the Irish experience, Commins and Kelleher (1973) provide a graphic example of the impact of the economic context on inheritance patterns. Before the agricultural revolution, where the predominantly tenant farmers in Ireland faced high rent demands in relation to the productivity of land under the prevailing livestock systems, it was not possible to support two generations on the same farm so normal practice was to delay the transfer of ownership until the father's death. Increased productivity in the eighteenth century, following the introduction of intensive arable production including potatoes, led to a new tradition of earlier, partible inheritance which encouraged the subdivision of farms, earlier marriage and bigger families. However, the collapse of the corn price and the potato famine in the early nineteenth century made subdivision and early marriage too risky a strategy to follow and inheritance norms reverted to those of the earlier era. Thus, by the beginning of the twentieth century, 'a pattern of late succession and late marriage had become truly institutionalized in the Irish rural economy'.

In the UK, it now seems likely that the prevailing inheritance norm of impartibility is coming under growing pressure as a result of increased owner-occupation and the rapid escalation of land prices in the 1970s. Five-fold increases in land values made many heirs inheriting quite average-sized farms into paper millionaires not only with resulting capital tax problems but with associated family tensions. Traditionally, the father may have left the land to one child and helped out others with the purchase of livestock or machinery, but the land is now so valuable that equal treatment is much more difficult. The essence of the problem is not land prices *per se* but the relationship between land prices and farming incomes. If the latter do reflect the former, single heirs might still be able to pay out their siblings from accumulated profits. But as Sandford concludes:

> Farmers everywhere have become wealthy but illiquid and, therefore, at risk both from capital taxation and, to an even greater extent, from the possibility of weakening family ties and loyalties.

(Sandford 1976: 111)

A recent survey of English farmers shows only 40 per cent of those owning land were in favour of passing it intact to a single heir (Errington and Tranter 1991). A similar proportion favoured division of the farm or some other strategy while the remainder were unsure what to do or had given no thought to it as yet. The relatively small proportion favouring strict impartibility is striking, but it should be recognized that these are only expressed intentions; as yet, no evidence exists to show what actually happens to UK farms as they pass from one generation to the next. The survey did however show that a higher proportion of the younger respondents favoured impartibility and it may be that farmers modify their commitment to a single heir as their children grow up. If so, the proportion of English farmers currently passing the entire farm to a single heir may be even less than the 40 per cent referred to above.

There is some evidence to suggest that the tradition of primogeniture was never universal in the UK among what might be termed 'yeomen' farmers (as distinct from the large landowners). Regional variations indicate that inheritance patterns might have been linked to the profitability of farming and the availability of alternative ways of making a living, again illustrating that the resolution of the inheritance dilemma depends on the economic context. In parts of northern England in the eighteenth and nine-teenth centuries, alternative employment in textile mills or lead mines, or as outworkers to local factories, made the inheritance of a viable full-time farm less crucial. It was quite possible to support a family from a combination of part-time farming and this alternative occupation. In Rossendale, the prevalence of part-time farming has long been associated with a tradition of partibility among local farmers. Farming was initially combined with hand-loom weaving in the farmhouse and then with paid employment in the textile factories which sprang up along the valley during the Industrial Revolution (Rossendale Groundwork Trust 1986).

In sum, then, we can see that partibility and timing are the two main variables characterizing different inheritance patterns in the farm family business. Actual patterns result from the interaction of the legal and fiscal framework, social norms and economic context as well as the particular circumstances of individual actors. There is therefore immense scope for variation, though there have been some attempts at simplifying generalization. For example, a recent study by Perrier-Cornet *et al.* (1991) identifies three main patterns currently found in the EC. First there are the Mediterranean countries such as Greece, Italy, Spain and Portugal, where strict partibility continues despite legal constraints designed to prevent it. This results in the continued existence of many small farm businesses and a lot of part-time farmers. Second, there are those countries (UK, Ireland, Germany, and to a some extent The Netherlands) where the legal framework, tax law and social norms all encourage strict impartibility. Finally, there are those countries such as France, Belgium and Denmark where there is impartibility in practice but the tax law and the requirement for successors to buy the farm from their parents or 'pay out' their siblings places a substantial burden of debt on young farmers. However, the evidence provided earlier in this chapter suggests that such country-wide generalizations are unlikely to be a reliable guide to the inheritance pattern exhibited by individual farm businesses. Still less do they provide an explanation of the actual process by which the assets of a particular farm family business are transferred from one generation to the next, a subject to which we will return in the next chapter.

PATTERNS OF SUCCESSION

We have argued above that, while obviously related, succession (the transfer of managerial control) is conceptually distinct from inheritance (the transfer of ownership). This distinction is particularly important in countries such as the UK where farm family businesses are sufficiently large to allow two or even three generations to be drawing their livelihood from the business at one time. In such a business it is possible for the incoming generation to acquire some degree of managerial control even though legal ownership still resides with the previous generation. This implies that in some farm family businesses there may be a significant separation of ownership from managerial control *within the family*. While again recognizing the enormous variation in practice between different farm family businesses, it is useful to identify a number of 'ideal types' in the patterns of succession.

Four Ideal Types

The literature describes many different patterns for the transfer of the managerial control of the farm family business from one generation to the next. One involves the establishment of a separate (usually small) enterprise on a separate farm in which the potential successor is able to exercise full authority, to learn from her mistakes and to develop her skills before returning to the 'home' farm. Another involves the successor working alongside his father on the home farm, often as a replacement for a hired worker. He is given no responsibility or status and precious little pay but remains in this position for most of the remainder of his father's life, still being introduced to visitors as 'the boy' until he is well into his 50s.

These are just two of the many examples derived from empirical studies of farm succession in different places and different times. There appear to be two key distinctions in all these examples, namely the amount of responsibility exercised by the successor in taking decisions on the home farm and the extent to which she is able to run an autonomous enterprise. Figure 7.2, which provides a generalized framework for classifying these examples, generates four ideal types of succession pattern. Much of the empirical evidence found in the literature can be related to one or more of these patterns.

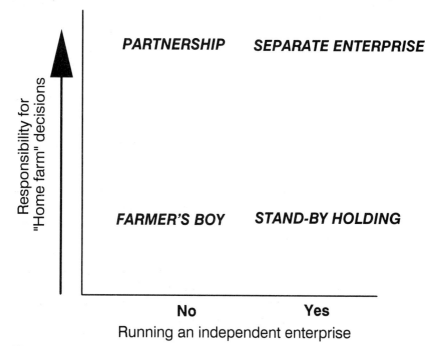

Figure 7.2. Patterns of succession.

In the case of the **stand-by holding** (Blanc and Perrier-Cornet 1992), the potential successor is set up by the father on a separate farm where he works for a number of years, developing his own husbandry and managerial skills. He may share machinery with the home farm and there is likely to be some co-operative labour-sharing at peak times, but he is substantially independent of his father. The successor's financial independence is important since the additional holding provides a source of income; the 'home farm' is not required to support two generations and the successor can even begin to build up a separate capital base with which to pay out parents or siblings. Eventually, his father retires and the son's holding may be amalgamated with the home farm or he may simply swap farm (and farmhouse) with his parents who move on to this farm which now functions as a 'retirement holding'.

In the case of the **separate enterprise**, the home farm is itself large enough to give the potential successor enough scope to develop her own enterprise, perhaps a pig unit or sheep flock. Once again, she has a good deal of autonomy in the development and management of this enterprise, thus developing skills which she is increasingly able to apply to the main enterprises on the farm on which she works alongside her father. The separate enterprise also gives the successor a degree of financial independence and may again allow her to develop her own capital base. The French phrase to describe this arrangement, *association et autonomie*, provides an apt description of its two essential components.

Even where he does not have his own enterprise, the potential successor may gradually acquire considerable responsibility for particular aspects of the management of the home farm. A particular expertise with machinery, for example, may lead his father to first involve him in discussions over machinery replacement and eventually leave such decisions to the successor himself. In this way, the potential successor works in a **partnership** which may eventually be cemented in a formal partnership agreement, such as the Dutch *Maatschap* described earlier in this chapter.

In the case of the pattern labelled **farmer's boy**, the potential successor may spend many years working with (or more accurately 'for') his father on the family farm but he has very little involvement in managerial activities and is mainly used as a source of manual labour. Because of this he has little opportunity to develop the managerial skills he will eventually need to take over the family business. To all intents and purposes he is simply a hired worker, though he may not even enjoy the hired worker's wage, and continue to be provided with an allowance on the grounds that his reward will be his eventual ownership of the family farm (the *salaire différé* to which French authors refer). Managerial control comes suddenly with his father's death or retirement and he may be ill-prepared for the management of the farm. The French term *aide familiale* aptly describes the role and status of the individual in this pattern of succession.

These four cases represent ideal types; in reality, the patterns of succession are many and varied and each may have some element of more than one ideal type. Indeed, a particular individual may move from one category to another in the course of his life. As with the patterns of inheritance there is both geographic and temporal variation in the prevalence of particular patterns. Once again, the fiscal and legal framework as well as the prevailing social norms all play a part, but in this case, it is probably the economic environment and its role in defining opportunities and constraints that has the greatest influence.

Succession Patterns in Practice

At the time of their survey in Ireland (the late 1960s), Commins and Kelleher (1973) suggested that the process of setting up sons on a separate holding was common, facilitated by the fact that 35 per cent of all farms had two or more holdings and this rose to 45 per cent among larger farms (over 100 acres). But they were already recognizing the increasing difficulty of following this traditional approach as land prices began to rise rapidly in the early 1970s. By the 1980s both Hastings (1984) and Hutson (1987) were explaining that the pattern of the 'stand-by holding' had become much less widespread in England and Wales because of increasing land prices and the reduction in new tenancies following the 1976 legislation and the decline in the number of County Council smallholdings. Indeed, this lack of suitable holdings coupled with the high cost of 'start-up' capital is now a significant constraint on all new entrants whether or not they come from a farming background (Errington *et al.* 1988).

While such changes have occurred and undoubtedly had a substantial impact on the patterns of succession in UK farming, this analysis understates the importance of regional variation and it is perhaps no coincidence that both Hastings and Hutson concentrated their fieldwork on particular localities. Differences in farm size and enterprise can have a major impact on the opportunity to incorporate a potential successor into the workforce while still remaining economically viable. For example, Hine and Houston (1973) showed that among the farm businesses in their two study areas, the 'stand-by holding' was much more common in Devon, while in the Midlands, the successor was more likely to have to work alongside the father on the home farm. The substantial difference between the prevalent 'stand-by holding' pattern reported by Williams in 1963 and the high proportion of successors incorporated into large, highly capitalized businesses in a 'partnership' model reported by Symes and Marsden 1983, probably owes as much to the regional difference between Devon and the eastern arable farming areas as it does to the economic changes of the intervening twenty years.

As the opportunities for using the 'stand-by holding' pattern in the UK have generally declined in the last two or three decades, more farm family businesses have been forced to explore the alternatives. There has probably been an increase in the number of sons now working alongside their fathers on a 'two generation' holding (the 'partnership' pattern in Figure 7.2), though the recent increase in formal partnerships in UK farming probably owes more to the conditions of Capital Transfer Tax (introduced in 1973) and the 1976 tenancy legislation than it does to a change in patterns of succession.

But as Hutson (1987) points out, new circumstances have encouraged a move away from a process of 'generational fragmentation' on separate farms to one of 'generational incorporation' on the home farm. Pembrokeshire farmers, like many elsewhere, are faced with a land constraint on opportunities to provide the successor with independent managerial experience and an independent income through the establishment of a separate farming business. They have therefore turned to expansion or intensification. As many as 40 per cent of the farmers covered in Hutson's survey had bought land to expand the farm, and half of these had bought it specifically to provide a living for their children. This echoes Hine and Houston's (1973) earlier finding that farm expansion in Nottinghamshire in the mid-1960s was more common among farmer–son partnerships than among other farms.

Farm diversification has also provided an increasingly attractive vehicle for development of the farm family business in line with the 'separate enterprise' pattern. Anecdotal evidence throughout the UK certainly points to an increasing number of agricultural contractor businesses run by farmers' sons from the home farm (NatWest Bank 1992). All these separate enterprises are important since they allow the successor to develop managerial skills without undermining the father's financial control of the farm family business as a whole.

Farm expansion, intensification or diversification may thus provide opportunities for the operation of an independent enterprise within the home farm. However, there is no firm empirical evidence on the proportion of successors on two generation farms who *are* responsible for their own enterprise, though Hastings (1984) cites some individual cases from his small exploratory sample and Commins and Kelleher (1973) found that nearly 60 per cent of the Irish successors currently farming alongside their fathers had run their own enterprise at some stage. It is interesting to note that these latter respondents stressed the importance of such enterprises as a source of financial independence rather than pointing to the status, responsibility or managerial experience they confer.

A recent French study (Perrier-Cornet *et al.* 1991), comparing practice across the EC as a whole, suggests that the 'partnership' pattern has only developed in the UK, The Netherlands, and to a smaller extent France (through use of a distinctive business form, the *Groupement Agricole d'Exploitation en Commun* or 'GAEC'). Limited farm size with its associated shortage of adequate income and accommodation to support the two generations is identified as the main constraint, currently solved either by a *détour professionelle* in which the successor pursues an independent career away from the farm before eventually returning to take it over, or by systematic selection of the youngest son as successor so that his parents are nearing retirement when the child is old enough to take over. Referring to Figure 7.2, the *détour professionelle* may be regarded as a variant of the 'stand-by holding' pattern while the selection of the youngest child may fall into the 'farmer's boy' category, particularly at a time of increased longevity, earlier marriage and reducing family size. There is little systematic empirical evidence on the prevalence of the *détour professionelle* in the UK apart from Nalson's (1968) description of Staffordshire farming in the 1960s. Anecdotal evidence from agricultural colleges and the universities, however, suggests that it is widespread, though the substantial decline in the agro-ancillary industries in the current recession may have significantly reduced opportunities and led to the absorption of additional children in the farm family business with a resultant increase in under-employment and family tensions (see Chapter 5).

SUMMARY AND IMPLICATIONS

This chapter has introduced the related concepts of inheritance, succession and retirement in the farm family business and has suggested a number of factors which help to account for variations in the prevalent patterns of inheritance and succession. Varying legal, social and economic circumstances lead to a rich variety of inheritance patterns but these can be differentiated in terms of partibility and timing. Four ideal types of succession were also identified – the **partnership**, the **farmer's boy**, the **separate enterprise** and the **stand-by holding** models.

Clearly, there is a relationship between patterns of inheritance and succession and these both relate back to the objectives of the farm family business. As Chapter 4 has shown, business survival and continuity can feature among the objectives of those involved in the farm family business but there is an important difference between systems of inheritance and succession that aim to keep the family name on the land as opposed to those merely seeking to keep the family in farming. These rather different objectives and their associated patterns of inheritance and succession may have somewhat different consequences for the farm family business itself.

Continuity in the sense of keeping the name on the land means that the structure of land holding is a constant to which the organization of the family has to adjust. Family relationships and individual aspirations may have to be sacrificed in the interests of the family business. Continuity is typically achieved by shedding some family members in each generation. Daughters are expected to marry or find work elsewhere. Non-inheriting sons might be forced to emigrate or remain in the home area as landless labourers. Historically in some parts of Finland and in the Tyrol, it was the custom for non-inheriting siblings of the farmer who remained in the farmhouse not to marry but to work for their brother and eventually his son.

The aspirations of the son chosen to inherit might also be thwarted in the pursuit of family goals. In the west of Ireland at the turn of the century, it was usual for farm parents to sanction the marriage of the inheriting son well in advance of their retirement from active life on the farm. This chapter has noted how the norms changed over the years with the changing prosperity of Irish agriculture. By the late 1960s, the trend was for permission for the son to marry being withheld until much later in the father's lifetime. If the father died suddenly, the decision about the son's marriage would pass to the widowed mother. Her reluctance to share her home with a stranger could cause further postponement of the marriage. Hence the mean age of men at marriage rose and so did the incidence of bachelor households (Symes 1973).

The ideal of setting up all sons in farming means adjusting the pattern of land holding to family structure. Family goals are given priority over attachment to a particular farm, although the practice of primogeniture could still result in a very uneven distribution of land between children. Taken to its extreme, the farm business might be sacrificed in the interests of family solidarity. Equity in the treatment of daughters or non-farming sons might be placed above the efficiency of maintaining a large farm business intact.

These different patterns of succession and inheritance aptly illustrate one of the central themes of this book. The fact of being a **family** business can constrain the choices open to the farmer and introduces an additional dimension to forward planning and strategic decision-making not encountered by the employed manager of a public company. At the same time, the existence of the farm **business** and the desire to maintain its continuity can seriously constrain the behaviour and life-chances of individual members of the farm family.

A second theme running through the book is the impact of the changing economic, social, legal and political environment in which the farm family business must operate. This chapter has illustrated the effect which such changes may have on patterns of inheritance and succession in the farming community. However, it has also shown the scope for individual action and illustrated the varied response that is still open to the actors involved. By concentrating on the processes of retirement and succession within the farm family business, our next chapter focuses more closely on the individual actors themselves.

8

THE PROCESSES OF SUCCESSION AND RETIREMENT

INTRODUCTION

> I started to work for my father, then with my father; now he works for me.
>
> (Hutson 1987: 221)

Our definition of the farm family business emphasizes that ownership and managerial control are combined, and that both must eventually be transferred to the next generation if continuity is to be achieved. While the previous chapter has concentrated on the patterns of inheritance and succession showing how they are moulded by the economic and social circumstances in which the individual farm business operates, this chapter will focus more narrowly on the process by which managerial control is transferred. But once again, aspects of the process, such as the speed with which it takes place, will vary between farm families under the influence of economic and social circumstances, mediated through the perceptions and attitudes of the individuals concerned.

Like any processes, succession, inheritance and retirement can be managed, i.e. planned for, monitored and controlled. Indeed, the ultimate survival of a particular farm family business may lie as much in the effective management of these transitions as it does in the management of the farming enterprise itself. As we explained at the beginning of the previous chapter, in the farm family business, retirement can be seen simply as the mirror image of succession: as one generation moves out of the driving seat, another moves in. This chapter therefore considers the manner in which successors are first identified and then brought into an increasingly central role in the business. But it also examines how the farmer and his wife prepare themselves for their eventual retirement from the farm family business.

Once again, we attempt to bring together the available empirical evidence, concentrating on the UK but drawing on other OECD countries where appropriate. However, our reliance on these secondary sources tends to introduce biases of which the reader should be aware. In the first place, we concentrate on retirement from managerial activity rather than manual work. Secondly, we tend to concentrate on the (usually male) farmer and his (usually male) successor with much less attention being paid to the role of the farmer's (usually female) spouse.

IDENTIFYING THE SUCCESSOR

Dombey was about eight-and-forty years of age. Son about eight-and-forty minutes.

(Dickens 1868b: 1)

The potential successor may be identified very early in life. A recent survey of English farmers suggests that on farms where there is at least one son in the family, a quarter have identified a successor by the time the oldest son is ten years old and nearly half have done so by the time he is sixteen (Errington and Tranter 1991). On farms where there are only daughters the identification of a successor comes much later.

The extent to which the successor has freedom to exercise his own choice in the matter is probably impossible to establish empirically, though a recent New Zealand study has begun to shed some light on this under-researched area (Keating and Little 1991). On the one hand, some observers refer to the 'nebulous' process of selection where a 'natural' successor simply emerges. Others envisage a long period of socialization which minimizes the risk that the best candidate for succession will choose a different career path. Marx may have been right when he said 'It is not the son who inherits the farm; the farm inherits the son' but any initial choice of successor is likely to be so tested and reinforced by subsequent socialization (of which both the successor and his parents are barely aware) that it would be impossible either to confirm or deny the statement. By its very nature difficult to measure, many farming parents deny the existence of socialization, emphasizing the need to 'leave it up to the children' and 'not to push them'. However, observers such as Anderson and Rosenblatt (1985) and Voyce *et al.* (1989) point to the differential help that is given to particular children in learning farm skills or in setting up their own small 'hobby' enterprise while still at school.

THE SUCCESSION LADDER

The empirical evidence suggests that, in the UK at least, more cases are following the 'partnership' or the 'separate enterprise' patterns described in

Chapter 7, in which the successor gradually comes to share managerial control of the home farm with her father. A growing body of evidence from such farms points to the existence of a 'ladder' of responsibility which the successor will climb, gradually becoming more and more involved in the management of the farm.

The ladder was first identified in Commins and Kelleher's (1973) major study of Irish inheritance and succession. They hypothesize three distinct stages in the transfer of managerial control. In the first, the successor simply works on the farm, providing manual labour, and with no direct involvement in management. Next, he may take responsibility for routine and repetitive tasks such as buying and selling livestock and thus become involved in some managerial decision-taking. Finally, he assumes full managerial control, i.e. 'control over all the decisions, planning and use of resources including the capital or finances necessary to implement plans and decisions'. While recognizing that not all respondents would be conscious of the gradual transition from one stage to the next, the Irish researchers established that less than a third believed they had begun to 'make major decisions in running the farm' before they were twenty and depending on farm size, between 40 per cent and 56 per cent did not reach this stage till they were over twenty-five years old. Between 32 per cent and 39 per cent did not achieve full managerial control till they were over thirty-five years old but again this was dependent on farm size with nearly half the respondents on the smallest farms reporting that they did not reach this stage till they were over thirty-five.

While the age at which each successive level of responsibility was attained tended to come later on smaller farms, the time gap between the two managerial stages narrowed so that on the smallest farms about half the respondents reached both stages simultaneously, in contrast to the more gradual process of transition on larger farms. Commins and Kelleher also identified lack of managerial responsibility as the most common source of dissatisfaction among sons working alongside their fathers, more common, even, than complaints on lack of financial independence or the lack of their own enterprise.

The main conclusion reached by the Macra na Feirme study group that drew on the findings of the Irish research project, was that the transfer of managerial control on Irish farms happens later than it does in some other European countries such as The Netherlands and Denmark, and far too late so far as the study group was concerned. In the final report (Commins and Kelleher 1973) the study group deplore the lack of planning for systematic progress up the ladder and make clear their view that most Irish farmers' sons do not climb it quickly enough for their own good, for the good of the farm or for the good of Irish agriculture as a whole. Their comments imply that the main problem is the son's lack of power which results from his dependent status. Indeed, less than 10 per cent of the sons working with their father received a regular wage or share of the profits. The largest single source of income was 'pocket money'. The group conclude:

> There is not any rational, planned and gradual transfer of functions from father to son. Thus, sons must wait until they acquire ownership to achieve managerial and operational control of the farm, and transfer means that fathers and sons change rather abruptly dominant and subservient positions in their relationships with one another ... there is no formal transfer of managerial or decision-making authority; what occurs is an imperceptible process whereby sons acquire responsibility but without any real power in the crucial aspects of farm management.
>
> (Commins and Kelleher 1973: 87)

This view is echoed by David (1987) who argues that a major problem in French farming is the son's status as *aide familial* remaining financially dependent on his father and only paid for all the work he puts into the farm when he eventually receives his inheritance – *le salaire différé*. David puts the case for giving the son professional status through the formation of formal partnerships such as GAEC (see Chapter 7).

Empirical studies elsewhere confirm the existence of a succession 'ladder'. From their New Zealand work Keating and Little (1991) identify a number of stages in a son's involvement in the farm business. For manual work, men graduate from 'half farm hand' through 'boy' to 'farmer'. In respect of management the stages are 'silent partner', 'jury' (who responds to parents' plans), 'partner' and 'manager'. Similarly in ownership, successors pass through several stages from non-owner to full owner (no doubt helped by New Zealand's well-developed tradition of share-farming). One of the points confirmed by this study is that men and women enter farming by different routes, with men typically beginning their careers at a higher level of involvement than women.

In the UK, Errington and Tranter (1991) built on the pioneering work of Hastings (1984) to examine the transfer of managerial control on 800 English farms. Box 8.1 is based on the analysis of completed questionnaires from the 250 farmers who had an identified successor aged 16 or more already actively involved in the business. The results, which are very similar to those obtained in Hastings' original survey, point to the existence of a ladder of responsibility which successors climb *en route* to the acquisition of full managerial control.

The decisions most commonly delegated concern work methods, the type and make of machines and equipment to be bought, the supervision of staff and the type and level of feed/sprays/fertilizers and drugs used. Three of the four are thus concerned with the organization and use of *existing* farm resources. Decisions least likely to be delegated all involve financial transactions such as negotiating loans and finance or deciding when to pay bills or sell produce.

Box 8.1. The sharing of decisions/activities. Source: Errington and Tranter 1992: 114

Activity/decision	Ranking	Mean Score
Decide when to pay bills	1	3.5
Identify sources and negotiate loans/finance	2	4.2
Negotiate sales of crops/stock	3	5.0
Decide when to sell crops/stock	4	5.2
Decide and plan capital projects	5	5.4
Recruit and select staff	6	5.6
Negotiate purchase of machines and equipment	7	5.7
Decide when to take on additional staff	8	5.7
Decide long-term balance and type of enterprise	9	5.8
Make annual crops/stock plans	10	6.0
Decide amount and quality of work expected	11	6.2
Plan day-to-day work	12	6.2
Decide timing of operations/activities	13	6.5
Decide work method/way jobs are done	14	6.5
Decide type and make of machines and equipment	15	6.5
Supervise staff at work	16	6.6
Decide type and level of feed/spray/ferts/drugs used	17	6.8

Score: 1 = Decision/Action by Farmer alone.
        5 = Shared equally
       11 = Decision/Action by Successor alone

The first areas in which a successor may achieve high levels of responsibility – the first steps on the succession ladder – are those in which he possesses specific technical expertise such as decisions about machinery purchase. Errington (1986b) describes this as 'internal information' whose value is recognized by the farmer and brought into the decision-making process. Decisions on the use of fertilizers, feed, sprays and drugs may either reflect similar recognition of specific expertise or the fact that the successor has been given substantial responsibility for the day-to-day management of an individual enterprise following the 'separate enterprise' pattern described in Chapter 7.

The proportion of successors with substantial involvement in financial matters is uniformly low except in the case of negotiations over new machinery, where the earlier point about specialist expertise provides a possible explanation. Hastings speaks of the cheque-book as the 'last bastion of father's control' but recognizes the reasons for his reluctance to let go:

Retention of these four items clearly gives fathers an ideal monitoring and control mechanism. They control the cheque book and deal with the bank. The father also controls sales from the farm and any negotiations that are required. It would be inappropriate to create a picture of despotic financial controllers, whose intention is purely to control and manipulate. When sons first return to the home farm, few are interested in the financial aspects of the business. As father grows older he will spend less time on physical work and his natural role is to spend more time on pure management and administrative duties. Thus handling bills and paperwork, judging the market and negotiating with contacts known for thirty plus years is seen as an excellent way of passing time.

(Hastings 1984: 199)

While recognizing that different successors of the same age will be on different rungs at any given point in their career, it is possible to consider the situation of the 'average' successor by taking an arbitrary point on the responsibility scale. Figure 8.1 takes the point at which responsibility is shared equally between respondent and successor and identifies the average age at which the successor reaches this point. Responsibility for deciding when to pay bills appears at the top. All too frequently it is beyond the top rung to which the successor can aspire during his father's lifetime.

In their small study in north-east Scotland, Anderson and Hepworth (1980) also highlighted the fact that financial control was the last area to be transferred, suggesting that farmers retain the financial reins for fear of being 'pushed aside' and sons are therefore deliberately 'kept in ignorance of the business management of the farm'. Hastings highlights the problems that this might entail:

The danger lies in the unprepared son. As reported earlier, the son's greatest concerns on final takeover are for the financial activities and decisions usually retained by father. College training on financial management has largely decayed over ten to fifteen years and fathers appear to make little attempt to train or give experience to their sons in financial management.

(Hastings 1984: 199)

Stages in the Succession Process

Five distinct stages in the succession process can be identified (see Box 8.2). Few farm businesses are completely static, however, and it is likely that the transfer of responsibility will overlay other changes in the business itself so that new areas of activity emerge for which the son may have particular responsibility. Thus Hutson (1987) introduces another stage into the succession process where a new venture is planned – and later implemented by the son – in order to take full advantage of the additional managerial

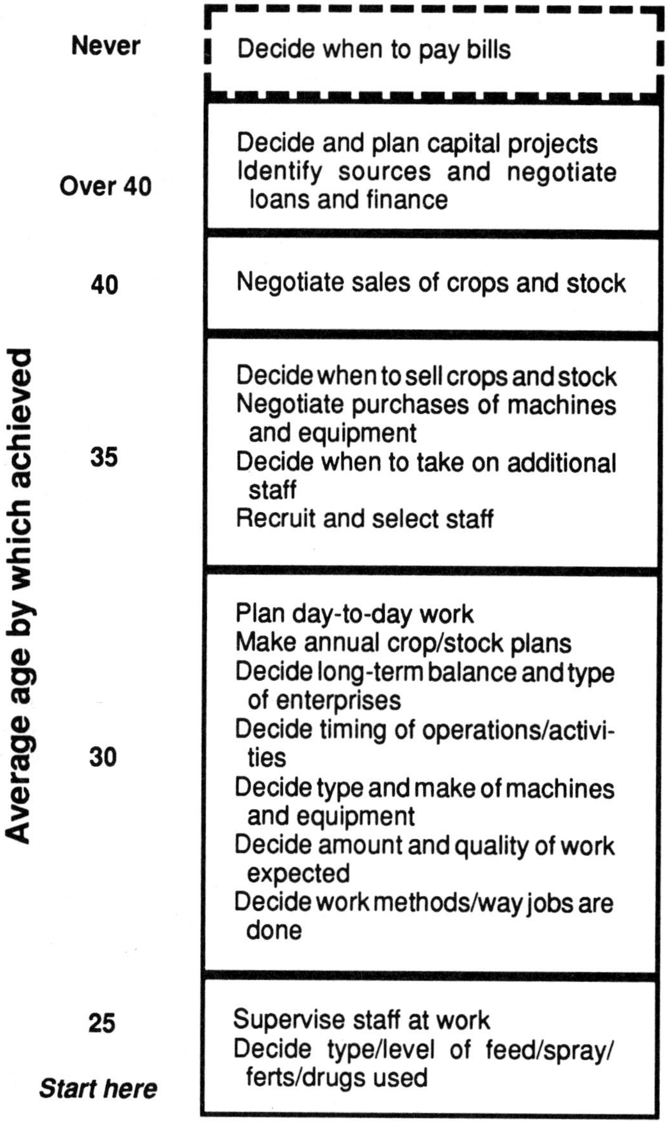

Average age by which achieved		
Never	Decide when to pay bills
Over 40	Decide and plan capital projects Identify sources and negotiate loans and finance
40	Negotiate sales of crops and stock
35	Decide when to sell crops and stock Negotiate purchases of machines and equipment Decide when to take on additional staff Recruit and select staff
30	Plan day-to-day work Make annual crop/stock plans Decide long-term balance and type of enterprises Decide timing of operations/activities Decide type and make of machines and equipment Decide amount and quality of work expected Decide work methods/way jobs are done
25 **Start here**	Supervise staff at work Decide type/level of feed/spray/ferts/drugs used

Figure 8.1. The succession ladder. Source: Errington and Tranter 1992: 121

capacity of the farm and to ensure adequate income is available to support the two generations. While Hastings' analysis of the succession ladder fits the 'partnership' pattern in Figure 7.2 (p. 204), Hutson's additions are relevant to the 'separate enterprise' pattern which may become increasingly common as farming incomes come under pressure.

It is important to recognize that the 'partnership' stage identified by Hastings in Box 8.2 does not necessitate a formal partnership in the legal sense, and indeed the growth of formal farming partnerships in the UK owes at least as much to the search for tax efficiency as it does to a growing desire for planned succession (Marsden *et al.* 1989). Some authors argue, however, that formal partnerships are important in countries such as France and Australia, not only because they confer status but because they allow the successor to build up his investment in the farm, so minimizing inheritance tax and providing him with funds to buy out sibling stakes in the business (David 1985; Voyce 1989).

The stages identified by Hastings concentrate on the changing responsibilities of the successor; there are, of course, reciprocal changes on father's side. Retirement is now increasingly regarded as the transition to a new role rather than easing out or giving up. So what is the farming father's new role after his son becomes 'Controller'? As we explained in Chapter 1 the decision process involves gathering all the relevant information and advice

Box 8.2. Stages in the succession process. Source: Hastings 1984: 229

Start here SOCIALIZATION		Extends from birth to working at home full time. The sons develop their personality and attitudes to family and farm life and as a result of working on the farm between school may learn many of the basic farm skills.
TECHNICAL APPRENTICESHIP		Extends from starting work to achieving 30–40 per cent involvement in management after working at home for four to six years, by which time the father is in his mid-50s. Main role consists of general farm work, some day-to-day planning, supervision of staff and helping decide makes of machines and equipment.
PARTNERSHIP	A.	Starts when father is in his mid-50s and continues until father is in his early 60s. Sons are increasingly involved in technical management decisions particularly related to crop and stock treatments and the planning of long-term projects.
	B.	Starts when father is in early 60s and extends to mid to late 60s. Sons take more responsibility for staffing, crop planning and enterprise balance. At this stage sons have up to 65 per cent of managerial responsibilities.
CONTROLLER		Son becomes increasingly involved in buying and selling as father's age and health decline in his late 60s. Final transfer to controller unlikely to take place until age and health retires the father.

as well as using personal judgement to choose between two or more courses of action. The work of Hastings (1984) and of Errington and Tranter (1991) suggests that in some decision areas, such as machinery purchase, sons moving up the succession ladder may 'graduate' from simply providing information and advice to using their own judgement to take the decision themselves. It may be that the process of succession in the farm family business is increasingly associated with role reversal, so that father now becomes the adviser to his decision-taking son. This role of 'elder statesman' has been identified in the wider business world by Barnes and Hershon (1976) who suggest that the older manager shifts into a new role of 'advise and teach' rather than 'control and dominate'.

The Rate of Ascent

While the rungs on the succession ladder might be identical on different farms, the speed at which the successor ascends the ladder varies considerably and a number of factors appear to influence this – characteristics of the father, of his successor and the relationship between them as well as the characteristics of the farm itself. In the first place there is father's assessment of his son's ability, of the changes he may make in the business and of the consequences for his own financial security and that of his wife (Clarke *et al.* 1976). Commins and Kelleher found that where father and son were working together on the same farm, three quarters of the sons felt they knew enough to run the farm on their own before the age of 24, but only half the farmers had the same estimation of their son's capabilities.

Next, there is the strength of father's desire to preserve the challenge, independence, status and feeling of responsibility which comes from being in control of one's own business. Finally, there is the opportunity cost of father's continued involvement which will be influenced by the other possible uses of his time. In farming this opportunity cost may be low where farmers may have done little in their working lives to develop interests outside the farm. Thus, Commins and Kelleher conclude that 'Farmers who have invested their whole careers in farming with little development of other interests or activities probably find it more difficult to part with the ownership or managerial control of the farm'.

The rate of ascent up the succession ladder on English farms is certainly related to farm size, though the relationship appears to be curvilinear with greatest delegation to successors occurring on the smallest (under 100 acre) as well as the largest (more than 400 acre) farms (Errington and Tranter 1991). Enterprise mix may also be important since a farm specializing in only one product may present few opportunities for identifying a discrete area of the business for which the son can be wholly responsible. The type of enterprise may also be important. Hutson (1987) cites the example of early potatoes with their requirement for one person to take a closely-related sequence of decisions, offering little scope for delegation. In such circumstances 'sons can feel very much under their father's thumb'. While the characteristics of the farmer, his potential successor and the farm itself may be the underlying factors that influence the rate of progress up the succession ladder, particular events, such as an accident, a serious illness or marriage, may precipitate rapid movement to another rung.

We have already seen that the consequences of late succession in the farm family business include the lack of opportunity for the successor to develop initiative and responsibility, the perpetuation of low social status for 'dependent' successors and, assuming youthfulness is associated with progressiveness, less progressive farming practice. Certainly, the sons that Commins and Kelleher met who had achieved full control of the farm felt that the most important benefit was that they 'could plan for their own future and put their ideas into practice'.

While there is considerable agreement in the literature that a sudden or unduly late transfer of managerial control (perhaps only on the death of the farmer) can have detrimental effects on the business, on the efficiency of resource use and on the economic welfare of the community as a whole, it is important to be aware of assumptions underlying this conclusion. For example, Anderson and Hepworth (1980) assert that 'The older generation have more experience, are more conservative, often value status and a quiet life more than cash income, and often wish to retain control of the business. The younger generation has often had a larger and more recent education ... are more progressive and are thirsty for responsibility and innovation'. Certainly, there is some empirical evidence (Jones 1967; Commins and Kelleher 1973) to support these assumptions and there do tend to be more major changes on two-generation farms where the son has taken over full managerial control but there is unlikely to be a perfect correlation between age and 'progressive' farming practice.

To summarize, the empirical evidence points to the existence of a ladder of increasing responsibility which the successor will climb at a rate depending not only on his own characteristics and those of his father but on the characteristics of the farm itself. There are significant disadvantages in late succession, both to the individual farm family business and to society at large. But whatever the circumstances in particular farm businesses, the higher rungs of the ladder invariably concern responsibility for financial matters so there is a grave danger that the successor will be insufficiently prepared to deal with the financial aspects of management when his father eventually retires or dies.

At the beginning of Chapter 7, we described succession as the mirror-image of retirement. In many respects it does simply reflect either the gradual or the rather sudden process by which the successor acquires control over, and responsibility for, the farm family business. However, in order to understand the nature of the process, and in particular the part which the farm family business may continue to play in meeting the older generation's needs for financial security, for accommodation and for personal fulfillment, it is now necessary to switch perspective from that of the successor to that of the retiring generation.

RETIREMENT FROM THE FARM FAMILY BUSINESS

> Retirement can be seen . . . as not an individual act but an extended sequence of transitions.
>
> (Rosenblatt and Anderson 1981: 154)

The idea of retirement as 'giving up work' is the product of an urban industrial culture that has little relevance to the farm family business, at least in the UK. In the context of urban employment it has come to be associated with a single point in time, a 60th or 65th birthday when the presentation of carriage clock or golf clubs marks the rite of passage from full-time employment into a world of permanent leisure. But the self-employed face a much wider range of opportunities (Keating and Marshall 1980) and in an occupation such as farming, the single term 'retirement' acquires many different connotations. In some cases it may indeed refer to the process of selling up, quitting the industry and giving up work. In others it may simply refer to the farmer's withdrawal from particular aspects of farm work such as milking cows. Rosenblatt and Anderson's view, cited above, is particularly useful when considering retirement in the context of the farm family business. Taking their basic assertion that retirement involves a sequence of transitions between different states, we can begin to identify a variety of retirement paths.

Many paths will start with the farmer fully involved in both the manual and managerial aspects of farm work on a full-time basis. It may finish with his complete **retirement from the farming industry** when he sells the farm and moves away to a retirement cottage by the sea. But more often it ends with him living on or close to the farm, giving occasional help to his successor, perhaps providing an extra pair of hands in an emergency or giving advice on difficult management decisions in the 'elder statesman' role described earlier in this chapter. As he moves from full involvement in the farm family business to this form of **retirement in farming**, he may pass through any number of intervening states in which he gradually withdraws from manual or managerial work on the farm. Each of these intervening states represent different forms of **semi-retirement in farming**. For example, a dairy farmer may gradually begin to reduce his involvement in particularly onerous manual tasks such as milking once his son returns from college, while over the next few years he drops a few more such tasks. Once he and his son have adjusted to the new working arrangements, he may begin to involve him in some managerial activities, delegating a number of decisions to him. As time goes on progressively more managerial responsibilities are handed over until the farmer reaches the state of retirement in farming which may eventually be accompanied by a move out of the farmhouse or even off the farm.

Any number of factors may intervene to alter the speed or direction of a particular individual's path into retirement. Failing health may force earlier withdrawal from manual activities or election to the District Council may necessitate a rapid transfer of day-to-day managerial responsibility to a successor. Alternatively, the path may follow a steady and carefully planned progress moving through semi-retirement to full-retirement in farming over a period lasting many years (Keating and Marshall 1980).

Even this picture with its many alternative paths is a simplified representation of the retirement process since it concentrates on only two of the actors involved, making no reference to hired farmworkers or to other family members. It does however serve to illustrate three terms that will be used frequently in the remainder of this chapter, for while there might be an infinite number of paths, we can distinguish three distinct states through which they run. First, there is the state currently occupied by farmers who have managed their own business in the past but are now **semi-retired in farming** – they still maintain some regular involvement in farming activity and the land continues to be farmed by their successor(s). Next, there are those who have **retired from farming** – they have ceased all farming activity, except on a very occasional basis, but the land continues to be farmed by their successor(s). Finally there are those who have **retired out of farming**. They have ceased all farming activity and the land is not farmed by their successor(s) – it has been sold, or surrendered to the landlord or to creditors.

As we have seen, an individual may pass through more than one of these states during his lifetime and there may even be some significant transitions within particular states as when a farming father gradually passes more and more managerial responsibilities to his son. While individual circumstances such as the farmer's health or his personality will determine the precise path followed, some generalizations may be made about the types of path that tend to be followed by substantial numbers of individuals. Once again these will be influenced not only by social norms and the legal and fiscal framework but by economic considerations. In particular, the move from full involvement in the farm to semi-retirement or full-retirement will be affected by the standard of living associated with each of these states.

This standard of living comprises more than just the monetary income received, and a plethora of non-monetary factors will give rise to what might be termed the 'psychic income' associated with particular states. For example, the farmer may attach a great deal of importance to the perceived status of retired farmers in the local community; he may derive a lot of satisfaction from the prospect of some continued involvement in farm work itself, or he may place a high value on living in a particular locality or even in a particular house.

We therefore consider several different aspects of retirement from the farm family business, first looking at the proportion of farmers retiring or intending to retire, the age at which they move from one state to another, and the factors that influence the timing of these moves. We then examine the monetary and psychic income associated with each succeeding state and finally consider the housing needs of farmers as they move towards full retirement.

DO FARMERS EVER RETIRE?

There is an old tradition that farmers never leave the land until they die, go broke or retire.

(Anderson and Hepworth 1980: 1)

According to Harrison (1975), about 3 per cent of English farmers 'retire' each year. Like many others, however, he fails to make a distinction between the different states described above and his estimate includes those who die or sell up as well as those handing the farm on to a successor. Among this latter group there is an important distinction to be made between retirement and semi-retirement even though farmers themselves may not recognize the distinction. Thus 'many farmers can only see retirement as a condition of decline, signifying the end of work, the onset of old age, or even impending death' while in fact agriculture 'offers possibilities for a positive kind of retirement, or more accurately, a diminished activity voluntarily undertaken with opportunities to develop a pattern of activities suited to advancing age' (Commins 1973; see also Selles and Keating 1989).

In their survey of English farmers in 1990, Errington and Tranter (1991) found that only one third expected to retire completely from farming while just over half said that they expected to 'become semi-retired at some stage'. The remaining 13 per cent declared that they would continue farming until their death, endorsing the statement: 'I expect I will never retire from farm work'. These proportions are similar to those found by Gasson (1984) in her survey of *Farmers Weekly* readers. In that study a further distinction was made between those planning to give up the decision-taking role in their semi-retirement while retaining some involvement in manual work and those planning to do the reverse. Taken together, these two surveys suggest that, out of every ten English farmers, one plans never to retire, three plan to become semi-retired and concentrate only on manual work, three to become semi-retired, concentrating only on managerial work, and three plan to retire completely.

Expectations vary between different groups of farmers, however. In the first place, both Gasson (1984) and Errington and Tranter (1991) found that older farmers were more inclined to say that they will retire completely, though it is unclear whether this indicates a fundamental change in norms or merely the fact that attitudes change as farmers get older. This is another example of the difficulty of distinguishing the vintage effect from the age effect in studies of the farm family business.

The characteristics of the farm seem to have as much, if not more, effect on plans than do the characteristics of the farmers. This is not surprising since the characteristics of the farm may severely constrain the farmer's options (Clarke *et al.* 1976; Keating 1991). Those with smaller farms are least likely to contemplate semi-retirement, either because they have no successor to take up the manual work and managerial responsibilities or because the farm provides insufficient scope and income for farmer and successor to work side by side. In this sense, semi-retirement and the gradual transfer of manual work and managerial control in partnerships of the type described in Chapter 7 is a luxury which not all farm family businesses can afford.

Retirement Age

Retirement norms may be changing, with progressively fewer farmers retaining full control over the farm till their death and more retiring 'normally' when they become eligible for the Old Age Pension (Gasson 1969). Increased longevity, earlier marriage, changing attitudes and a changing fiscal environment would all point to such a trend but the lack of longitudinal data on farm family businesses makes it impossible to test this hypothesis with any rigour. The very small amount of empirical data available does however seem to support the view that English farmers may be retiring earlier now than in the past. In their survey of small farmers in the early 1970s, Hine and Houston (1973) found that half the farmers aged 60–64 expected to retire within the next five years. Among the same age group in Errington and Tranter's 1990 survey the proportion was two thirds (though this may be more a reflection of the average size of farms covered in the two surveys than the result of changing norms).

Farmers with no children generally retire somewhat later than others – possibly because they have no successor to chivvy them out (Naylor 1982). Tenant farmers also tend to retire later, perhaps because of the difficulty of obtaining suitable accommodation in the area in which they have spent their working lives. They may therefore try to hang on as long as possible (Gasson 1984).

The average retirement age of English farmers appears to be older than that of counterparts in some other European countries, perhaps as a result of the conditions attached to the payment of state retirement pensions rather than to different social norms or economic circumstances. For example, Fennell (1981) reports that Dutch farmers tend to retire at an age where their successor is 27–30 while Commins and Kelleher (1973) refer to Danish practice where farmers retire at 60 and then return to work for their sons for a weekly wage.

Elderly Farmers

A particularly interesting group of farmers are those aged over 65, still engaged in farming and apparently with no plans to retire. Evidence from the EC Structure Survey (Eurostat 1991) suggests that these farmers may continue to make up a significant proportion of the total farming population (ranging from 29.8 per cent of all 'holders' in Portugal to 6.1 per cent in Germany; 22.3 per cent in the UK). However, these statistics are likely to contain many of those who are semi-retired and the farms may actually be run by a younger successor. Farm surveys that insist on only one person being designated as 'the holder' fail to do justice to the two-generation business common in some parts of the Community.

The high proportion of elderly farmers remaining in the industry beyond the 'normal' retirement age has long been a source of concern to policy makers in many EC countries. These farmers are believed to depress levels of productivity because they are less 'progressive' than their younger and better-educated counterparts and they are regarded as the most appropriate target for schemes designed to improve farm size structure by reducing the total number of holdings and increasing average farm size.

A recurrent feature of national and EC agricultural policies since the 1950s has therefore been schemes to encourage retirement **out of farming** and the subsequent amalgamation of small farms. These schemes are generally reckoned to have been unsuccessful (Gasson 1969; Hine and Houston 1973) with very few farmers taking up the retirement incentives offered. Thus only 0.1 per cent of UK farmers took up the pension annuities or lump sums offered in the EC Outgoers Scheme between 1975 and 1977. A large part of the explanation for such a low take-up may be found in the terms and conditions of the scheme. For example, the incentives offered were very small in relation to the current and expected value of land and there was an onus on the outgoers themselves to find suitable farms with which to amalgamate. But the general failure of such schemes highlights the social and psychological barriers to exit from farming. There is, for example, the social status and psychological well-being conferred by the ownership and operation of land to which Commins refers:

The typical farmer will have invested much of his own self in his farm by the time he is in his 60s or 70s; the attachment to the land is a strong sentiment with him and farm work gives him a feeling of self-worth and usefulness. To exchange these for the cash benefits of a retirement scheme would require a major personal adjustment in his established pattern of life.

(Commins 1973: 6)

While these socio-psychological factors are highlighted by researchers examining retirement out of farming, they are also important in explaining the rate and timing of transition from farming both to semi-retirement and to retirement in farming for, as we have already explained, the decision to move from one state to another is a function of psychic as well as money income.

SOURCES OF RETIREMENT INCOME

An assured stream of money income is a necessary prerequisite for successful retirement. Indeed, the first of Lachapelle's *Twelve Key Points in the Successful Transfer of a Farm* is 'ensuring parents have an adequate retirement income'. There is little empirical evidence on the level of income sought or obtained by retiring farmers even though policy measures are predicated on the perceived attractiveness of retirement incentives pitched at particular levels (such as the £370 per year offered in the 1973 UK Outgoer's Scheme to each married couple, equivalent to £1968 at 1990 prices). Errington and Tranter do however provide estimates of the *proportion* of their income which their respondents expected to obtain from various sources after retirement or semi-retirement in farming (see Figure 8.2).

The picture was substantially the same for those those anticipating semi-retirement as it was for those with full retirement in view, the largest single source (about 30 per cent) being a self-employed/private pension. The only substantial difference between the two groups was, not surprisingly, the proportion of income expected to flow from the farm itself. Where semi-retirement was contemplated this rose to almost a quarter, while for those planning to retire completely it was only about 10 per cent. The proportion of income expected from the sale of farm assets including land and livestock was a mirror image of this, with those intending to retire completely expecting about a quarter of their income from this source. Income from a state pension and income from investments was of roughly equal importance to both groups.

The proportion of the post-retirement income expected to come from an independent capital fund such as a private pension or other off-farm investments is particularly significant for the farm family business. Such

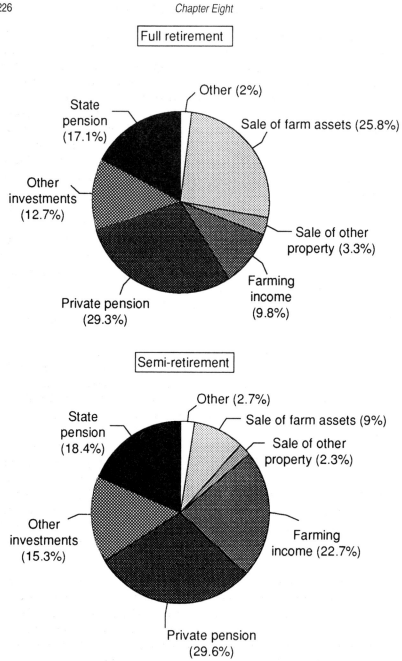

Full retirement

Other (2%)

State pension (17.1%)

Sale of farm assets (25.8%)

Other investments (12.7%)

Sale of other property (3.3%)

Private pension (29.3%)

Farming income (9.8%)

Semi-retirement

Other (2.7%)

State pension (18.4%)

Sale of farm assets (9%)

Sale of other property (2.3%)

Other investments (15.3%)

Farming income (22.7%)

Private pension (29.6%)

Figure 8.2. Sources of retirement income. Source: Errington and Tranter 1992: 86

funds can safeguard the succeeding generation against the drain on farm income and capital which might otherwise be required to finance the retirement of the out-going generation. Three quarters of the respondents to Errington and Tranter's survey were already contributing to a private pension scheme though there was some variation associated with farm size and the farmer's educational background. These findings stand in marked contrast to Commins and Kelleher's study of Irish farmers in the early 1970s, which revealed a marked lack of interest in pension schemes. The Irish study reports that, having explored the possibility of introducing a special pension scheme for farmers, an insurance company dropped the plan because the majority of farmers preferred to invest any surplus funds in their own farm. A survey of elderly English farmers in the mid-1970s (Ministry of Agriculture, Fisheries and Food 1978) also showed that 'only one third had made any kind of provision for retirement and even fewer had made plans to provide a supplementary income on retirement'. The markedly different situation in England in 1990 almost certainly reflects the impact of the fiscal framework which has not only offered income tax incentives to private pension contributions but induced many farmers to establish a separate fund from which to finance capital transfer or inheritance tax commitments associated with the farm.

Whatever the impact of the present tax system, the Irish study does highlight the dilemma faced by any businessman who has the option to invest in his own business. The pension fund simply provides an alternative destination for investible funds and some farmers will always feel that it is more sensible to invest these funds in their own business, thus making the farm itself their retirement 'nest-egg'. Under certain economic conditions this will be a quite rational decision but it is clearly important that the succeeding generation should be aware of these unwritten 'prior charges' on farm profits. Indeed, there may be circumstances where the post-retirement consumption needs of the retiring generation require a policy of disinvestment diametrically opposed to the successor's desire to expand the business. Unless handled well, the situation is fraught with difficulties and may lead to considerable tension between the generations. As Boehlje and Eisgruber observe:

> During the stage in the life cycle when most farm estate transfers take place, the processes of disinvestment (exit) and establishment (entry) are occurring simultaneously. Parents are usually attempting to relieve themselves of the managerial and financial burden of operating the farm business. At the same time, an operating heir may be aspiring to establish a resource base and entrepreneurial competence in the agricultural industry. If the two processes of entry and exit are not well co-ordinated, personal conflicts can arise and significant social costs are incurred.
>
> (Boehlje and Eisgruber 1972: 471)

In short, whether he is moving into retirement or semi-retirement the farmer is likely to expect the family business to continue to provide at least some of his income. The smooth transfer of ownership and control in the farm family business therefore requires sufficient financial planning to ensure that the provision for the welfare of the older generation does not undermine the continuing viability of the farm family business itself.

THE IMPORTANCE OF PSYCHIC INCOME

Retirement for him (the farmer) is not just making land available for productive use or giving up his customary source of income; it is also likely to mean a change in his established relationships with his neighbours and relatives, a change in the way these people evaluate or treat him, thus affecting his own feeling of well-being, a change in the pattern of his activities, interests and time, and a change in the meaning which his surroundings have for him.

(Commins 1973: 45)

As previous chapters have stressed, monetary considerations only form part of the explanation of individual behaviour in the farm family business. Depending on their own particular goals and values, many farmers (and their spouses) will derive psychic income from particular aspects of farming that they may have to forgo when they take the path to retirement or semi-retirement. For example, Commins (1973) emphasizes the importance of the status of the working farmer both in his own eyes and those of the local community. In general there is no recognized retirement role in farming and Commins concludes that the principal reason for rejecting the Farm Outgoers schemes was 'the farmer's conception of himself as an active working farmer'.

By asking farmers what they would most miss and what they would be happy to give up when they retire, Errington and Tranter (1991) threw some light on the psychic income which farmers will unconsciously bring into the account when facing the prospect of retirement. Asked what they would most miss, it was noticeable how often they mentioned the intrinsic aspects of their work, such as working with livestock. This again underlines the farmer's predominantly intrinsic orientation to work highlighted in Chapter 4. For a smaller group it was the location of the job, rather than the job itself that would be most missed, though it should be recognized that for many, semi-retirement or even full retirement would not necessarily mean that they would have to forgo these pleasures. Chapter 4 also emphasized the importance of independence among farming values. Like any other small businessman, the farmer values the freedom to manage his own affairs and to take his own decisions. Thus one respondent contemplating retirement said that he would miss 'The fact that you can please yourself what you do and when to do it, as long as it gets done' while another spoke of 'The freedom, pleasure and satisfaction of running my own business in the country in league with, yet also against, nature'.

Such replies make it clear that the farmer's retirement decision is based on much more than a crude monetary computation. But his dissatisfactions with his present job will also be taken into account. When Errington and Tranter asked their respondents what they would be happy to give up when they retired, the most commonly-mentioned factors all related to the hardships of farm work, especially the long, unsocial hours often working in bad weather. These long hours are often combined with the particular 'tie' to the farm especially where livestock are concerned and many respondents said that they would be very happy to escape this constant commitment on their retirement.

In explaining the failure of various financial incentives to induce Irish farmers to retire early, Commins (1973) comments that the farmer 'may seek to maximize on the more intangible satisfactions in his life'. The results from Errington and Tranter's survey certainly suggest that Commins was right to emphasize the intangible factors, though recent research findings from the United States suggest that he might be wrong when he cites the maintenance of active contacts with relatives as a prime example of this. Dorfman *et al.* (1988) conclude that the level of post-retirement satisfaction among rural households is most closely related to the maintenance of good health and an adequate income. Frequency of contact with relatives was not linked to either the husband's or his wife's level of satisfaction. Moreover, while continuing contact with his own friends was positively related to the husband's level of satisfaction, the number of his wife's contacts with her friends was *negatively* related to his satisfaction in retirement. Meanwhile, the number of close relatives seen at least once a month by the husband contributed to his wife's dissatisfaction!

RETIREMENT HOUSING

When Daryl went into farming in partnership with his dad in 1968, he was under the impression that someday soon he and Marilyn would move into the big house and the folks would take the little one, the one that Grandpa Tollerud built when he came from Norway. But nothing had been said about this for a long time. The little house would be fine for an older couple, who tend to sit quietly and not tear around chasing each other. But the old folks sit quietly in the big house, with four empty bedrooms upstairs. 'We really need a larger house,' Daryl says. 'Well,' his dad says, 'Soon as we get the pig barn built, we'll see about adding on to it.'

(Keillor 1989: 174–175)

One of the defining characteristics of the farm family business is that home and workplace are synonymous but what happens when the older generation retires? The availability of adequate alternative accommodation for either the retiring parents or the successor and his family is clearly an essential prerequisite for the smooth transition of the farm family business from one generation to the next. Indeed, Clarke *et al.* (1976) found that it had a major bearing on the timing of retirement since:

> It was not always possible to achieve a gradual transfer of control.
> Often the holding was too small to support two families, the parents
> had insufficient means to support an early retirement and, indeed, *had*
> *nowhere to move to* to make way for the incoming son.
>
> (Clarke *et al.* 1976: 7)

In Ireland, Commins and Kelleher found that 60 per cent of their respondents would not want to share the farmhouse with a married son and daughter and most believed that the timing of transfer, inheritance as well as retirement, was related to availability of alternative accommodation. The authors refer to the 'problems of two women sharing the same kitchen' and suggest the construction of second homes on family farms which can be let to tourists at times in the farm family cycle when they are not required for members of the family. Indeed Winter (1987) has established that the main reason given by farmers for refurbishing and letting farm cottages is to retain the property in family ownership until it is needed for retirement or for a newly-married son.

In other European countries various solutions have been adopted to overcome the accommodation problem associated with retirement or semi-retirement in farming. In The Netherlands, the succeeding son moves to the local village on his marriage and later swaps farmhouse with his parents as they retire. In Denmark only 2 per cent of farms have two generations living together in the same house; in most cases, the older couple moves into a house in the village on their retirement. In Lower Saxony and Finland, the tradition has been to build a separate dower extension on to the farmhouse at the time of the successor's marriage while Arensberg and Kimball (1968) refer to the Irish tradition of making the 'west room' available to the parents as they enter the sunset of their lives.

Errington and Tranter's survey of English farmers again throws light on their current attitudes and intentions. Figure 8.3, which refers to all respondents contemplating retirement or semi-retirement, shows that the majority (59 per cent) expected to move but in most cases to another house either on the farm or close to it. The decision whether to move out of the farmhouse varied considerably between different parts of the country, perhaps reflecting the differences in farming structure and local housing markets. It is not surprising that these accommodation plans vary with the characteristics of the farm since these will influence both the *need* to move

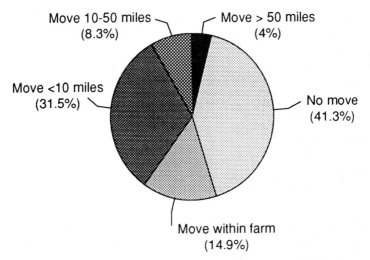

Move 10-50 miles (8.3%)

Move > 50 miles (4%)

Move <10 miles (31.5%)

No move (41.3%)

Move within farm (14.9%)

Figure 8.3. Plans to move house on retirement. Source: Errington and Tranter 1992: 73

and the *opportunity* to do so. Thus, those on the smallest farms (less than 100 acres) were least likely to move out of the farmhouse (only 47 per cent were planning to do so) perhaps reflecting the lack of opportunity to move elsewhere, while many of those on the largest farms were expecting to move out of the farmhouse but remain on the farm, implying that alternative housing was already available on the home farm.

MANAGING THE PROCESSES OF INHERITANCE, SUCCESSION AND RETIREMENT

> Not only does Old Man Tollerud hate to commit himself to trips, he also likes to stay loose in regard to drawing up a will or some other legal paper that gives Daryl and Marilyn some right to the farm that they've worked on for fifteen years. When Daryl mentions it, his dad says, 'Well, we'll have to see. We'll talk about it in a few months.' Daryl is forty-two years old and he's got no more ownership of this farm than if he'd gone off and been a drunk like his brother Gunnar. Sometimes he gets so mad at the old man, he screams at him. But always when he's on the tractor in the middle of the field with the motor running.
>
> (Keillor 1989: 87)

Inheritance, succession and retirement are all processes that can be managed. The aim will usually be to ensure the survival and continued prosperity of the family business while at the same time minimizing family conflict. All three processes involve role changes and task realignments which are potentially very stressful since:

> the younger generation may be striving for self-respect, autonomy, and a greater share of responsibility, while the older generation is striving to maintain control of decision-making and respect for past accomplishments
> (Russell *et al.* 1985: 361)

Indeed, Hedlund and Berkowitz (1979) reported inter-generational transfer problems among 75 per cent of the farmers in their sample.

Some exploratory research suggests that inheritance matters may give rise to greater tension in farming than in non-farming families because they concern more than just cash and capital values. The children may have been strongly socialized to be interested in farming – it may be that all of them want to be involved in the family business but it is simply not large enough to make this possible. There is some evidence (Russell *et al.* 1985) that the younger generation tends to be more stressed by the process of inter-generational transfer than the parent generation, probably because they have less control in the situation. Moreover, the successor will be much more aware than his parents of the tensions between himself and those siblings who resent the differential treatment they are receiving.

The parents may also be subject to stress, but for somewhat different reasons. In the first place, farmers tend to have had little experience of incorporating leisure into their lives (Keating 1991) and, since few people ever adopt new leisure activities in retirement, this may present consider-able problems. As one respondent commented to Errington and Tranter (1991), 'Having spent 50 years here working and having very few interests, its going to leave a very big hole to fill'. In the final analysis it may be this factor, rather than income, accommodation or health that makes it so difficult for many farmers to 'let go' of the farm and leave their successor to get on with the job. There may also be tensions between the retiring farmer and his wife. While Anderson and Hepworth (1980) argue that the transition to retirement will be easier for farmers because they have always worked from home, there may in fact be much greater potential for territorial conflict between the farmer and his wife since their respective roles tend to have been very clearly defined before retirement and much of the household space identified as her territory (see Chapters 1 and 6).

Much of the existing literature suggests that the resolution of the tensions created by the 'critical transitions' of inheritance, succession and retirement lies in careful planning aided by appropriate advice from outsiders and the discussion of these plans between family members. The farmer's wife often plays a crucial mediating role as Chapters 5 and 6 have shown. She is variously described in the literature as 'referee', 'bridge' or 'switchboard' between the generations and between siblings, which can in itself be a very stressful role.

Planning the Transition

Successful farm inheritance can only be achieved through a transfer of both management responsibility and ownership where there is a harmonious relationship between all members of the family. Panic measures taken to avoid death duty could create unnecessary tensions within the family, thus harming the inheritance process.

(Commins and Kelleher 1973: 99)

In order to manage the processes effectively, the first requirement is for the family to be aware of all the options open to them and their likely consequences. In particular, tax law can have a major influence on the timing of transfers, the size of the residual estate over which the beneficiary has eventual control and the appropriate strategy to follow. Inadequate tax planning or the wrong decision taken at a critical point in time can have a huge impact on capital tax liability. In most countries these legal and fiscal provisions have grown up over a number of years, sometimes introduced by governments of quite different political complexions and with quite different objectives. In all cases therefore, the fiscal and legal framework is likely to be so intricate, so complex and so liable to sudden change that farmers must rely on up-to-date professional advice when contemplating the transfer of their business to the next generation.

Just over half the respondents in both the *Farmers Weekly* survey and Errington and Tranter's study said that they had talked over their retirement plans with someone outside the family. Figure 8.4 summarizes the results of the latter survey, showing the proportion of farmers receiving advice from each source. Clearly, the accountant is the main source of retirement advice in English farming, having been approached by almost half the respondents, whereas the bank manager and solicitor had been approached by only about one in ten. This may simply reflect the fact that most farmers will be in contact with the accountant at least once a year over the farm accounts, while a special meeting would need to be arranged with the bank manager or solicitor. But the fact that the accountant was the one professional adviser consulted by so many respondents may also suggest that pre-retirement discussions outside the family tend to be primarily concerned with questions of tax efficiency.

Half the farmers covered by Gasson's (1984) survey believed that sufficient help and advice on retirement matters was already available and only one in five thought that it was not. While there is the need for 'a continuing review of the creation-transfer plans by accountants and management specialists as well as lawyers ... to ensure proper management of the estate during the parents' lifetime as well as after their deaths' (Boehlje and Eisgruber 1972), others emphasize the considerable interpersonal skills required by such specialists:

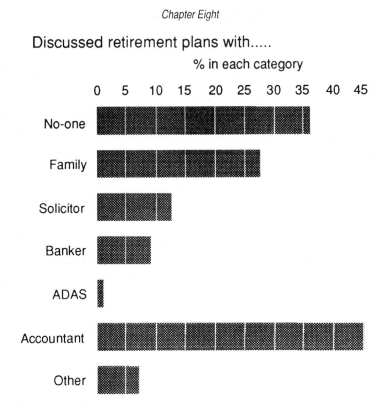

Figure 8.4. Discussion of retirement plans. Source: Errington and Tranter 1992: 69

> Professionals such as attorneys, farm management organizations and
> estate planners need to be aware that critical psychosocial transitions
> are occurring within the farm family at the same time that economic
> transitions are occurring within the farm business.
>
> (Russell *et al.* 1985: 375)

What does appear to be lacking in the UK are impartial advisers who can
cover the range of both financial and legal issues associated with retirement,
succession and inheritance and at the same time possess the skills to deal
with family sensitivities and conflicts. The same deficiency has also been
noted by Gamble *et al.* (1992) in Australia.

Both Denmark and The Netherlands have advisers who specialize in
dealing with all aspects of farm inheritance work, including the drawing up
of formal agreements between farming fathers and their successors. In some
respects the Socio-Economic Advisory Service established in the UK in
response to EC Directive 72/161 fulfilled this role. However, much of the
energy of these advisers was subsequently channelled into farm diversification advice and grant scheme administration. There may thus be a gap in

the consultancy market which will eventually be filled by one or more of the professions. Indeed, Blacksell *et al.* (1987) suggest that solicitors might eventually return to the central role that they once played in the UK's rural areas if they succeed in developing multi-disciplinary partnerships.

Effective planning will normally entail making a will as soon as the farm is inherited. This is particularly important in countries such as the UK where there is little legal prescription for the treatment of intestate farmland. The small amount of empirical evidence available reveals substantial differences in the proportion of farmers making a will at different times and in different countries. Among Commins and Kelleher's (1973) farmer respondents 82 per cent had not yet made any arrangements for the transfer of the farm and only 42 per cent of these had even thought about making a will though many said that on reflection they thought it a good idea to do so. The researchers conclude that 'while there is general acceptance of the desirability of making timely arrangements this is not followed through in practice, even though there are no particular obstacles to doing this'. Thus, the 'planning for the future transfer is a haphazard or non-existent activity'.

These Irish findings from the early 1970s stand in marked contrast to some other studies. For example, Abrahams (1991) reports that 60 per cent of farm transfers in Finland occur when both parents are still alive, and only 5 per cent when both are dead. While no directly comparable figures are available for the UK, evidence from recent surveys suggests that most English farmers do plan ahead, at least by making a will (Gasson 1984; Errington and Tranter 1991). Over three quarters of respondents to both these large-scale surveys had already made a will and though the proportion was smaller on small farms and among younger farmers, it was still close to 60 per cent both on farms less than 100 acres and among farmers not yet 40 years old.

Family Discussions

Il est préférable de régler la transmission d'exploitation à froid quand les parents sont chauds qu'à chaud quand les parents sont froids.
(Traditional French saying)

According to Keating and Marshall (1980), farmers actually start planning their retirement earlier than non-farm rural businessmen, the financial planning for example starting on average at 48. But the mean age at which these farmers began to discuss these matters with their spouse was 52, and it is likely that other members of the family will have only become involved still later. However, not all the available evidence points to the absence of family discussion over matters of retirement, inheritance and succession. Russell *et al.* (1985) found that many UK farmers recognize the potential for family tensions in this area and deliberately use family discussion as a key means of reducing stress. This finding stands in stark contrast to that of Commins and Kelleher (1973) in Ireland, who reported that 44 per cent of the farmers they interviewed had never talked about inheritance or succession with their parents. The authors went on to conclude that 'Transfer ... is often late simply because it is never even a matter of discussion. Initiating the discussion may be more of a problem than achieving a mutually satisfactory settlement'.

Among their small sample of Australian farmers, Gamble *et al.* (1992) found that parents were less likely to talk things over where their children were already married. On farms where there were married children back on the home farm, 42 per cent of the fathers had not even spoken about inheritance and succession matters to their wives, 63 per cent had not spoken to their children and 84 per cent had not involved their daughter-in-law in any such discussions. There was also considerable discrepancy between the generations in their perceptions of how much discussion had gone on. Parents were much more likely to say such discussions had taken place than were their children.

Successful Succession

There is some consensus in the literature that successful succession requires the planned and gradual transfer of managerial responsibilities over a long period of time. This gives the successor adequate opportunity to develop the necessary skills through guided practice and planned experience. Ideally, this will include the opportunity to take on full responsibility for some discrete aspect of the business either in one functional area or in one particular enterprise.

Perhaps as a result of the detailed research work in the early 1970s, the Irish Agricultural Advisory Service designed a 'Farm Development Card'. In consultation with the advisor, the farmer is asked to indicate on the card when he plans to give his successor progressively more managerial control. He is also encouraged to decide when he plans to get him involved in the financial aspects of the business, starting with 'Information Collection and Recording' and moving ultimately to the use of his own bank account for farm business transactions.

There is also some consensus that education and training (for both generations) can aid the transfer process but the timing of formal courses and systematic help may be crucial. Given the tendency to increased longevity and improved health, few existing farmers will regard themselves as being close to retirement when their successor leaves school or college. Russell *et al.* (1985) emphasize the need for creating distance between father and son if stress is to be minimized. As we have already seen, one well-established way to achieve this distance, and also allow the family business to benefit from the resulting experience, is to encourage the potential successor to embark on a *détour professionelle* in which he spends a number of years working on another farm or in a related industry; Keating and Little (1991) refer to the 'Overseas Experience' of young New Zealand farmers. When the successor has returned home and been there for a number of years, it may be time for his father and mother to go on their own *détour professionelle*, spending time off the farm developing and pursuing their own interests. In the UK there are numerous examples of farming fathers becoming more involved in local government or NFU activities when their son returns home. Some Illinois farming fathers even take off-farm jobs or establish a small separate business in order to allow their successors to take over the farm early. Farming families planning for succession would do well to take note of this industrial manager encountered by Barnes and Hershon:

> I left my own father's company and swore I'd never subject my own children to what I had to face. Now my son is getting good experience in another company in our industry before coming in to take over this one. Within five years of the day he walks in that door, I walk out. And everyone knows it – even me.

(Barnes and Hershon 1976: 114)

SUMMARY AND IMPLICATIONS

This chapter has described the processes of succession and retirement in the farm family business. In the UK at least, farming successors tend to be identified very early in their lives and enter a period of socialization that begins while they are still at school. Recent surveys identify a ladder of managerial responsibility which the successor will eventually begin to climb. The lower steps involve areas of technical decision-making where the successor may already have distinctive expertise but the highest steps invariably involve financial decisions. While the ladder itself appears to be the same on different farms, the rate at which it is climbed will vary considerably according to the characteristics of the farmer and his successor as well as the farm itself.

Retirement is recognized as a series of transitions between different states – full-time work in farming, semi-retirement in farming, retirement in farming, and retirement from the farming industry. Most UK farmers favour semi-retirement in farming. Factors influencing the transition from one state to another are not only monetary income but a number factors broadly categorized as 'psychic income' as well as the availability of retirement accommodation. There are significant differences between (and probably within) OECD countries in the processes of succession and retirement. Finally, we recognize that the processes of succession and retirement (and indeed inheritance) can be managed to ensure continuity of the farm family business while minimizing intra-family conflict. There appears to be some consensus in the literature that adequate planning aided by professional advice, family discussion and appropriate education and training for all generations can facilitate a smooth transition of the farm family business from one generation to the next.

Clearly, if succession is the mirror-image of retirement, anything which inhibits retirement is likely to hinder the transfer of managerial control from one generation to the next. The question remains why so many farmers with successors already identified hang on till the last moment before they retire? In part, it must reflect the intrinsic satisfactions of the job, the status and the psychic income which it affords. But it must also relate to their need to secure control over what might be the major source of income and accommodation in their old age. Where this leads to a reluctance to retire, the situation can only be eased by sufficient forward planning (or government intervention) to provide the older generation with a 'lifeboat' that will remain afloat whatever happens to the farm family business under its new management. As we have seen, this figurative lifeboat needs to be large for it must contain not only an adequate and assured income, but a house (which may be increasingly difficult to find in countries such as the UK facing a rural housing shortage) and sometimes even a 'retirement small-holding' from which the retiring generation can continue to derive many of the satisfactions that were so important to the earlier part of their farming lives. Indeed, the 'retirement smallholding' formed an integral part of the French scheme for early retirement – the *Indemnité Viagère de Depart* (IVD) – which allowed those taking advantage of the scheme to retain one sixth of their holding.

Various European governments have long played an active role in the design and implementation of schemes to encourage retirement out of farming. EC Directive 72/160 which introduced the Voluntary Retirement Scheme followed, rather than led, a variety of national schemes such as the UK Outgoers Scheme of 1967 and the associated Farm Amalgamation Scheme and Boundary Adjustment Grant. Similar schemes were established in Germany by 1957, The Netherlands by 1964, and Sweden by 1967. All the schemes sought to improve the structure of farming by 'accelerating the flow of older farmers on smaller farms out of the industry'. The EC scheme encouraged farmers aged 55-65 to retire and either make their land available by sale or long-term lease to other farmers operating a development plan, or to put it to non-agricultural use such as wildlife conservation, leisure or afforestation. The retiring farmers were to receive an annual annuity and in the EC's designated priority regions the national government could reclaim 65 per cent of these costs from FEOGA.

The impact of the various national schemes has not been impressive. Numbers taking up the EC-wide Farm Amalgamation Scheme declined from

15,693 holdings in 1975 to 9115 in 1977, accounting for only 0.3 per cent of registered agricultural holdings during this period (Anderson and Hepworth 1980). There is considerable debate over the causes of this failure. Some attribute it to the level of compensation offered or the administrative complexity of the schemes while others point to the policy-makers' failure to take into account the non-tangible benefits that are associated with land-ownership and farming. As early as 1973 Commins had commented:

> Both social and economic needs must be catered to, and ideally a policy for structural reform in agriculture should be an integral part of a more comprehensive set of policies for aged and retired people in rural communities.
>
> (Commins 1973: 45)

What is required is 'an appropriate concept of retirement for agriculture itself rather than the adoption of what prevails in other sectors of the economy'.

By focusing on retirement and succession this chapter has been concerned primarily with the internal dynamics of the farm family business as it moves through the family cycle. It has concentrated primarily on the actors involved and their response to some of the perennial changes that face any family business. But as we emphasized in Chapter 3, the farm family business does not operate in a vacuum. It must respond to changes in the environment in which it operates. The smooth transition through time from one generation to the next is certainly a prerequisite for the survival of the individual farm family business but what of the survival of farm family businesses in general? Our final chapter looks to the future and considers the strengths and weaknesses of the farm family business as it responds to changes in the economic, social and political environment in which it must operate.

THE FUTURE OF THE FARM FAMILY BUSINESS

INTRODUCTION

> The suggestion offered here is that finality in farming progress has not and can never be reached, that whatever the economic circumstances, the producer has before him a way to adjust himself to them if only he can find it.
>
> (Orwin 1930: 119)

The farm family business has certain strengths and weaknesses in comparison with the non-family farm. Its strengths can be summed up in one word, 'flexibility', which enables it to survive in certain situations where a non-family farm would fail. Much of the early literature on the family farm portrayed it as unchanging, a focus of stability, conservatism and tradition-alism. Its internal solidarity, built upon kinship and emotional ties, generational continuity and family links with a particular plot of land, was not expected to withstand the encroachment of a rational, contractual, profit-oriented modern agricultural industry. The message of this chapter is that family farming is far more resilient than previously supposed, but that the cost of survival is change. Farm family businesses are seen to be adapting in a great variety of ways to the pressures for change, both the insistent demands and challenges coming from the wider economy and the needs and aspirations of family members from within.

In this chapter we review the range of responses to the economic imperative. We go on to argue that to survive, the farm business must be capable of reproducing itself and responding to the challenges of the environment. The farm household too must be able to reproduce and meet the needs and aspirations of its members. Many types of adaptive response are found in practice and a number of examples are assessed against these requirements. For policy-makers and for society as a whole, the question to be asked is not whether we should save the family farm, but what kind of family farming do we want to encourage and what are the associated costs and benefits. The chapter ends by considering three different interpretations of 'saving the family farm' and comes down in favour of keeping the occupation open to newcomers.

STRENGTHS AND WEAKNESSES OF THE FAMILY FARM

> How does the relationship of the family to the farm affect its productivity, efficiency, and ability to survive adversity? Are family-operated farms more likely to provide the commitment needed for long-term productivity and continuity in the face of natural and economic adversity?
>
> (Wilkening 1981a: 35)

By its very nature, the farm family business has certain strengths which give it an advantage in comparison with the non-family farm. These strengths are implicit in the way the family farm has been defined. At the same time, each strength can be paired with a weakness. For example, the first condition is that business ownership is combined with managerial control. There is no 'leakage' due to conflicting loyalties, as where employed managers pursue their own objectives in the business rather than those of shareholders. In a farm business with a sole proprietor, conflicting objectives still have to be resolved, but within the farmer's own mind or in consultation with family members rather than round the boardroom table. Pride of ownership, the desire for independence, enjoyment of pleasurable tasks, may cloud the farmer's judgement when crucial business decisions have to be taken. In non-family businesses where the functions of ownership, management and labour are separated, it is more likely that the cost of pursuing objectives which result in sub-optimal profits, will be reckoned with. In a family business the farmer himself has to make judgements about how to allocate his time between the various functions of ownership, management and manual work. There may be a tendency to leave managerial tasks until more 'pressing' manual work is done (Chapters 4 and 5).

The second condition, that business principals are related by ties of kinship or marriage, gives the farm family business a certain tenacity which the non-family farm does not have. Chapter 1 suggested that the pooling of resources, division of labour, unity of production and consumption activities, family ties and obligations, marital responsibilities and affective relationships, are mutually reinforcing in farm households and likely to be more enduring than relationships based on economic interest alone. The family farm may therefore weather difficult passages and survive where the non-family farm business would be wound up. The converse may be that business problems can put a strain on marriage and family relationships and that family strains in a farm household may destroy the business.

Family members including business principals provide capital and do farm work. In the past the strength of family farming lay in its access to unpaid family labour, which is likely to be more flexible than hired labour as regards working hours. It is an advantage for the farmer to be able to employ members of his own family rather than recruit non-family labour whose qualities are unknown. Family members are likely to be highly motivated and Chapter 5 has underlined the importance of the 'motivation calculus' for labour productivity. When times are hard, family members may be prepared to work for less than the market wage and accept a low return on their own capital, enabling them to survive where the non-family business might be forced to quit and obtain only the salvage value of its assets. Family members may even subsidize the farm business by setting up diversified enterprises or working off the farm. As Chapter 3 showed, part of the cost of reproducing the farm family workforce is met by consumption of home produce and by the unpaid domestic labour of wives and children, giving a cost advantage over non-family firms which have to pay for all goods and services.

Weaknesses of using family labour mirror these strengths. While the farmer may prefer to recruit members of his own family whom he knows, the pool is small and the family labour force is not necessarily rich in talents and skills. Family members may be highly motivated but they may also be exploited, obliged to work hard for meagre returns to satisfy the goals of husband or father, which may not be their goals. Tightening belts and working harder in difficult times is a cost imposed on farm household members, not necessarily with their agreement. If the farm household subsidizes part of the cost of reproducing the labour force, it is because farmers' wives are willing to provide these services, usually without pay or recognition as Chapter 6 has shown. Because family labour does not have to be accounted for at a realistic rate, it may be used wastefully on the family farm when it would make better economic sense to transfer some to outside employment.

The family labour supply is prone to fluctuations over the course of the family cycle, though this becomes less of a drawback as mechanization and various forms of temporary labour are used to iron out the peaks and troughs (Chapter 5). Although usually regarded as a negative feature, cyclical variation of development and maintenance phases in the farm family business could actually aid survival. The cycle creates periodic pressure for innovation, which keeps the enterprise from stagnating, and it creates periods of resistance to innovation when debts and risks are minimized. Thus there is no point at which even a majority of family farms will be over-extended or vulnerable to a sudden downturn in profitability (Reinhardt and Barlett 1989).

Having the family living on the farm is a source of strength in that business managers are usually close at hand to monitor and control crop and livestock systems and take swift action if a crisis threatens (Chapter 1). Non-family farms with livestock or sensitive crop enterprises would normally also have staff living on the farm, though not necessarily with full authority to take quick decisions. Drawbacks for the family can be isolation and having to cope with constant intrusions of the business into family life – straw and mud in the house, business callers at inconvenient times, having to drop everything at a moment's notice regardless of what is in the oven. The business tends to take precedence over family life. Farming crises can mean family outings and holidays being cancelled.

Inter-generational transmission of the family farm creates a longer time horizon than is usual in a non-family business tied to short-term profit goals. The family business *can* be more entrepreneurial precisely because it is a family business. On the other hand, succession on the basis of kinship rather than promotion on merit is not a recipe for excellence in management. Farmers stepping into family businesses are typically less well qualified and have had less varied work experience than hired managers. As Chapter 7 suggested, a farmer may choose as his successor the son he feels he can work best with, or even the child in most need of protection or the one who will be the last to chivvy him out of his job. A running-in period for retiring father and successor son has obvious advantages but if the succession process is too protracted, the son may lose patience and move away. Or, by the time he is fully in control, he may be too old to make imaginative changes in the business (Chapter 8).

With all its strengths and weaknesses, the farm family business is essentially a flexible organization. The interweaving of family relationships with business objectives and activities gives it a resilience, tenacity and durability which enables it to respond to pressures from without and from within, pressures which could break the non-family business. In the final analysis this may be its greatest strength. It helps to explain why, when subjected to apparently overwhelming pressures from the outside world, family farming has survived. The following section reviews the evidence for the survival of the farm family business within advanced capitalism.

MACROECONOMIC TRENDS

The main thrust of this book has been to study the internal structure and workings of the farm family business but it is important not to overlook the constraints which the development of capitalism imposes on the farm family's options. Chapter 3 dealt with trends in the wider economy, the context within which individual farm family businesses have to operate. As that chapter showed, the disciplines of economics and sociology approach the topic in quite different ways.

Economists conceive of the rational entrepreneur, free to act in the best interests of his firm in competition with other firms. They hold that farming and food production everywhere is subject to Engel's Law, which states that as incomes rise, proportionately less of them is spent on food. This means that if personal incomes rose without any significant change in the structure of production and the state of technology in agriculture and other industries, a declining share of total disposable income would find its way to the farming sector. Individual farm households will endeavour to maintain parity of incomes with other households, sustaining their social status and level of living, by expanding production. Increasing output from a given area of land – **intensification** – against a stable demand has the effect of pushing down product prices, thereby leading to another round of expansion. Increasing output by taking on more land – **extensification** – means fewer, larger farms and the disappearance of weaker units. Either way, some farms will go out of business.

When the principal resource of the family farm was labour, the scope for expansion at either the intensive or the extensive margin of production was limited by the labour which the family could supply. Today the farm family business can mechanize to increase the productivity of family labour and thereby operate on a larger scale. Mechanization, intensification and acquiring additional land increase the farm's dependence on outside sources of capital. The treadmill of technology similarly increases dependence and hastens the trend towards farm enlargement. As a commercially-minded businessman, the farmer should borrow to finance expansion so long as the anticipated return on capital exceeds the cost of borrowing.

Sociologists lay emphasis on the powerlessness of the individual in opposition to the interests of capital. In Marxist terms, the agricultural sector is being penetrated by financial and industrial capital, stimulating the direct and indirect subsumption of the labour process. Indirect subsumption implies that producers become increasingly dependent upon sources of capital outside their own control. This can be brought about through provision of credit, growing reliance on purchased technological inputs and increased dependence on external marketing links. Direct subsumption means the farm family losing ownership and control of the means of production; typically land, labour, capital and management are supplied by unrelated individuals as a pure business venture.

Chapter 3 concluded, on the evidence of various empirical studies, that while farm businesses are undoubtedly being penetrated by outside sources of capital and this trend is increasing, levels of *direct* subsumption are generally low. Large numbers of family farms are apparently managing to resist being taken over by external capital. **Indirect** subsumption of farm businesses by external capital sources is widespread, though the extent to which this is undermining the integrity of the family business is unclear. The **survival** school of thought emphasizes barriers to the capitalist transformation of agriculture, which hinge on nature, land and space. Where these barriers do not operate, where capital substitutes for land-based processes, direct subsumption soon follows.

One perspective on the future of farming under capitalism seems to be shared by economists and sociologists. Observing trends in the size of holdings and individual farm enterprises, a number of researchers have predicted a growing polarization of structures: 'Time seems likely to further polarize farm structure and reduce the number of small family farms because large farm businesses have advantages in acquiring land and financing improvements' (Furness 1983: 36). Polarization is expected to result in a bimodal structure of very large and very small farms coupled with the rapid marginalization of medium-sized farms, the phenomenon of the 'disappearing middle' (Buttel 1983).

The polarization thesis may appeal intellectually to political economists supporting a certain perspective of structural change under advanced capitalism and ideologically to those opposed to the loss of the traditional family farm. Persuasive as the argument is, Munton and Marsden (1991) were not able to verify it empirically using British data. They suggested the explanation was too mechanistic, paying inadequate attention to the range of responses to be found among farm households. These researchers drew attention to the social dynamics which condition individual and group responses – family structure, the presence or absence of a successor, family aspirations, the social and economic means of acquiring land and the size and period of debts currently being serviced. They concluded that as previous strategies developed by farm families become redundant during the phase of post-productionist agriculture, it may be the family's skill in responding to opportunities outside farming which will hold the key to continued occupancy of the land.

While the polarization theory, like all the other explanations, is plausible and can be substantiated to a certain extent, it is felt to be too rigid, implying a rather passive acceptance on the part of farm families of their inevitable demise. More recent thinking stresses the flexibility of farm families, the range of responses they are able to make to the encroachment of capital. Family farms are not only unique but continually changing, both in their internal relations and in their external relations with sources of capital (Marsden *et al.* 1986a, 1986b, 1987). The following section explores the variety of strategies that farm families have developed in response to the changing demands of capital.

First, though, the suggestion that external threats to the farm family business are somehow unique to the late twentieth century and entirely related to capital, needs to be dispelled. On the basis of his study of family farming in eastern Finland, Abrahams (1991) argues that there is nothing new in farm families being subjected to external pressures and controls. Nor is capitalism the only force to be reckoned with, for the feudal system and the Christian church each have their own record of oppression. It is therefore misleading to draw a contrast between farming today, embedded in large-scale, complex, modern society and some earlier form of 'natural' domestic economy in which rural communities were immune from the demands and pressures of the outside world. As Abrahams puts it, the ground rules under which the people of Karelia lived and farmed for centuries were largely laid down for them by the succession of political regimes under which they lived. While these regimes, varying in times of peace or war, had a powerful influence on domestic settlement and land use patterns, the people themselves have a long history of adaptation to such pressures.

If external forces were all-powerful, the study of family farming systems would simply be a branch of the study of law and the state and their interaction with religious and economic forces. People are not, however, just passive recipients of rules from above. They are typically adaptive and manipulative in their reactions to the influences which impinge on them. The forces of alienation and commercialization are present and active in the farmer's world. Yet farmers can still assert fundamental values about farming as an occupation and a way of life, in which they can ideally look after themselves and their families and collaborate with others without losing their identity and integrity as productive individuals (Abrahams 1991).

PATTERNS OF ADAPTATION

Whilst the survival and subsumption positions imply rather a passive stance on the part of farm families, the adaptation perspective emphasizes the range of responses which farm families are able to make. Encroachment by external sources of capital may be seen as a threat but it may also offer new opportunities to farm families. If farm family businesses are to some extent adapting to the pressures and demands of capitalism, it needs to be asked what forms that adaptation is taking and what consequences it may have for the business and the household.

Chapter 3 depicted family farms in a state of flux, continually changing both in their internal relations of production and their relations with external sources of capital. Among the **financial** strategies which farmers may adopt in order to remain competitive are various partnerships, corporate arrangements or trusts which help to lighten the burden of taxa- tion, secure family continuity and encourage a flow of working capital. Sale and leaseback was used, when farmland was an attractive investment to financial institutions, to free some of the capital locked up in land (Marsden *et al.* 1986a, 1986b, 1987).

Turning to **household** responses, Marsden *et al.* (1986a) identified three broad strategies adopted by farm families in the face of growing pressure to capitalize the farm business: accumulation, survival and hobby farming. **Accumulation** can be achieved by transferring income from other businesses under the family's control or through integration with larger companies. **Survival** strategies are pursued by families mainly dependent on inadequate incomes from farming. Options are to diversify activities, either from the farm base or through off-farm employment, to reduce personal consumption or to rely upon pensions and savings. The **hobby farming** strategy means income is mainly obtained from non-farm employment or other business interests.

When this classification was applied to the sample of 85 farm businesses in the Metropolitan Green Belt in 1985, 34 per cent of households were found to be wholly dependent on farm sources of income, 26 per cent were following a strategy of accumulation, 31 per cent were pursuing survival strategies and 9 per cent were hobby farms or the household head was retired. While farmers pursuing a strategy of accumulation were generally judged to be commercially successful and well in control of their business interests, those in the survival groups were losing control of the management of their farm businesses (Marsden *et al.* 1986a).

In a subsequent project Marsden *et al.* (1992) classified the farms in their five study areas according to the course of their businesses since 1970 (Table 9.1). Here the three categories were **accumulators** with steady or increasing profits, **survivors** whose profits have declined and now need new sources of income, and **marginalized** farms where losses occur regularly so that they cannot survive as independent full-time family businesses. Accumulators were the dominant type among the large arable farms of Bedfordshire. Survivors made up the largest category in upland Staffordshire and Cumbria. Elsewhere farms were more evenly spread across the three categories.

Table 9.1. Distribution of farms in five study areas by economic status categories.

Economic status	Bedford	Dorset	Cumbria	Stafford	Green Belt
			(per cent of farm businesses)		
Accumulators	70	43	21	7	29
Survivors	23	31	59	71	30
Marginalized	7	26	20	22	41
All farms	100	100	100	100	100
Numbers	99	86	79	88	70

Source: Marsden *et al* 1992, Table 1

As new typologies of farm family businesses are devised, increasing emphasis is laid on alternative sources of income, whether from earnings, pensions or savings. One which has been used extensively in the past classifies farmers, farm households or farm businesses into full-time, part-time Class I and part-time Class II according to the importance of farming (OECD 1978). Full-time farmers or households devote all or most of their time to farming and/or derive most or all of their income from it, Class I depend mainly on the farm for employment and income while Class II are mainly dependent on off-farm or non-farm sources. This typology has proved useful in capturing a large amount of variation in business and household structure, activities and attitudes (Gasson 1988; Gasson *et al.* 1992b). Its value for present purposes is limited because it is static and historical. It does not help us to predict how the farm business will respond in the future to the macroeconomic forces impinging on it.

The Arkleton Trust has recently completed a large-scale survey of farm household pluriactivity, that is the activities and sources of income of members of farm households. The survey was both longitudinal and cross-sectional. Random samples of 300 farm households were drawn in each of 24 study areas across western Europe, chosen to represent a range of farming conditions and labour market opportunities. Data were collected from all households at the beginning and end of the five-year study period, providing a basis for monitoring change. From analysis of the initial baseline data, three broad categories of farm household adjustment were identified (Arkleton Trust 1990).

1. **Professionalization**. Increasing importance is attached to the farm in the economic life of the household. Professionalizers consciously manipulate the means at their disposal (technological and economic management, uptake of policies encouraging production) in order to expand their output and market share.

2. **Disengagement**. Declining importance given to the farm as a focus for economic activity. Over time farmers produce less, market less efficiently and are less responsive to many forms of agricultural policy. This may be a consequence of declining farm income, due to the farmer's increasing age or disability, or the growing importance of other sources of income.

3. **Stable reproduction**. Households in the third category appear to be relatively constant in their dependence upon agriculture as a source of income. Their commitment to farming goes as far as maintaining existing levels of income but does not extend to expanding the enterprise or raising productive capacity.

More than the OECD classification, this approach tries to capture the kinds of responses and adaptations which farms make to the demands of the wider economy but it still does not address the question of how the households arrived in that category or where they are going. Implicitly it focuses on the individual rather than the domestic group and it makes no reference to succession. A more illuminating typology was devised to account for different forms of **household** pluriactivity observed in the three French study areas of the Arkleton Trust project (Campagne *et al.* 1990).

1. Picardy. Faced with the crisis in agricultural markets, some of the large arable farms of Picardy are able to maintain their incomes within agriculture but others are diversifying their businesses in the sense of finding alternative investment opportunities for family capital – financial investment outside farming, investment in the non-farm sector (transport, construction etc.). This can be termed 'business pluriactivity'.

2. Languedoc. In the wine-growing region of southern France, capital requirements of farming rose steeply after the Second World War. New machinery was often obtained by the farmer or other household members finding off-farm work, typically in manufacturing industry. Outside earnings might be used for household consumption so that farm income could be ploughed back into the business, but the objective of pluriactivity is 'to maintain the farming activity'.

3. Savoy. Pluriactivity in the mountainous Savoy region is largely 'pluriactivity for survival'. Growth of the tourist industry has provided new opportunities for farm household members to find off-farm employment (for example in winter sports resorts) and also to develop new enterprises on the farm (tourist accommodation).

SYNTHESIS OF HOUSEHOLD RESPONSES

These are but a few examples of the many classification schemes which researchers have devised to help them make sense of the range of farm household responses to the economic pressures of the outside world. The term **household strategies** needs to be used with care since it seems to imply more rational decision-making and more conscious implementation of collective action than is likely to occur in practice. While households are certainly not incapable of collective action, their behaviour is shaped by many factors and not normally preceded by formalized decision-making. Another problem with this concept is the tendency to assume that whatever action a household takes is its 'strategy'.

> Given this uncritical perspective, anything less than the complete dissolution of a household would qualify as a 'strategy'. But such reasoning leaves no room for 'non-strategic' change or for patterns of individual behaviour that is obviously not germane to household maintenance and development.
>
> (Schwarzweller and Clay 1992: 6)

Through the diversity of responses which have been classified in various ways and given a multitude of different names, certain general trends seem to emerge. Typologies often begin with the **professionalizing, full-time farmer** or farm household which is swimming with the tide, following the main economic impetus in agriculture, which involves accumulating capital in order to expand the business and keep up with technological change. Like Fairweather and Keating's **dedicated producer**, the farmer or household is highly committed to farming as an occupation and to narrow productivist goals. Also farming on a large scale but with different objectives are those entrepreneurs accumulating capital by merging farming with other businesses. In this category are the large-scale cereal growers of Picardy following a strategy of **business pluriactivity**. A third familiar type is the middle-scale farm household firmly attached to farming but willing to diversify its activities in response to capital or income needs of the farm business or the household or in order to provide employment for family members. The Languedoc wine growers and the New Zealand **flexible strategists** come into this category, together with those seeking **survival through diversification**.

Next comes the **disengaging, marginalized** or **sub-marginal producer** on a small farm. Households in this category typically have low or falling farm incomes but are limited in their farming responses by a harsh environment, shortage of capital, or by an incomplete household or lack of successors. Depending upon the availability of other jobs and opportunities for farm diversification, some of these households may be able to pursue a strategy of **pluriactivity for survival** as in the Savoy valleys or Cumbria. Typically farming on a limited scale like the marginalized producer but contrasting in other ways is the **hobby farmer** or **lifestyler**, not making a living from farming but with another substantial source of earned or unearned income, for whom the farming activity is oriented towards consumption rather than production.

CONDITIONS FOR SURVIVAL

The family firm is a dynamic institution but also a vulnerable one.
(Symes and Marsden 1983a: 100)

To survive and be successful, a farm family business must be able to meet a number of conditions. It must be capable of responding to the pressures and challenges of the economic environment and reproducing itself as a business. It must also be able to satisfy the needs and aspirations of family members and reproduce itself as a domestic group. Fulfilling all these conditions is a necessary condition for the continuation of the existing family farm in a recognizable form, that is to say with present household members or their descendants farming on the same land or in the same locality. Failure to meet the conditions may sever the link between a particular household and farm business but it need not spell total disintegration; a family may stay together but move out of farming; a farm may change hands but continue to be run as a family business. We explore some of these possibilities later in the chapter.

Survival of the Farm Business

In order to survive a farm business must be able to respond to the challenges of the wider economy and reproduce itself. This means generating sufficient income at least to cover current costs of production, including servicing the labour force, paying rent and interest and meeting the costs of depreciation on capital assets. Pressures to adopt new technology and increase production (termed 'expanded reproduction') involve raising additional capital to buy land, machinery, stock, industrial inputs and so on, and hence to higher interest charges.

Farm businesses can be regarded as 'autonomously reproductive' if they do not depend on off-farm sources of income for their reproduction. 'Non-reproductive' units are those subsidized by off-farm earnings, investment income, savings, pensions or transfer payments (Djurfeldt 1992). In this strict sense, only the category of large full-time farm businesses are capable of self-sustaining reproduction and even their ability may be compromised when farm incomes are under pressure. At such times family drawings from the business may be reduced to a minimum, depreciation payments deferred and expansion plans shelved.

Farm businesses which do not generate an adequate income through farming alone but *do* when farming is combined with other farm-based enterprises such as tourism, food processing, direct retailing, agricultural contracting, could be regarded as autonomously reproductive in the above sense because they do not rely upon *off-farm* sources of income. This is a fine distinction to make, however. As the dependence of farm businesses upon external sources of capital has grown and farming incomes have declined in real terms, the capital generated through farming has become less self-sufficient to satisfy the income needs of the family and the investment needs of the business. With increasing complexity of farm businesses and family financial arrangements, 'it becomes difficult to gauge how far these businesses are self-contained generators of capital and income (i.e., individual capitals in the true sense, capable of reproduction unaided)' (Marsden *et al.* 1986a: 273).

To what extent can farm businesses be regarded as capable of surviving if they draw on other household sources of capital? Business survival seems assured for the cereal-growers of Picardy who switch capital between the farm and other businesses which the family manages, and for the 'accumu-lators' described by Marsden *et al.* (1986a). Their later work suggests that capital accumulation and diversification of income sources can be comple-mentary strategies in lowland areas with buoyant labour markets and other business opportunities and ample scope for on-farm diversification. In the harsher upland environment where labour markets are weaker, diversifi-cation is more often associated with the *survival* of marginal businesses and family occupancy of the holding than with capital accumulation. On larger upland farms where capital penetration is more extensive, diversification plays a decreasing role (Marsden *et al.* 1992).

Farm businesses which do not generate sufficient income to support a family and maintain a level of production are 'non-reproductive' in Djurfeldt's terms. In other words, the farming activity can only continue so long as members of the farm household are willing to subsidize it from other sources. The extent to which farm households have sought alternative sources of income, by diversifying or supplementing farm income with off-farm earnings of family members, is a measure of their willingness to compromise with external capital in order to stay in business (Marsden *et al.* 1986a). The difference between 'pluriactivity to maintain farming' and 'pluriactivity for survival' is that the first strategy enables the business to respond to the challenges of its environment while the second does not. There is little evidence to show which strategy is more widespread but studies on the North Island of New Zealand suggest the second. While many households were pluriactive, off-farm income was used for general household support rather than to prop up the farm (Le Heron 1988; Le Heron *et al.* 1991). Both strategies imply a conscious choice by household members to forgo part of their income, a choice which may be willingly made in order to stay in farming or to enjoy the amenities of a farm lifestyle. When the sacrifice is no longer acceptable and potential earners withdraw financial support or leave the household, or when other sources of income dry up, the farm ceases to be viable and becomes a sub-marginal unit.

At one extreme, then, a farm ceases to be a farm family business in our terms when there is no sustainable commercial farming activity. Examples would be a retired farmer with no successor who had run the business down and no longer farmed, a hobby farming household using land for horses or some other non-agricultural purpose. At the other extreme, a farm family business may lose its identity by merging with other capital funds, even if controlled by the same family. For example a farm family may diversify from arable farming into agricultural contracting and thence into plant hire contracting, quarrying or construction, or from dairying via a golf course to a country club or hotel complex. These may still be run as family businesses but they are no longer recognizably *farm* businesses.

Besides facing up to the threat of takeover by external capital, the farm business has to be able to synchronize critical stages in the family cycle with external events. The business may develop its own cycle of growth and decay, set off initially by the family cycle but gaining its own momentum and strongly influenced by events in the wider economy and in the context of inexorable pressures to increase investment. The failure of the two cycles to mesh at the appropriate times and to respond to the needs of capital can signal the break-up of the family business. Relations between the farm business and external capital are in a constant state of interaction:

> The needs of capital and the family have to be synchronized ... To invest at the 'wrong' moment in terms of swings in the macro-economy may lead to consequences that cannot be rectified without progressive loss of family control, however apposite the timing seemed from the family 'stage' point of view.
>
> (Marsden *et al.* 1992: 418–9)

Imposition of milk quotas, for example, dealt a particularly hard blow to family farms which were in process of expanding their herds because a son was coming into the business. To take another example, the opportunity to acquire a neighbouring holding might only occur once in a farmer's lifetime and be hard to resist, even though the timing might not be prudent in relation to his own business or stage in the family cycle. As Marsden and his colleagues conclude,

> ... the social *co-ordination* of exchange and commoditized relations on the one hand, with the longer time horizons of family-based use values on the other, is an increasingly important activity for farm families if they are to maintain continuity. The price of failing is not an abrupt extinction through subsumption, but displacement by those families who have been able to synchronize rather better the demands of capital and their own aspirations to land occupancy.
>
> (Marsden *et al.* 1992: 426)

Reproduction of the Farm Household

For the farm family business to be successful and to survive, it is not sufficient that the *business* respond to the challenges of its economic environment and reproduce itself. The household must also respond to the needs and aspirations of family members and reproduce itself as a domestic group. Household reproduction means that the family workforce is maintained in a productive state, which implies not just sustaining present members but providing replacements. Household reproduction therefore covers marriage, raising children and socializing and training successors.

Household members need as a bare minimum food and shelter, then above this some disposable income for personal use, a reserve for emergencies, savings for old age. Besides these material needs individuals want to feel that they are usefully employed, that their work is recognized and valued by others, that they have a chance to develop their potential and achieve their objectives. For farmers these objectives may include being a farmer, maintaining independence, keeping control of the farm business, in due course handing it on to a successor. Other family members may not share these objectives. Wives may for instance aspire to greater personal autonomy, a chance to share decision-making power and control in the family business, status as a business partner, recognition for their contribution to the family enterprise. Wives may also place a high value on maintaining harmonious family relationships. Salient objectives for farmers' children might include freedom to choose a career, control of their own destiny, responsibility for areas of the farm business, a chance to make and follow through decisions.

The large and expanding full-time farm family business that is accumulating capital from farming or other family enterprises, has the potential to satisfy most family needs and reproduce a viable household. Income should be adequate to finance the transfer of the business to a successor, covering accommodation for the retiring couple and some financial settlement for non-succeeding children. The farmer's objectives of 'being a farmer' and controlling his own business are met, although increasing links with hired labour, landlords, banks and credit agencies, firms supplying inputs and marketing products, may compromise his sense of independence. Critical qualities for continuing the business are technical knowledge, openness to expert advice, a readiness to innovate, which by their nature increase dependence on outside capital.

Producing a successor helps to satisfy the farmer's desire for family continuity. Prospects for bringing children into the business depend on its being large enough to support at least two families. A farm with several enterprises offers scope for delegating responsibility to younger family members. Smaller businesses may expand by acquiring more land in order to accommodate children wishing to farm. As the Pembrokeshire and Humberside studies showed, the extended family can provide a very positive framework for commercial expansion in the larger farm business, the family labour force becoming a management team (Symes and Marsden 1983a; Hutson 1987).

The upper limit is reached when the farm business is too large to be owned and managed by a family, so that control passes to shareholders outside the family and to salaried management. This limit need not be reached if nuclear family units split off from the large family-owned company and continue as independent family businesses. This could happen when two brothers, or perhaps cousins, each have businesses large enough to compete effectively and with the potential for further development by incorporating sons in their turn.

Losers in the process of family business expansion may be non-farming children and wives. Transferring a large farm business with adequate working capital intact to a son or sons will most likely mean that other sons or daughters receive a smaller share of the inheritance, a dilemma described in Chapter 7. Leaving non-successor children shares in the farm only postpones the problem, since farming children may be forced to buy out their siblings at a time when the capital cannot easily be realized. If on the other hand greater weight is given to family solidarity, the farm business may have to be sacrificed so that all children can receive equal shares.

The position of wives in large farm businesses can be a source of dis-satisfaction, as Chapter 6 showed. Especially where the husband is in partnership (and on good terms) with his father, brother or son, the wife tends to be excluded from business discussions. On highly mechanized, labour-employing farms her manual labour is not needed either. To a growing extent wives on large farms are seeking status and recognition, personal fulfilment and autonomy off the farm, pursuing their own careers or becoming involved in voluntary work (Symes and Marsden 1983b; Bouquet 1985; Symes 1991). Dissatisfaction on the part of wives or children can spell the disintegration of the household and the severing of ties with the farm; divorce settlements may result in the farm being sold.

Farm households which pursue a conscious strategy of pluriactivity so that the farming activity can continue, may satisfy the wife's needs for autonomy and status rather better. Critical qualities for success in this case include a flair for spotting new opportunities and a good marketing strategy. Off-farm employment or running a diversified enterprise on the farm may give wives the chance to achieve positions of influence and earn income in their own right (Bouquet 1985). Pluriactivity may ease the process of succes-sion too, the successor being able to accumulate some capital, gain experi-ence and exercise responsibility in a diversified enterprise of his own; the son waiting to take over the farm who builds up a contracting business, for example. Husbands may not fare so well, for men enjoy public status as farmers, gaining their identity through farm work rather than off-farm work (Keating *et al.* 1987).

The integrity of the farm family business may be threatened if the wife or son's enterprise is seen to be significantly more successful than the farm. In business terms the diversified enterprise would have a stronger claim on any surplus capital than the farm itself. In human terms increasing dependence upon the earnings of other members could challenge existing power relations within the farm household, although supporting evidence is rather meagre (Gasson and Winter 1992). The limits of a farm family business may be reached where other enterprises engulf or dwarf the farming activity. The family may end up running a hotel, a wildlife park or a gravel works. Such enterprises are no less and probably more prone to penetration and take-over by outside capital, so once again the distinctive *family* element in the business may be lost.

Reproduction of the household in a marginal farm business is less assured. The farmer can call on family members as loyal, unpaid workers but satisfying the farmer's needs to remain in farming and enjoy independence may mean the family working harder and accepting a lower standard of living. The crucial quality in this case is family solidarity. If there is no scope for outside employment, family members can be exploited, tied to the farm, involved in unremitting hard work within the framework of family relationships and parental authority (Hutson 1987). If off-farm work is available, the household's level of living may rise but more farm work now devolves on the remaining family members. Survival of the household may depend on one member's off-farm earnings, which could signal a re-negotiation of power relations within the household.

Family succession in marginal farms is threatened on several counts, as discussed in Chapters 6 and 8. Children who have experienced such a hard living may not be anxious to make it their career. In particular, girls growing up on marginal farms and observing the conditions under which their mothers worked, may be unwilling to marry farmers. Besides this, the farm may be too small for farmer and successor to work in harness, so the successor (son) may have to find another job until his father retires. By this time he will have gained experience of other work and farming may seem less attractive. Finally, there is the problem of housing two families on a small farm, discussed in Chapter 8.

The future of households on sub-marginal farms is therefore uncertain. Elderly farmers without successors and middle-aged unmarried farmers are prevalent. The family may continue to occupy the farm so long as other suitable employment is available for one or more members but the balance between family and farm is precarious and could be upset by the employed member giving up or losing her/his job or leaving the household. From the family standpoint, the lower limit for a farm family business is reached when the household is no longer engaged in farming or where the farm couple retires without a successor. This is the logical outcome on sub-marginal holdings.

Farm families on sub-marginal units are commonly replaced by hobby farmers. Farming activity may dwindle to insignificance. Consumption needs of the household are met, usually very adequately, by non-farm sources of income (salaries, directorships, investment income). The critical element in this case is an adequate and secure outside source of income. Reproduction of the household on the farm is, however, less likely to occur. A small farm is less attractive as an inheritance, in capital and income terms, than a larger business. Besides this, hobby farmers are usually professional or businessmen and likely to encourage their children in that direction rather than into farming. Further, hobby farmers typically purchase their holdings in middle age when their children have left home, so the younger generation would have no particular emotional links with the farm. Two studies quoted in Chapter 7 indicate a close association between the household's dependence on farm income and the likelihood of succession.

This section has traced various routes which the farm family business may follow in response to the pressures of the capitalist economy. Pursued to its logical conclusion each response – accumulation, diversification, hobby farming, belt-tightening – may sever the link between the household and the farm business. Either the business or the household may be incapable of reproduction. Even within the boundaries of a family-owned and managed business, a limit may be reached where the family ethos is completely submerged by the interests of capital. Formal subsumption of the labour process may split the farm from the family, demanding a change in 'traditional' family relations. The family may continue to provide labour but becomes increasingly irrelevant to business decisions.

FARM HOUSEHOLD REPRODUCTION UNDER SUBSUMPTION

As a farm business moves towards capitalist relations of production, so its ties with the family are expected to loosen. A recent study by Marsden and colleagues (1992) has attempted to test this hypothesis directly, relating the social reproduction of the farm family to measures of subsumption. The central issue is seen to be the conflict between the need of capital to dominate and the family's desire to maintain its control over the ownership and management of the farm business from one generation to the next. The difficulties of financing the inter-generational transfer of the farm are exacerbated by any increase in penetration by capital.

Respondents in the five study areas were asked a number of questions about family structure and their expectations about succession. Over half of the farmers saw succession as likely while nearly a third said it was definitely ruled out. The rest either had no children or very young children, or were uncertain whether succession was a viable option. Positive responses were highest among the predominantly large-scale arable farms in Bedfordshire and the dairy farms of Dorset, lowest in the two upland areas (Table 9.2).

On the basis of these answers and other information about family links with the farm in the past and future plans, five categories of 'family commitment' were defined:

1. Strongly established families where succession is planned and the family has occupied the farm for at least two generations.
2. Establishers where future succession has not been ruled out, and the farm has been in the family at least two generations; or a first generation farm where succession is definitely planned; or a first generation farm where succession is possible and the farmer belongs to a local farming network.

Table 9.2. Farmers' expectations about succession in five areas of England.

Is succession expected?	Bedfordshire	Dorset	Cumbria	Stafford	Green Belt	Total
			(per cent)			
Yes	58	58	47	41	50	53
No	17	32	31	34	35	30
Unsure, other	25	10	22	25	15	17
All farms	100	100	100	100	100	100
Numbers	80	99	88	70	86	423

Source: Marsden *et al.* 1992, Table 3

3. Potential establishers – first generation farms where succession has not been ruled out but the farmer does not belong to a local farm family network.

4. Uncommitted families where succession has been ruled out, often because children are unwilling to take over the farm.

5. Non-family farms managed by an employee on behalf of a company.

One third of the farms across the five study areas were strongly established and another third judged to be establishers on the criteria chosen. One family in four was defined as uncommitted. The highest proportion of strongly established farm families was found among the arable farms of Bedfordshire, which also had the fewest uncommitted. Upland Cumbria had the fewest strongly established families. The larger the farm, the stronger the family's commitment to continuity tended to be. Supporting evidence can be found in Chapter 7, which showed that family continuity was positively associated with the household's level of dependence on farm income, and by implication with size of business.

The key question for the researchers was the relationship between the 'social trajectories' of farms in terms of family commitment to continuing farming in that place, and their position on the subsumption matrix. Cross-tabulating farming commitment against the ideal types of family farm from the subsumption matrix, they were able to demonstrate commitment to family continuity increasing as farms become more dependent on external capital. Strongly committed families were the dominant type among family business farms and establishers formed the largest group among transitional units. Nearly half the family labour farms had ruled out inter-generational succession, compared with 22 per cent of the transitional units and only 14 per cent of the family business farms (Table 9.3). Family continuity appears to be under greatest threat where reliance on outside sources of capital is

Table 9.3. Social trajectories of ideal types of family farm.

Social trajectory	Family labour farm	Transitional unit (per cent)	Family business farm	Subsumed unit
Strongly established	22	36	41	17
Establisher	25	40	27	16
Potential establisher	5	2	14	0
Uncommitted	48	22	14	17
Non-family farms	0	0	4	50
Total	100	100	100	100
Numbers	81	118	22	6

Source: Marsden *et al.* 1992, Table 5

least. The likelihood of farm family businesses surviving into the next generation is seen to increase as they become more engaged with outside capital through technology, credit and marketing links and develop more complex structures.

These results suggest that family relationships and market mechanisms can be mutually reinforcing in directing agricultural development. Stability and commitment in family relations are as much in the interests of capital as they are of the farm family. Establishment of complex relationships of dependence on outside capital does not necessarily diminish family values but may provide a means to attain more socially-oriented goals of family continuity and succession.

CONTINUITY OF FAMILY FARMING

There have always been Starkadders at Cold Comfort.

(Gibbons 1973: 47)

One of the themes running through this book has been the continuity of family farming. Marsden and colleagues took continuity to be the central issue in the social reproduction of the farm family. Implicit in the definition of a farm family business was the condition that the farm should be handed down within the same family and in Chapters 7 and 8 the processes of farm inheritance, succession and retirement were discussed in detail. As Chapter 4 showed, to be able to hand on the farm to the next generation is a guiding principle for many farmers. Chapter 3 dealt with the resilience and survival of family-run farms within a capitalist economy. The present chapter has placed more emphasis on the positive response which farm families make in adapting to the pressures upon them. It concludes that survival is not consonant with unbroken continuity in the sense of an absence of change. 'Saving the family farm' can be interpreted in a number of ways. The remainder of this chapter asks what kind of family farming we want to encourage, what form of continuity would be most desirable for society as a whole.

From the literature, three distinct meanings can be associated with the 'continuity' of family farming:

- keeping the name on the land;
- keeping farming in the family;
- maintaining farming on a family scale.

Chapter 3 refers to continuity in the third sense of retaining the option of farms being run as family businesses. Macro-level data like agricultural census results can only indicate trends at this level of generality; whether over time the numbers of one- to two-man farms are being maintained, or the proportions of farmers inheriting their farms or expecting succession are remaining about the same. Nothing is implied about the links between particular families and farms or the persistence of farming in certain families. Such links can only be revealed by detailed studies at the individual farm/household level. The research by Marsden and colleagues described above, tracing the course of individual farm households over a fifteen-year period, has provided valuable insights. Their classification of 'social trajectories' of families gives one measure of the degree of family continuity in farming.

'Keeping the name on the land', if taken to the extreme described by Arensberg and Kimball for the west of Ireland, tends to produce a fossilized structure of small holdings. The family makes sacrifices in order that one son shall inherit each holding – the 'farmer's boy' pattern described in Chapter 7. No allowance is made for farms to expand. Marriage to young or middle-aged farmers on smallholdings who may still be under the domination of one or both parents is not an attractive prospect for young women and so these farmers are liable to remain single, without direct successors. The consequences for society of this kind of attitude are a run-down agriculture of small, inefficient farms with elderly, impoverished operators. Perversely, the problems of over-production in western agriculture may show such farmers in a kinder light. Their more extensive farming practices help to reduce surpluses and may provide conservation benefits for society at large (Potter and Lobley 1992).

Continuity in the second sense of 'keeping farming in the family' means setting up more than one son in a viable farm business. The growing capital requirements of modern farming have produced significant changes in the way this type of continuity is achieved. The ideal of 'generational fragmentation' as in Ashworthy, where each child is established in a viable but separate farm, has given way to one of consolidation, incorporating members of the next generation to form an extended unit. If the business is large enough, sons wanting to farm can remain working on the home farm in a father–son partnership, possibly with responsibility for separate enterprises – two of the patterns described in Chapter 7. On smaller farms or where more sons wish to remain with the family business, the firm's capital may be used to acquire additional holdings. Typically these become the home and responsibility of the son but remain within the parent business structure, dependent upon a common source of capital – the 'stand-by holding' model. In these successful, dynamic farm families, kinship is now concentrated within the business rather than being spread widely to create a supportive network between families. The family used to act as a pool of labour, often deficient to farm requirements at some stages of the family and farming cycles and surplus at others. Today on the larger, family business type of farm it functions more as a management team, whose skills must extend to commercial and financial expertise, obtaining loans, planning capital investment, controlling skilled and casual labour (Symes and Marsden 1983a: Hutson 1987). The success of such teams depends on having the right combination of skills among the members (Chapter 5).

One consequence is a change in significance of **inheritance** and **succession**. The process of farm inheritance, the transfer of legal ownership, used to be crucial. Decisions had to be made about which child should take on the family holding in return for looking after the parents, which children were to be set up on their own with what shares of property. The process of succession, the transfer of management control, now assumes greater importance and takes on new forms with the growing complexity of modern farm businesses, as described in Chapter 8.

Keeping farming in the family as a viable occupation, whether by setting up sons in farms of their own or incorporating them into an existing family business, implies expansion. The cost of some families continuing to farm is the absorption of other family holdings. There is therefore an in-built contradiction between **survival** and **continuity** for family farming as a whole. Whereas Marxist interpretations see non-farm finance and industrial capital as the main threat to the family farm, agricultural economists stress competition for land within the farming sector. Cochrane (1979) spoke of the 'cannibalism' of ambitious farmers buying the farms of their less competitive neighbours and operating them with larger equipment. 'The dominant force in this potential trend toward fewer and larger farms is that of large family units growing even larger' (Ball and Heady 1972: 380). When Essex University researchers interviewed a cross-section of Suffolk farmers in the 1970s, two out of three were keen to expand their own farms. Yet many of them were hostile to the idea of their bigger neighbours buying up small holdings and thus putting small farmers out of business (Newby *et al.* 1981).

If families are large, pursuit of this objective can mean intense competition for land. Such a situation can be observed among Amish communities in the United States today. Strongly-held ethno-religious norms dictate that families are close-knit with many children. Keeping the family together in farming means that farmers must constantly be on the lookout for additional land to enlarge their holdings. When all the farmland in the home area is in Amish hands, family groups have to move away and colonize new areas.

Continuity and Family Influence

> The approach to farming is mainly by 'social inheritance', i.e., birth and upbringing in farming families.
>
> (Ashby 1953: 98)

Even if the extent to which families continue occupying the same parcel of land has been exaggerated, the fact remains that family influence is usually instrumental in gaining a foothold in farming. The claim made by Ashby was based on his extensive knowledge of farming in Britain between the wars, when 80 per cent of farmers in England and Wales were farmers' sons (Chapman 1944). In the light of soaring land prices and working capital requirements, a shrinking rented sector and the sale or amalgamation of statutory smallholdings, it is becoming progressively harder for individuals to establish themselves in farming by savings and hard work alone. The Suffolk survey revealed that 74 per cent of a representative sample of farmers were farmers' sons and almost 80 per cent had inherited either land or the money to buy land. Only a minority had established their own businesses by dint of thrift, hard work and bank borrowing and even in the mid-1970s this was becoming harder. Over time the family is therefore likely to become even more important as a means of entry to farming (Newby *et al.* 1981). Confirmation comes from Harrison's national survey in the late 1960s which suggested that 83 per cent of English farmers were from farming origins (Harrison 1975). As Harrison observed,

> The overall weight of evidence served only to emphasize the narrowing of opportunities for entering farming unless strong and tangible links with the industry already existed. Usually these were family links ...
>
> (Harrison 1975: 21)

As a corollary of this, the larger the farm, the more likely it is that the farmer was established with family help. The Wartime Social Survey revealed, for example, that 72 per cent of the fathers of farmers with under 50 acre holdings were farmers, the percentage rising to 88 per cent in larger size groups (Ashby 1953). Essex University's study of farms over 1000 acres in East Anglia likewise demonstrated a link between farming inheritance and size of business; almost 80 per cent of these large-scale farmers were

Table 9.4. Backgrounds of farmers in eastern England.

	1000+ acre sample*	Suffolk sample* (per cent of farmers)	Small farm sample+
Sons of a farmer	80	72	65
Grew up on present farm	48	33	27
Inherited farm	70	56	50
Number in sample	105	57	102

Sources: *Newby *et al.* 1978; +Gasson 1969

sons of farmers, 70 per cent had inherited their farms and a further 11 per cent had been helped by relatives to start farming (Newby *et al.* 1978). Comparing these results with their Suffolk sample and with an earlier survey of small (one- and two-man) farms in eastern England reveals a consistent pattern; farm birth, upbringing and inheritance are more common on larger farms (Table 9.4).

Looking to the future, Chapter 7 showed that the larger the farm and the greater the household's reliance on farming as a source of income, the greater the likelihood of family succession. The family, then, is highly functional for launching sons into farming, especially on a large scale. On the debit side, the successor's experience of other jobs, even of other farms, may be limited. Two thirds of farmers in England and Wales in the 1940s, according to Ashby, had had no previous occupation. Even in the 1970s, the Essex University researchers found that many large-scale farmers in East Anglia, among the most prosperous of farming regions in the EC, had had experience of only one farm, their own and their father's before them. Further questioning revealed that over half the brothers, over a quarter of the brothers-in-law and more than a third of the fathers-in-law of the respondents were also farmers. 'The stereotype of the farmer belonging to the somewhat enclosed and self-contained world of the farming fraternity therefore has some basis in reality' (Newby *et al.* 1978: 71).

Opportunities for Newcomers

A third meaning of 'continuity of family farming' is that farms continue to be operated by families, without specifying which families they are. It might in fact be judged desirable to give *different* families the opportunity of entering farming. While it is certainly very difficult for a young person in the UK to start farming without family help, some individuals will always find a means of entry on their own account. In the context of over-production in agriculture, it might be argued that young people, especially those who are strongly motivated and above average in productivity, should not be encouraged to enter the industry. Reading University researchers studying a group of young people who had started farming without family help, emphatically rejected this view. They were strongly of the opinion that some opportunity should be maintained for those from non-farm backgrounds. Any move towards a 'closed shop' in farming, they felt, was a recipe for stagnation and a worsening competitive position (Errington *et al.* 1988). The Northfield Committee considering trends in the acquisition and occupancy of farmland in the UK held a similar view:

> ... many believe that agriculture, like any other industry, needs a continuous infusion of 'new blood' from outside the industry to provide a fresh and innovative outlook, energy and drive. Some of those giving evidence argued that there were dangers in agriculture becoming a closed shop and that it would not be desirable if entry to farming were restricted solely to a privileged class of inheritors or to those few with large sums of capital to buy themselves in.
>
> (Northfield 1979: paras. 474–5)

This book has provided ample illustration of 'a privileged class of inheritors' occupying the larger farms and handing them on within the family. Commenting on this 'highly introverted selection process', Sandford (1976) observed that:

> There is nothing in the process of inheritance to ensure that the son of a businessman or farmer is necessarily the best person to carry on his father's enterprise. There is something to be said for property coming on to the market fairly frequently, for there must be a *prima facie* assumption that the person or organization prepared to pay the best price for it is able to put it to the most efficient use.
>
> (quoted in Harrison *et al.* 1982: 140)

Smaller farms foster a more open society where entry to farming is more likely to be achieved than ascribed, family influence being less crucial for success. *Because* entry to farming at a high level is so difficult, most of those coming into the industry from other walks of life start on a modest scale. Chapter 2 described how the onset of the Great Depression at the end of the nineteenth century facilitated the entry of artisans and ambitious farmworkers to smallholdings in Devon. For the past hundred years the statutory smallholdings offered by local authorities to selected tenants, have provided a possible route into farming. Despite reductions in the number of holdings available as a result of amalgamation and sale, a quarter of the young people studied by Reading University who had started farming without family help had used this route (Errington *et al.* 1988). To an increasing extent, though, small holdings which come on the market are purchased by families outside farming who rely mainly upon other sources of income.

Some Implications

From the individual farmer's point of view, farming continuity within the family is something to be valued, as Chapters 4 and 7 have shown. Other family members may have some reservations, believing their own needs and aspirations are more likely to be satisfied outside farming or free from the patriarchal dominance of the family. From society's point of view, there are certain advantages to be gained from having some turnover of families within farming. To caricature the alternatives, keeping the name on the land can result in a fossilized structure of non-viable farms. Maintaining a family's links with farming may mean more aggressive farms gobbling up their weaker neighbours. In neither case will there be a continuing element of vigorous, active, small and medium-scale independent family farmers in the rural population. Where there is some turnover of farms, there is at least a sense of farming being an open occupation, even if the failure rate is high.

Agriculture's increasing dependence on outside capital and new technology underlines the need for adequate education and training among farmers. The fact that access to the farming occupation is ascribed rather than achieved, helps to account for relatively low levels of education. For instance, the Essex University study found that 86 per cent of farmers in the Suffolk sample had received no formal education or training in agricultural subjects and even among the 1000 acre farmers, agricultural qualifications were by no means universal. With the passage of time, vocational training levels among the farming population are rising as younger farmers study at agricultural college or university or attend Agricultural Training Board courses. Even so, a recent survey found that only 52 per cent of a big sample of British farmers, biased towards the larger farm, had studied 'farming practice' in some form, implying that nearly half had had no formal training at all (NatWest Bank 1992). Levels of formal qualifications and training are much higher among employed farm managers and newcomers to farming, highlighting once again the distinctive nature of the farm family business where entry is determined largely by birth. New entrants can also bring new ideas, tap new sources of capital, find new market niches or forge new links with the urban population.

Family farming also has implications for the environment. For the population as a whole, it is important that the appearance of the countryside should be preserved. In Britain this means protecting the farmed country-side. Much of the quality and content of the landscape depends on the structure of holdings – the layout of fields in relation to farmhouse and buildings, the size and shape of fields and woods, the patchwork of crops, the quality and type of field boundaries and so on. Changes detrimental to the appearance of the countryside such as the removal of hedgerows and small woods, more uniform cropping patterns, frequently result from farm amalgamation. It follows that maintaining farming on a *family* scale will help to maintain the appearance of the landscape. Further, the economies of scale enjoyed by larger businesses may incur substantial social costs in terms of the externalities of pollution and environmental destruction. This is not an argument for increasing productivity or farming profitability but it might appeal to the growing numbers in the population who regard the country-side as place of consumption rather than production.

Family farms may make a greater net contribution to the welfare of society than much larger units run as non-family businesses. Family farms may prove to be more resilient in the face of agricultural recession and may provide an employment refuge for family members. Work on farms may be less alienating than in other sectors too since 'The majority of the (farm) labour force is still composed of men and women who can legitimately regard themselves as participants in decisions and processes that shape their lives' (Raup 1969).

CONCLUSION

The emphasis in this book on the perpetuation of the farm family business necessarily focuses on stability and continuity. In practice however there must be constant adaptation and change if individual farming families, and family farming as a whole, are to survive. First, the farm family develop-ment cycle imposes a pattern on the operation of the business. Birth, children leaving home, marriage, farm succession, retirement and death are associated with changes in the size and experience of the farm labour force, the personality of the principal decision-maker, the allocation of responsi-bility for business control, the size and distribution of the income stream, capital stocks and flows, occupation of the main farmhouse, the acquisition of other dwellings and so on. Second, the farm business may develop its own cycle of growth and decay, investment and entrenchment, set off by the family cycle but gaining its own momentum and subject to events in the wider economy. Synchronizing these two cycles may itself be crucial for the continuance of the farm family business.

Diversification of the activities of farm household members marks a kind of discontinuity, where the circuit of capital through the farm and household is widened. Diversification may be a strategy to accumulate capital for the farm business, to create employment or to supplement house-hold consumption. Off-farm employment goes one step further, widening the circuit beyond the farm base. Other transitions include the move to other forms of family business outside agriculture. A farm family business could move to another business form – a quoted company, share farming, vertical integration – becoming in effect a non-family firm. Another transition has the family remaining on the farm but no longer earning a living from farming. Self-sufficiency, alternative lifestyles, hobby farming, dependence on pensions, social transfers, investment income – a farm family but no longer a farm family business.

Where strategies of accumulation or diversification are insufficient to reproduce the farm business, the business may fail, representing a break between the family and the farm. Biological failure of the family to reproduce itself signals another kind of discontinuity. Business failure and biological failure may result in a family leaving farming or moving from a particular holding but this need not spell the end of farming as a family concern. Each gives an opportunity for a new family to enter. New links are forged between a farm household and a farm business and family farming continues.

REFERENCES

Abrahams, R. (1991) *A Place of Their Own: Family Farming in Eastern Finland.* Cambridge University Press.

Agriculture EDC (1972) *Agricultural Manpower in England and Wales.* London: HMSO.

Agriculture EDC (1973) *Farm Productivity.* London: NEDO.

Aines, R.O. (1972) Linkages in control and management with agribusiness. In: Ball, A.G. and Heady, E.O. (eds) *Size, Structure, and Future of Farms.* Ames, Iowa: Iowa State University Press, pp. 171–89.

Allan, V. (1985) *Southland Rural Women: An Aspect of Change.* New Zealand: Rural Education Activities Programme.

Almas, R. and Haugen, M.S. (1991) Norwegian gender roles in transition. *Journal of Rural Studies* 7, 79–83.

Anderson, R. and Hepworth, M. (1980) Retirement from farming: some economic and social considerations. *Farm Management Review* 13, 1–8.

Anderson, R. and Rosenblatt, P. (1985) Intergenerational transfer of farm land, *Journal of Rural Community Psychology* 6, 19–25.

Ansell, D.J., Giles, A.K. and Rendell, J. (1989) *Very Small Farms: A Neglected Component?* University of Reading, Department of Agricultural Economics and Management, Special Studies in Agricultural Economics, Report No. 5.

Ansell, D.J., Giles, A.K. and Rendell, J. (1990) *The Economics of Very Small Farms – A Further Look.* University of Reading, Department of Agricultural Economics and Management, Special Studies in Agricultural Economics, Report No. 9.

Arensberg, C.M. and Kimball, S.T. (1968) *Family and Community in Ireland,* 2nd edn. Cambridge, Massachusetts: Harvard University Press.

Arkleton Trust (1990) *Agrarian Change and Farm Household Pluriactivity in Europe: Second Research Report for the Commission of the European Communities on Structural Change, Pluriactivity, and the Use made of Structures Policies by Farm Households in the European Community. Vol. I: European Analysis.* ATR/90/19. Nethy Bridge, Inverness-shire: Arkleton Trust (Research) Ltd.

Ashby, A.W. (1925) The human side of the farming business. *Welsh Journal of Agriculture* 1, 16–22.

Ashby, A.W. (1953) The farmer in business. *Journal of Agricultural Economics* 10, 91–126.

Augustins, G. (1989) *Comment se Perpétuer? Devenir des Lignées et Destins des Patrimoines dans les Paysanneries Européennes* Nanterre: Société d'Ethnologie.

Ball, A.G. and Heady, E.O. (1972) Trends in farm and enterprise size and scale. In: Ball, A.G. and Heady, E.O. (eds) *Size, Structure, and Future of Farms*. Ames, Iowa: Iowa State University Press, pp. 40–58.

Ball, R.M. (1988) *Seasonality in the UK Labour Market*. Aldershot: Avebury.

Barnes, L.B. and Hershon, S.A. (1976) Transferring power in the family business. *Harvard Business Review* July–August, 105–114.

Bauwens, A.L.G. and Loeffen, G.J.M. (1983) *The Changing Economic and Social Position of the Farmer's Wife in The Netherlands*. Paper presented at the 12th European Congress for Rural Sociology, Budapest.

Becker, G.S. (1965) A theory of the allocation of time. *The Economic Journal*, 75, 493–517.

Belbin, M. (1983) *Management Teams*. London: Heinemann.

Bell, C., Bryden, J.M., Fuller, A.M., MacKinnon, N. and Spearman, M. (1990) *Economic and Social Change in Rural Europe: Participation by Farm Women in the Labour Market, and Implications for Social Policy*. Nethy Bridge, Inverness-shire: Arkleton Research, unpublished paper.

Bennett, J.W. (1982) *Of Time and the Enterprise*. Minneapolis: University of Minnesota Press.

Benvenuti, B. (1961) *Farming in Cultural Change*. Wageningen: Van Gorcum.

Beresford, T. (1975) *We Plough the Fields*. Harmondsworth: Penguin.

Berlan, M., Painvin, R-M. and Dentzer, M-T. (1980) *Life and Work Conditions of Women in French Farms*. Rennes: Regional Centre of Research in Rural Sociology and Economy.

Blacksell, M., Economides, K. and Watkins, C. (1987) Country solicitors; their professional role in rural Britain. *Sociologia Ruralis* 27, 181–96.

Blanc, M. (1987) Family and employment in agriculture; recent changes in France. *Journal of Agricultural Economics* 38, 289–301.

Blanc, M. and MacKinnon, N. (1990) Gender relations and the family farm in Western Europe. *Journal of Rural Studies* 6, 401–5.

Blanc, M. and Perrier-Cornet, P. (1992) *Farm Take-over and Farm Entrance Within the European Community*. Paper presented to the colloquium: La transmission des exploitations agricoles et l'installation des agriculteurs dans la CEE, ENSA, Dijon 10–11 December 1992.

Blood, R. and Wolfe, D. (1960) *Husbands and Wives*. New York: The Free Press.

Boehlje, M.D. and Eidman, V.R. (1984) *Farm Management*. New York: Wiley.

Boehlje, M.D. and Eisgruber, L.M. (1972) Strategies for the creation and transfer of the farm estate. *American Journal of Agricultural Economics*, 54, 461–72.

Bouquet, M. (1985) *Family, Servants and Visitors*. Norwich: Geo Books.

Bowers, J.K. and Cheshire, P. (1983) *Agriculture, the Countryside and Land Use*. London: Methuen.

Bradley, T. (1987) Poverty and dependency in rural England. In Lowe, P., Bradley,T. and Wright, S. (eds) *Deprivation and Welfare in Rural Areas*. Norwich: Geo Books.

Breimyer, H.F. (1965) *Individual Freedom and the Organization of Agriculture*. Urbana, Illinois: University of Illinois Press.

Britton, D.K. (1977) Some explorations in the analysis of long–term changes in the structure of agriculture. *Journal of Agricultural Economics* 38, 197–208.

Britton, D.K. (ed.) (1990) *Agriculture in Britain: Changing Pressures and Policies*. Wallingford: CAB International.

Britton, D.K. and Hill, B. (1975) *Size and Efficiency in Farming*. Farnborough: Saxon House.

Buccleuch and Queensberry, Duke of (1981) Smallfarming: A landowner's view. In: Tranter, R.B. (ed.) *Smallfarming and the Nation*. Reading: Centre for Agricultural Strategy, CAS Paper 9, pp. 21–6.

Buchanan, W.I., Errington, A.J. and Giles, A.K. (1982) *The Farmer's Wife: Her Role in the Management of the Business*. Reading University Farm Management Unit, Study No. 2.

Burrell, A.M. (1989) The microeconomics of quota transfer. In: Burrell, A.M. (ed.) *Milk Quotas in the European Community*. Wallingford: CAB International.

Buttel, F.H. (1982) Farm structure and rural development. In: Browne, W.P. and Hadwiger, D.F. (eds) *Rural Policy Problems: Changing Dimensions*. Lexington, Massachusetts: D.C. Heath, pp. 213–35.

Buttel, F.H. (1983) Beyond the family farm. In: Summers, G. (ed.) *Technology and Social Change in Rural Areas*. Boulder, Colorado: Westview Press, pp. 87–107.

Buttel, F.H. and Newby, H. (1980) Towards a critical rural sociology. In: Buttel, F.H. and Newby, H. (eds) *The Rural Sociology of Advanced Societies: Critical Perspectives*. London: Croom Helm, pp. 1–35.

Byron, R. and Dilley, R. (1989) Social and micro–economic processes in the Northern Ireland fishing industry. In: Jenkins, R. (ed.) *Northern Ireland: Studies in Social and Economic Life*. Aldershot: Avebury, pp. 56–65.

Campagne, P., Carrere, G. and Valceschini, E. (1990) Three agricultural regions of France: three types of pluriactivity. *Journal of Rural Studies* 6, 415–22.

Casson, M. (1982) *The Entrepreneur: An Economic Theory*. Oxford: Martin Robertson.

Cernea, M. (1978) Macrosocial change, feminization of agriculture and peasant women's threefold economic role. *Sociologia Ruralis* 18, 107–24.

Chapman, D. (1944) *Agricultural Information and the Farmer*. Wartime Social Survey. London: Central Office of Information.

Chayanov, A.V. (1966) *The Theory of Peasant Economy*. Translated and edited by Thorner, D., Kerblay, B. and Smith, R.E.F. Homewood, Illinois: Irwin Press.

Clarke, G.J., Vaughan, J.S. and Waud, L.M. (1976) *Elderly Farmers in the United Kingdom*. Ministry of Agriculture, Fisheries and Food, Agricultural Development and Advisory Service, Socio-economics Paper 4.

Cochrane, W.W. (1979) *The Development of American Agriculture: An Historical Analysis*. Minneapolis: University of Minnesota Press.

Colman, G. and Elbert, S. (1984) Farming families: the farm needs everyone. In: Schwarzweller, H.K. (ed.) *Research in Rural Sociology and Development volume 1*. Greenwich, Connecticut: JAI Press, pp. 61–78.

Commins, P. (1973) *Retirement in Agriculture. A Pilot Survey of Farmers' Reactions to EEC Pension Schemes*. Dublin: Macra na Feirme.

Commins, P. and Kelleher, C. (1973) *Farm Inheritance and Succession*. Dublin: Macra na Feirme.

Commission of the European Communities (1991) The development and future of the Common Agricultural Policy: Proposals of the Commission. *Green Europe* 2/91.

Coughenour, C.M. and Wimberley, R.C. (1982) Small and part-time farmers. In: Dillman, D.A. and Hobbs, D.J. (eds) *Rural Society in the US: Issues for the 1980s*. Boulder, Colorado: Westview Press, pp. 347–56.

Craig, R.A. (n.d.) *Role Conflicts of Australian Farm Women*. Unpublished paper.

Cyert, R.M. and March, J.G. (1963) *A Behavioural Theory of the Firm.* Englewood Cliffs, New Jersey: Prentice-Hall.

David, J. (1985) Observations sur le Phénomene du GAEC Pere–Fils. *Revue de Droit Rural* 136, 368–371.

David, J. (1987) Les Formes Contemporaines de la Transmission des Exploitations Agricoles. *Revue de Droit Rural* 152, 155–162.

Davies, E.T. (1969) *Tourism and the Cornish Farmer.* University of Exeter, Department of Economics, Report No. 173.

Davies, E.T. (1973) *Tourism on Devon Farms: A Physical and Economic Appraisal.* University of Exeter Agricultural Economics Unit, Report No. 188.

Davis, J.E. (1980) Capitalist agricultural development and the exploitation of the propertied labourer. In: Buttel, F.H. and Newby, H. (eds) *The Rural Sociology of Advanced Societies: Critical Perspectives.* London: Croom Helm, pp. 133–49.

Dawson, P.J. (1984) Labour on the family farm: a theory and some policy implications. *Journal of Agricultural Economics* 35, 1–19.

de Haan, H. (1992) *Patrimony or Commodity? The Cultural Mediation of Economic Constraints on Farm Succession.* Paper presented to the colloquium: La transmission des exploitations agricoles et l'installation des agriculteurs dans la CEE, ENSA, Dijon 10–11 December 1992.

Dexter, K. and Barber, D. (1961) *Farming for Profits.* London: Penguin.

Dickens, C. (1868a) Farm and College. *All the Year Round,* pp. 414–421.

Dickens, C. (1868b) *Dombey and Son.* London: Chapman and Hall.

Djurfeldt, G. (1992) *Family Farms on the Decline: Contemporary Swedish Farming in a Chayanovian Perspective.* Paper presented at VII World Congress for Rural Sociology, Penn State University USA, August.

Dorfman, L., Heckert, D., Hill, E. and Kohout, F. (1988) Retirement satisfaction in rural husbands and wives. *Rural Sociology* 53, 25–39.

Drucker, P.F. (1981) *The Effective Executive.* London: Pan Books.

Durkheim, E. (1933) *The Division of Labour in Society,* translated by Simpson, G. New York: The Free Press.

Engler-Bowles, C.A. and Kart, C.S. (1983) Intergenerational relations and testamentary patterns: an exploration. *The Gerontologist,* 23, 167–173.

Errington, A.J. (1980) Occupational classification in British Agriculture. *Journal of Agricultural Economics* 31, 73–81.

Errington, A.J. (1984) Adviser or decision–taker? The role of the consultant agronomist on Britain's farms today. *Agricultural Manpower* 9, 9–16.

Errington, A.J. (1986a) *The Farm as a Family Business: An Annotated Bibliography.* University of Reading Farm Management Unit, Agricultural Manpower Society.

Errington, A.J. (1986b) The delegation of decisions on the farm. *Agricultural Systems* 19, 299–317.

Errington, A.J. (1986c) *Introducing Farm Management: A tape–slide presentation.* Kenilworth: Royal Agricultural Society of England.

Errington, A.J. (1987) *Rural Employment Trends and Issues in Market Industrialized Countries.* Geneva: ILO, World Employment Programme Research Working Papers.

Errington, A.J. (1988) Disguised unemployment in British agriculture. *Journal of Rural Studies* 4, 1–7.

Errington, A.J. (1992a) Developing talents and team building. *Farm Management* 8, 101–10.

Errington, A.J. (1992b) *The changing size and structure of the agricultural and horticultural workforce in England and Wales.* Paper presented to the annual meeting of the Agricultural Economics Society, Aberdeen University, April 1992.

Errington, A.J. and Tranter, R.B. (1991) *Getting out of Farming? Part Two: The Farmers.* Reading University Farm Management Unit, Study No. 27.

Errington, A.J., Giles, A.K. and Oakley, P.C. (1988) *Getting Started in Farming.* Reading University Farm Management Unit, Study No. 15.

Eurostat (1991) *Agricultural Income 1990.* Luxembourg: Eurostat.

Fairweather, J. (1987) *Farmers' Responses to Economic Restructuring: Preliminary Analysis of Survey Data.* Canterbury NZ: Lincoln University Agribusiness and Economics Research Unit, Research Report No. 187.

Fairweather, J. (1992) *Agrarian Restructuring in New Zealand.* Canterbury NZ: Lincoln University Agribusiness and Economics Research Unit, Research Report No. 213.

Fairweather, J. and Keating, N. (1990) *Management Styles of Canterbury Farmers.* Canterbury NZ: Lincoln University Agribusiness and Economics Research Unit, Research Report No. 205.

Fassinger, P.A. and Schwarzweller, H.K. (1984) The work of farm women: a midwestern study. In: Schwarzweller, H. (ed.) *Research in Rural Sociology and Development* volume 1. Greenwich, Connecticut: Jai Press, pp. 37–60.

Fasterding, F. (1984) *Entwicklung der bestande an familienarbeitskraften in Landwirtschaftlichen betrieben.* ISBL Braunschweig-Volkenrode, Braunschweig.

Fennell, R. (1981) Farm succession in the European Community. *Sociologia Ruralis* 21, 19–42.

First-Dilic, R. (1978) The productive roles of farm women in Yugoslavia. *Sociologia Ruralis* 18, 125–39.

Friedmann, H. (1986) Family enterprises in agriculture: structural limits and political possibilities. In: Cox, G., Lowe, P. and Winter, M. (eds) *Agriculture: People and Policies.* London: Allen & Unwin, pp. 41–60.

Fuller, A.M. and Brun, A. (1988) Socio-economic aspects of pluriactivity in Western Europe. In: *Structural Policies and Multiple Job Holding in the Rural Development Process.* Nethy Bridge: Arkleton Research, pp. 147–67.

Furness, G.W. (1982) Some features of farm income and structure variations in regions of the United Kingdom. *Journal of Agricultural Economics* 33, 289–309.

Furness, G.W. (1983) The importance, distribution and net incomes of small farm businesses in the UK. In: Tranter, R.B. (ed.) *Strategies for Family-worked Farms in the UK.* Reading: Centre for Agricultural Strategy, CAS Paper 15, pp. 12–41.

Galeski, B. and Wilkening, E. (1987) Introduction. In: Galeski, B. and Wilkening, E. (eds) *Family Farming in Europe and America.* Boulder, Colorado: Westview Press, pp. 1–4.

Gamble, D., Blunden, S., White, L. and Easterling, M. (1992) *The Transfer of the Farm Family Business: Working Paper to Focus Group and Survey Participants.* University of Western Sydney-Hawkesbury, Faculty of Agriculture and Rural Development.

Gasson, R. (1969) *Occupational Immobility of Small Farmers.* Cambridge University Farm Economics Branch, Occasional Papers No. 13.

Gasson, R. (1973) Goals and values of farmers. *Journal of Agricultural Economics* 24, 521–37.

Gasson, R. (1974a) The future of the family farm: social and psychological aspects. In: *The Future of the Family Farm in Europe*. Wye College Centre for European Agricultural Studies.

Gasson, R. (1974b) Socioeconomic status and orientation to work: the case of farmers. *Sociologia Ruralis* 14, 127–41.

Gasson, R. (1980a) Roles of farm women in England. *Sociologia Ruralis* 20, 165–80.

Gasson, R. (1980b) Women on the farm. *Farmers Weekly* September.

Gasson, R. (1984) *Results of 'Farmers Weekly' Retirement Survey*. Unpublished paper.

Gasson, R. (1987) Careers of farmers' daughters. *Farm Management* 6, 309–17.

Gasson, R. (1988) *The Economics of Part-Time Farming*. Harlow: Longman.

Gasson, R. (1989) *Farm Work by Farmers' Wives*. Wye College Farm Business Unit, Occasional Paper No. 15.

Gasson, R. (1990) *The Hidden Workforce*. Cirencester: Women's Farm and Garden Association.

Gasson, R. (1992) Farmers' wives: their contribution to the farm business. *Journal of Agricultural Economics* 43, 74–87.

Gasson, R. and Winter, M. (1992) Gender relations and farm household pluriactivity. *Journal of Rural Studies* 8, 573–84.

Gasson, R., Crow, G., Errington, A., Hutson, J., Marsden, T. and Winter, M. (1988) The farm as a family business: a review. *Journal of Agricultural Economics* 39, 1–41.

Gasson, R., Rosenthall, P., Shaw, A. and Winter, M. (1992a) *Pluriactivity and the Work of Farmers' Wives*. Cirencester: Royal Agricultural College Centre for Rural Studies, Occasional Paper No. 18.

Gasson, R., Shaw, A. and Winter, M. (1992b) *Characteristics of Farm Household Pluriactivity in East and Mid Devon*. Cirencester: Royal Agricultural College Centre for Rural Studies, Occasional Paper No. 19.

Ghorayshi, P. (1986) The identification of capitalist farms: theoretical and methodological considerations. *Sociologia Ruralis* 26, 146–69.

Gibbons, S. (1973) *Cold Comfort Farm*. St Albans: Panther Books.

Giles, A.K. and Mills, F.D. (1971) *More about Farm Managers*. Reading University Department of Agricultural Economics and Management, Miscellaneous Study No. 49.

Giles, T. and Stansfield, M. (1990) *The Farmer as Manager*, 2nd edn. Wallingford: CAB International.

Goldstein, B. and Eichhorn, R.L. (1961) The changing Protestant ethic: rural patterns in health, work, and leisure. *American Sociological Review* 26, 557–65.

Goodman, D. and Redclift, M. (1981) *From Peasant to Proletarian: Capitalist Development and Agrarian Transitions*. Oxford: Basil Blackwell.

Goodman, D. and Redclift, M. (1986) Capitalism, petty commodity production and the farm enterprise. In: Cox, G., Lowe, P. and Winter, M. (eds) *Agriculture: People and Policies*. London: Allen and Unwin, pp. 20–40.

Gourdomichalis, A. (1991) Women and the reproduction of family farms. *Journal of Rural Studies* 7, 57–62.

Guillou, A. (1991) Food habits, the freezer and gender relations in the countryside. *Journal of Rural Studies* 7, 67–70.

Gunter, L. and Vasavada, V. (1988) Dynamic labour demand schedules for US agriculture. *Applied Economics* 20, 803–812.

Handy, C.B. (1981) *Understanding Organisations*. Harmondsworth: Penguin.

Hannan, D.F. and Breen, R. (1987) Family farming in Ireland. In: Galeski, B. and Wilkening, E. (eds) *Family Farming in Europe and America*. Boulder, Colorado: Westview Press, pp. 39–69.

Hannan, D.F. and Katsiaouni, L.A. (1977) *Traditional Families? From Culturally Prescribed to Negotiated Roles in Farm Families*. Dublin: Economic and Social Research Institute, Paper No. 87.

Harl, N.E. (1972) The family corporation. In: Ball, A.G. and Heady, E.O. (eds) *Size, Structure, and Future of Farms*. Ames, Iowa: Iowa State University Press, pp. 270–89.

Harris, J.R. and Todaro, M.P. (1970) Migration, unemployment and development: a two-sector analysis. *American Economic Review* 60, 126–42.

Harrison, A. (1972) *The Financial Structure of Farm Businesses*. Reading University, Department of Agricultural Economics and Management, Miscellaneous Study No. 53.

Harrison, A. (1975) *Farmers and Farm Businesses in England*. Reading University Department of Agricultural Economics & Management, Miscellaneous Study No. 62.

Harrison, A. (1981) *Factors influencing Ownership, Tenancy, Mobility and Use of Farmland in the UK*. Luxembourg: Commission of the European Communities, Information on Agriculture No. 74.

Harrison, A. (1982) Land policies in the Member States of the European Community. *Agricultural Administration* 11, 159–74.

Harrison, A. (1986) Financing farm businesses today. In: Giles, A.K. and Wiggins, S.L. (eds) *Management Matters in 1986*. Reading University, Farm Management Unit, Study No. 10, pp. 1–2.

Harrison, A. and Tranter, R.B. (1989) *The Changing Financial Structure of Farming*. Reading University Centre for Agricultural Strategy, CAS Report 13.

Harrison, A. *et al.* (1982) *Factors influencing Ownership, Tenancy, Mobility and Use of Farmland in the Member States of the European Community*. Luxembourg: Commission of the European Communities, Information on Agriculture No. 86.

Hastings, M. (1984) *Succession on Farms*. Cranfield Institute of Technology, unpublished MSc thesis.

Hastings, M. (1987/8) Farming wives as business managers. *Farm Management* 6, 309–15.

Heady, E.O. and Jensen, H.R. (1954) *Farm Management Economics*. New York: Prentice-Hall.

Hedlund, D. and Berkowitz, A. (1979) The incidence of social-psychological stress in farm families. *International Journal of Sociology of the Family* 9, 233–43.

Heffernan, W.D. (1982) Structure of agriculture and quality of life in rural communities. In: Dillman, D.A. and Hobbs, D.J. (eds) *Rural Society in the US: Issues for the 1980s*. Boulder, Colorado: Westview Press, pp. 337–46.

Hill, B. (1989) *Farm Incomes, Wealth and Agricultural Policy*. Aldershot: Avebury.

Hill, B. (1990) In search of the Common Agricultural Policy's 'agricultural community'. *Journal of Agricultural Economics* 41, 316–26.

Hill, B. (1991) Measuring farmers' incomes and business performance: farm-level (FADN) data analysis, present and future. *Green Europe* 3/91.

Hill, B. (1992) *Total Income of Agricultural Households: 1992 Report*. Luxembourg: Eurostat.

Hill, B. and Gasson, R. (1984) *Farm Tenure and Performance.* Wye College School of Rural Economics.

Hine, R.C. and Houston, A.M. (1973) *Government and Structural Change in Agriculture.* Report prepared by Universities of Nottingham and Exeter for Ministry of Agriculture, Fisheries and Food.

Hobbs, D.J., Beal, J.M. and Bohlen, J.M. (1964) *The Relation of Farm Operator Values and Attitudes to their Economic Performance.* Ames, Iowa: Iowa State University, Department of Economics and Sociology, Rural Sociology Report No. 33.

Hughes, A. (1980) *The Diary of a Farmer's Wife 1796–1797.* London: Allen Lane.

Hunt, K.E. (1976) The concern of agricultural economists in Great Britain since the 1920s. *Journal of Agricultural Economics* 27, 285–96.

Hunter-Smith, J.D. (1982) Opening address. In: Marshall, B.J. and Tranter, R.B. (eds) *Smallfarming and the Rural Community.* Reading: Centre for Agricultural Strategy, CAS Paper 11, pp. 9–11.

Hutson, J. (1987) Fathers and sons: family farms, family businesses and the farming industry. *Sociology* 21, 215–29.

Hutson, J. (nd) The Farm as a Family Business. Unpublished paper.

Jenkins, D. (1971) *The Agricultural Community in South-West Wales at the Turn of the Twentieth Century.* Cardiff: University of Wales Press.

Jollans, J.L. (1983) (ed.) *Agriculture and Human Health.* Reading: Centre for Agricultural Strategy, CAS Paper 14.

Jones, C. and Rosenfeld, R.A. (1981) *American Farm Women: Findings from a National Survey.* Chicago: National Opinion Research Center, NORC Report No. 130.

Jones, G.E. (1967) The adoption and diffusion of agricultural practices, *World Agricultural Economics and Rural Sociology Abstracts* 9, 1–34.

Keating, N.C. (1991) *Aging in Rural Canada.* Toronto: Butterworths Canada.

Keating, N.C. and Little, H.M. (1991) *Generations in Farm Families: Transfer of the Family Farm in New Zealand.* Lincoln University, Agribusiness and Economics Research Unit, Research Report No. 208.

Keating, N.C. and Marshall, J. (1980) The process of retirement: the rural self-employed, *The Gerontologist* 20, 437–43.

Keating, N.C., Doherty, M. and Munro, B. (1987) The whole economy: resource allocation of Alberta farm women and men. *Canadian Home Economics Journal* 37, 135–9.

Keillor, G. (1989) *Leaving Home.* London: Faber and Faber.

Laband, D. and Lentz, B. (1983) Occupational inheritance in agriculture, *American Journal of Agricultural Economics* 65, 311–14.

Laslett, P. (1972) Mean household size in England since the sixteenth century. In: Laslett, P. and Wall, R. (eds) *Household and Family in Past Time.* Cambridge: Cambridge University Press.

Lawrence, G. (1990) Agricultural restructuring and rural social change in Australia. In: Marsden, T., Lowe, P. and Whatmore, S. (eds) *Rural Restructuring: Global Processes and their Responses.* London: David Fulton, pp. 101–28.

Le Heron, R. (1988) State, economy and crisis in the 1980s: implications for land-based production of a new mode of regulation. *Applied Geography* 8, 273–90.

Le Heron, R., Roche, M., Johnston, T. and Bowler, S. (1991) Pluriactivity in New Zealand's agro-commodity chains. In: Fairweather, J. (ed.) *Proceedings of the Rural Economy and Society Section of the Sociological Association of Aotearoa (NZ).*

Lincoln University, Canterbury NZ: AERU Discussion Paper No. 129.

Lifran, R. (1988) *Land Ownership Structures of Farms and the Wealth of Farmers.* Montpellier: Station d'Economie et Sociologie Rurales, unpublished paper.

Lifran, R. (1989) *The Interaction Between the Size and Sex Composition of the Progeny: The Case of French Farmers.* Paper presented to the Third Annual Conference of the European Society for Population Economics, Paris, 8–10 June.

Lloyd, D.H. (1970) *The Development of Farm Business Analysis and Planning in Britain.* Reading University, Department of Agriculture, Study No. 6.

Long, N. (1984) Introduction. In: Long, N. (ed.) *Family and Work in Rural Societies: Perspectives on Non-Wage Labour.* London: Tavistock, pp. 1–29.

Lund, P.J., Morris, T.G., Temple, J.E. and Watson, J.M. (1982) *Wages and Employment in Agriculture: England and Wales 1960–1980.* London: Ministry of Agriculture, Fisheries and Food, Government Economic Service Working Paper No. 52.

Madden, P.T. (1967) *Economies of Size of Farming.* Washington DC: USDA Agricultural Economics Report 107.

Mann, S. and Dickinson, J. (1978) Obstacles to the development of capitalist agriculture. *Journal of Peasant Studies* 5, 466–81.

Marsden, T. (1984) Land ownership and farm organization in capitalist agriculture. In: Bradley, T. and Lowe, P. (eds) *Locality and Rurality: Economy and Society in Rural Regions.* Norwich: Geo Books, pp. 129–45.

Marsden, T., Whatmore, S., Munton, R. and Little, J. (1986a) The restructuring process and economic centrality in capitalist agriculture. *Journal of Rural Studies* 2, 271–80.

Marsden, T., Munton, R., Whatmore, S. and Little, J. (1986b) Towards a political economy of capitalist agriculture: a British perspective. *International Journal of Urban and Rural Research* 4, 498–521.

Marsden, T., Whatmore, S. and Munton, R. (1987) Uneven development and the restructuring process in British Agriculture: a preliminary exploration. *Journal of Rural Studies* 3, 297–308.

Marsden, T., Munton, R., Whatmore, S. and Little, J. (1989) Strategies for coping in capitalist agriculture: an examination of the responses of farm families in British agriculture. *Geoforum* 20, 1–14.

Marsden, T., Munton, R. and Ward, N. (1992) Incorporating social trajectories into uneven agrarian development. *Sociologia Ruralis* 32, 408–32.

Marsh, J., Green, B., Kearney, B., Mahé, L., Tangermann, S. and Tarditi, S. (1991) *The Changing Role of the Common Agricultural Policy.* London: Belhaven Press.

Maslow, A.H. (1954) *Motivation and Personality.* New York: Harper.

Mendras, H. (1970) *The Vanishing Peasant: Innovation and Change in French Agriculture.* Translated by Jean Lerner. London: MIT Press.

Mingay, G.E. (1962) The size of farms in the eighteenth century. *Economic History Review* 14, 469–88.

Mingay, G. (1990) British rural history: themes in agricultural history. In: Lowe, P. and Bodiguel, M. (eds) *Rural Studies in Britain and France.* London: Belhaven Press, pp. 76–89.

Ministry of Agriculture, Fisheries and Food (1990) *Agriculture in the United Kingdom.* London: HMSO.

Moore, C.V. and Dean, G.W. (1972) Industrialized farming. In: Ball, A.G. and Heady, E.O. (eds) *Size, Structure, and Future of Farms.* Ames, Iowa: Iowa State University Press, pp. 214–31.

Morkeberg, H. (1978) Working conditions of women married to selfemployed farmers. *Sociologia Ruralis* 18, 95–106.

Munton, R. and Marsden, T. (1991) Dualism or diversity in family farming? Patterns of occupancy change in British agriculture. *Geoforum* 22, 105–17.

Nakajima, C. (1986) *Subjective Equilibrium Theory of the Farm Household.* Amsterdam: Elsevier.

Nalson, J.S. (1968) *Mobility of Farm Families.* Manchester University Press.

NatWest Bank (1992) *NatWest National Farm Survey: Summary Report and Tables.* London: National Westminster Bank.

Naylor, E. (1982) Retirement policy in French agriculture. *Journal of Agricultural Economics* 33, 25–36.

Neville-Rolfe, E. (1984) *The Politics of Agriculture in the European Community.* London: Policy Studies Institute.

Newby, H., Bell, C., Rose, D. and Saunders, P. (1978) *Property, Paternalism and Power.* London: Hutchinson.

Newby, H., Rose, D., Saunders, P. and Bell, C. (1981) Farming for survival: the small farmer in the contemporary class structure. In: Bechhofer, F. and Elliott, B. (eds) *The Petite Bourgeoisie: Comparative Studies of the Uneasy Stratum.* London: Macmillan, pp. 38–70.

Nikolitch, R. (1969) Family-operated farms: their compatibility with technological advance. *American Journal of Agricultural Economics* 51, 530–45.

Nikolitch, R. (1972) The individual family farm. In: Ball, A.G. and Heady, E.O. (eds) *Size, Structure, and Future of Farms.* Ames, Iowa: Iowa State University Press, pp. 248–69.

Norman, L. (1986) How do farmers and managers spend their management working time? *Farm Management* 6, 175–82.

Northfield, Lord (1979) *Report of the Committee of Inquiry into the Acquisition and Occupancy of Agricultural Land.* Cmnd. 7599. London: HMSO.

Olsson, R. (1988) Management for success in modern agriculture. *European Review of Agricultural Economics* 15, 239–59.

Organisation for Economic Co-operation and Development (1978) *Part-time Farming: in OECD Countries: General Report.* Paris: OECD.

Orwin, C.S. (1930) *The Future of Farming.* Oxford: Clarendon Press.

Office of Technology Assessment (1986) *Technology, Public Policy, and the Changing Structure of American Agriculture.* Washington D.C.: OTA.

Pahl, R.E. (1984) *Divisions of Labour.* Oxford: Basil Blackwell.

Pearson, J. (1979) Note on female farmers. *Rural Sociology* 44, 189–200.

Perkin, P. (1992) An Investigation into the Relationship between Farm and Farmer Characteristics and Objectives among a Sample of Berkshire Farmers. University of Reading, Department of Agriculture, unpublished PhD thesis.

Perrier-Cornet, P., Blanc, M., Cavailhes, J., Dauce, P. and Le Hy, A. (1991) *La Transmission des Exploitations Agricoles et L'installation des Agriculteurs dans la CEE.* Dijon: INRA.

Peters, G.H. and Maunder, A.H. (1983) Equity and agricultural change with special reference to land tenure in Western Europe. In: Maunder, A. and Ohkawa, K. (eds) *Growth and Equity in Agricultural Development.* Aldershot: Gower.

Peterson, M. (1990) Paradigmatic shifts in agriculture: global effects and the Swedish response. In: Marsden, T., Lowe, P. and Whatmore, S. (eds) *Rural Restructuring:*

Global Processes and their Responses. London: David Fulton, pp. 77–100.

Petrini, F. (1969) The goals of farmers – a pilot study. Supplement to *International Journal of Agrarian Affairs* 5, 175–84.

Petit, M. (1982) Is there a French school of agricultural economics? *Journal of Agricultural Economics* 33, 325–37.

Pile, S. (1990) *The Private Farmer.* Aldershot: Dartmouth.

Planck, U. (1987) The family farm in the Federal Republic of Germany. In: Galeski, B. and Wilkening, E. (eds) *Family Farming in Europe and America.* Boulder, Colorado: Westview Press, pp. 155–91.

Ploeg, J.D. van der (1985) Patterns of farming logic, structuration of labour and impact of externalization: changing dairy farming in northern Italy. *Sociologia Ruralis* 25, 5–25.

Pollack, R.A. (1985) A transactionist approach to families and households. *Journal of Economic Literature* 23, 581–668.

Pomeroy, A. (1987) *The 'Rural Crisis' in Perspective: Family Farming in Australia and New Zealand.* Paper presented at SAANZ Conference, University of New South Wales, Sydney.

Potter, C. and Lobley, M. (1992) Ageing and succession on family farms: the impact on decision making and land use. *Sociologia Ruralis* 32, 317–34.

Raup, P. (1969) *What Policies should we have towards Corporations in Farming?* St Paul, Minnesota: University of Minnesota Staff Paper.

Raup, P.M. (1972) Societal goals in farm size. In: Ball, A.G. and Heady, E.O. (eds) *Size, Structure, and Future of Farms.* Ames, Iowa: Iowa State University Press, pp. 3–17.

Redclift, N. and Whatmore, S. (1990) Household, consumption and livelihood: ideologies and issues in rural research. In: Marsden, T., Lowe, P. and Whatmore, S. (eds) *Rural Restructuring: Global Processes and their Responses.* London: David Fulton, pp. 182–97.

Rees, A.D. (1971) *Life in a Welsh Countryside.* Cardiff: University of Wales Press.

Reid, I.G. (1974) Legal and economic aspects of the future of the family farm enterprise and its role in the rural areas. In: *The Future of the Family Farm in Europe.* Wye College Centre for European Agricultural Studies.

Reinhardt, N. and Barlett, P. (1989) The persistence of family farms in United States agriculture. *Sociologia Ruralis* 29, 203–25.

Robinson, M.A. (1984) *Farmers' Objectives 1983.* Harper Adams Agricultural College Occasional Paper 84/1.

Rodefeld, R.D. (1978) Trends in US farm organizational structure and type. In: Rodefeld, R., Flora, J., Voth, D., Fujimoto, I. and Converse, J. (eds) *Change in Rural America: Causes, Consequences, and Alternatives.* St Louis, Missouri: The C.V. Mosby Company, pp. 158–77.

Rodefeld, R.D. (1982) Who will own and operate America's farms? In Dillman, D.A. and Hobbs, D.J. (eds) *Rural Society in the US: Issues for the 1980s.* Boulder, Colorado: Westview Press, pp. 328–36.

Rodefeld, R.D., Flora, J., Voth, D., Fujimoto, I. and Converse, J. (1978) *Change in Rural America: Causes, Consequences, and Alternatives.* St Louis, Missouri: The C.V. Mosby Company.

Rogers, S.C. (1991) *Shaping Modern Times in Rural France. The Transformation and Reproduction of an Aveyronnais Community.* Princeton: Princeton University Press.

Romero, C. and Rehman, T. (1984) Goal programming and multiple criteria decision-making in farm planning: an expository analysis. *Journal of Agricultural Economics* 35, 177–90.

Rosenblatt, P.C. and Anderson, R.M. (1981) Interaction in farm families: tension and stress. In: Coward, R.T. and Smith, W.M. (eds) *The Family in Rural Society.* Boulder, Colorado: Westview Press, pp. 147–66.

Rossendale Groundwork Trust (1986) *Grass Routes.* Rawtenstall: The Groundwork Trust.

Ruane, J.B. (1973) Fathers and sons: the process of transfer and succession. In: Commins, P. and Kelleher, C. (eds) *Farm Inheritance and Succession.* Dublin: Macra na Feirme, pp. 50–67.

Russell, C., Griffin, C., Flinchbaugh, C., Martin, M. and Atilano, R. (1985) Coping strategies associated with intergenerational transfer of the family farm. *Rural Sociology* 50, 361–76.

Sachs, C.E. (1983) *The Invisible Farmers.* Totowa, New Jersey: Rowman and Allanheld.

Sachs, C.E. (1991) Women's work and food. *Journal of Rural Studies* 7, 49–55.

Salamon, S. (1985a) An anthropological view of land transfers. In: D.D. Moyer and G. Wunderlich (eds) *Transfer of Land Rights: Proceedings of a Workshop on the Transfer of Rural Lands.* Washington DC: Department of Agriculture Economic Research Service, pp. 123–44.

Salamon, S. (1985b) Ethnic communities and the structure of agriculture. *Rural Sociology* 50, 323–40.

Salamon, S. (1988) *Variability among Persistent Family Farms in the US Corn Belt.* Paper presented at World Congress for Rural Sociology, Bologna, Italy.

Salamon, S. (1992) *Prairie Patrimony: Family, Farming, and Community in the Midwest.* Chapel Hill: University of North Carolina Press.

Salamon, S. and Davis–Brown, K. (1986) Middle–range farmers persisting through the agricultural crisis. *Rural Sociology* 51, 503–12.

Salamon, S. and Davis–Brown, K. (1988) Farm continuity and female land inheritance: a family dilemma. In: W.G. Haney and J.B. Knowles (eds) *Women and Farming: Changing Roles, Changing Structures*: Westview Press, Boulder, Colorado, pp. 195–210.

Sandford, C. (1976) The taxation of personal wealth. In: Jones, A. (ed.) *Economics and Equality.* Oxford: Philip Allan, pp. 102–21.

Schmitt, G. (1991) Why is the agriculture of advanced Western countries still organized by family farms? *European Review of Agricultural Economics* 18, 443–58.

Schwarzweller, H.K. and Clay, D.C. (1992) *Conceptualizing and Researching Household Survival Strategies.* Paper presented at VII World Congress for Rural Sociology, Penn State University, USA, August.

Scully, J. (1971) *Agriculture in the West of Ireland.* Dublin: Department of Agriculture and Fisheries.

Selles, R. and Keating, N. (1989) La transmission des fermes par les Albertainages d'origine Hollandaise. In: Santerre, R. and Meintel, D. (eds) *Veiller au Quebec, en Afrique et Ailleurs.* Laval, Quebec: University of Laval Press.

Shaver, F.M. (1991) Women, work and the evolution of agriculture. *Journal of Rural Studies* 7, 37–43.

Sheridan, R. (1982) Women's contribution to farming. *Farm and Food Research* 13, 46–8.

Shucksmith, D.M., Bryden, J., Rosenthall, P., Short, C. and Winter, D.M. (1989) Pluriactivity, farm structures and rural change. *Journal of Agricultural Economics* 40, 345–60.

Siiskonen, P., Parviainen, A. and Koppa, T. (1982) *Women in Agriculture. A Study of Equality and the Position of Women engaged in Agriculture in Finland in 1980.* Espoo: Pellervo Economic Research Institute, No. 27.

Simon, H.A. (1957) *Models of Man: Social and Rational.* New York: Wiley.

Sparrow, T. (1972) The use of agricultural manpower. *Journal of Agricultural Labour Science* 1, 3–10.

Stanworth, J. and Curran, J. (1981) Growth in the small firm. In: Gorb, P., Dowell, P. and Wilson, P. *Small Business Perspectives.* London Business School: Armstrong Publishing.

Stockdale, J.D. (1982) Who will speak for agriculture? In: Dillman, D.A. and Hobbs, D.J. (eds) *Rural Society in the US: Issues for the 1980s.* Boulder, Colorado: Westview Press, pp. 317–27.

Streeter, D.H. (1988) Farmland preservation: the role of off-farm income. *Landscape and Urban Planning* 16, 357–64.

Suits, D.B. (1985) US farm migration: an application of the Harris–Todaro model. *Economic Development and Cultural Change* 33, 815–28.

Symes, D.G. (1972) Farm household and farm performance: a study of twentieth century Ballyferriter, southwest Ireland. *Ethnology* 11, 25–38.

Symes, D.G. (1973) Stability and change among farming communities in southwest Ireland. *Acta Ethnographica Academiae Scientarium Hungaricae* 1, 89–105

Symes, D.G. (1990) Bridging the generations: succession and inheritance in a changing world. *Sociologia Ruralis* 30, 280–91.

Symes, D.G. (1991) Changing gender roles in productionist and post-productionist capitalist agriculture. *Journal of Rural Studies* 7, 85–90.

Symes, D.G. and Appleton, J. (1986) Family goals and survival strategies: the role of kinship in an English upland farming community. *Sociologia Ruralis* 36, 345–63.

Symes, D.G. and Marsden, T.K. (1983a) Family, continuity and change in a capitalist farming region. *Acta Ethnographica Academiae Scientiarum Hungaricae* 32, 77–101.

Symes, D.G. and Marsden, T.K. (1983b) Complementary roles and asymmetrical lives: farmers' wives in a large farm environment. *Sociologia Ruralis* 23, 229–41.

Tarver, J.D. (1952) Intra-family farm succession practice. *Rural Sociology* 17, 266–71.

Taylor, J.P. (1983) Policy and the family farm in Wales: prospects and proposals. In: Tranter, R.B. (ed.) *Strategies for Family-worked Farms in the UK.* Reading: Centre for Agricultural Strategy CAS Paper 15, pp. 187–90.

Twain, M. (1984) *Life on the Mississippi.* Harmondsworth: Penguin.

Voyce, M. (1989) *Handing Down The Family Farm.* New South Wales: Macquarie University, published mimeo.

Voyce, M. *et al.* (1989) *The Transfer of the Family Farm: A Community Response.* Richmond, NSW: University of Western Sydney, Hawkesbury, published mimeo.

Warren, M. (1989) *Farming Change in Devon and Cornwall: The Implications for Training and Advice.* Newton Abbot: Faculty of Agriculture, Food and Land Use, Polytechnic South West, Seale Hayne.

Westermarck, N. (1986) Gender partnership: a postulate for socioeconomically viable family farms. *Acta Agriculturae Scandinavica* 36, 429–34.

Whatmore, S. (1991a) *Farming Women.* Basingstoke: Macmillan.

Whatmore, S. (1991b) Life cycle or patriarchy? Gender divisions in family farming. *Journal of Rural Studies* 7, 71–6.

Whatmore, S., Munton, R., Little, J. and Marsden, T. (1987a) Towards a typology of farm businesses in contemporary British agriculture. *Sociologia Ruralis* 27, 21–37.

Whatmore, S., Munton, R., Marsden, T. and Little, J. (1987b) Interpreting a relational typology of farm businesses in southern England. *Sociologia Ruralis* 27, 103–22.

Whitener, L.A. and Munir, R.A. (1990) Hired farm labour. In: Barse, J.R. (ed.) *Seven Farm Input Industries.* Agricultural Economic Report No. 635, USDA Economic Research Service.

Wilkening, E.A. (1954) Techniques of assessing farm family values. *Rural Sociology* 19, 39–49.

Wilkening, E.A. (1981a) Farm families and family farming. In: Coward, R.T. and Smith, W.M. (eds) *The Family in Rural Society.* Boulder, Colorado: Westview Press, pp. 27–37.

Wilkening, E.A. (1981b) *Farm Husbands and Wives in Wisconsin.* Madison, Wisconsin: University of Wisconsin–Madison College of Agricultural and Life Sciences.

Wilkening, E.A. and Bharadwaj, L. (1966) *Aspirations, Work Roles and Decision-Making Patterns of Farm Husbands and Wives in Wisconsin.* Madison, Wisconsin: Wisconsin Agricultural Experiment Station Research Bulletin 266.

Wilkening, E.A. and Guerrero, S. (1969) Consensus in aspirations for farm improvements and adoption of farm practices. *Rural Sociology* 34, 182–96.

Wilkening, E.A. and Lupri, E. (1965) Decision-making in German and American farm families: a cross-cultural comparison. *Sociologia Ruralis* 5, 366–85.

Williams, W.M. (1956) *The Sociology of an English Village: Gosforth.* London: Routledge and Kegan Paul.

Williams, W.M. (1963) *A West Country Village: Ashworthy.* London: Routledge & Kegan Paul.

Williams, W.M. (1973) The social study of family farming. In: Mills, D.R. (ed.) *English Rural Communities.* London: Macmillan.

Winter, M. (1984) Agrarian class structure and family farming. In: Bradley, T. and Lowe, P. (eds) *Locality and Rurality: Economy and Society in Rural Regions.* Norwich: Geo Books, pp. 115–28.

Winter, M. (1986) The development of family farming in West Devon in the nineteenth century. In: Cox, G., Lowe, P. and Winter, M. (eds) *Agriculture: People and Policies.* London: Allen and Unwin, pp. 61–76.

Winter, M. (1987) In: Bouquet, M. and Winter, M. (eds) *Who From Their Labours Rest?* Aldershot: Avebury.

Young, J.A. (1984) Small-scale farmers. In: Applebaum, H. (ed.) *Work and Market in Industrial Societies.* Albany, NY: State University of New York Press, pp. 150–63.

Young, K. (1978) Changing economic roles of women in two rural Mexican communities. *Sociologia Ruralis* 18, 197–216.

Index

accommodation
  problems in succession and
    retirement 229–31
  for visitors 164–5
accountant as advisor 233–5
accumulator as an ideal type 247
adaptation of family farms to external
    capital 76–7
administration of farm business 157–8
advice for planning inter-generational
    transfer 233–5
age of farmers
  and levels of education and training
    138
  see also elderly farmers
agricultural contractors 118–19
agricultural economists' approaches 4–6
  explanations of capital-labour
    substitution 69–70
agricultural policy see government
    intervention
Agricultural Training Board 138–9, 180
Arkleton Trust survey 188, 248–9
artisan as an ideal type 102
aspirations of family members 107
Australia 193, 217, 234, 236
autonomy, wife's desire for 178–9, 254–5

background of farmers and wives see
    social background
backward-sloping supply curve for
    labour 124
bank manager as adviser 233–4

batchelor farmer see single farmer
biological failure to secure succession
    190
borrowing
  farmers' attitudes to 106
  see also credit, debt
business see farm business
business cycle
  and farm business reproduction 253
  implications for labour productivity
    129–30
business principal 25

Canada 15, 156
capital
  assets owned by farmers 43–4
  borrowing trends 54–5
  grants 80
  ownership 21
  substitution for labour 69–70
  taxation and property transfer
    198–9
Capital Transfer Tax 78, 160, 199
capitalist influence
  on manual work by wife 155–7
  and trends in wife's role 176–8
capitalist production 15, 17, 60
Chayanov 58, 85
children
  causes of tension in family farming
    140
  wife's role in socializing 166
  working on family farm 118–20, 125

classical entrepreneur as an ideal type 102

classification schemes
    taxonomic approach 12
    see also ideal types, typology

'closed shop' 264

coalition, as a means of solving management conflict 141

Code Napoleon 196–7

Common Agricultural Policy 2
    reform of 2, 3, 5, 28, 143

conflict
    between spouses 168
    in family workforce 140–1
    over objectives 107–10
    resolving 110–11

consumption
    needs 37
    objectives 92

continuity of family farming 184, 259–67
    conflict with farm enlargement 261–2
    and family influence 262–3
    and farm size 262–3
    means of achieving 189–90
    value attached to 259

contract farming, as a form of indirect control by capital 68–9

controller, as a stage in succession process 215–7

co-operation, as a means of spreading fixed costs 84

credit 55
    as a form of indirect control by capital 68
    see also borrowing, debt

cultural norms 90

data on farm family businesses 42–3
    weaknesses of 44

daughters
    likelihood of inheriting farms 195–6
    marriage prospects 147
    social norms of inheritance 201
    succession rights in Norway 178, 196

daughter-in-law
    position in family business 159, 179, 181

debt
    numbers of indebted farmers 54–5
    see also borrowing, credit

decision process 26

decision-making in farm family business 25–7
    delegation of 117, 136
        to successor 212–5
    wife's involvement 158–62

dedicated producer as an ideal type 103–4, 250

definition of farm family business 18

Denmark 45, 165–6, 196, 197, 203, 212, 224, 230, 234

detour professionelle 129, 138, 208, 237

disciplines, academic 3
    multi-disciplinary approach 8–9
    rival perspectives 69–72

disengagement
    as a household strategy 248

disguised unemployment 132–4

diversification 164–6
    and farm business development 207, 252
    and wife's autonomy 178
    see also part-time farming, pluriactivity

division of labour 34–5, 135–6
    gender division 51–7

divorce 9, 179, 181
    influence on timing of inheritance 193
    see also family breakdown

dowry 164, 195

economies of scale 66

education of farmers and family workers 137–9, 265

elderly farmers 224–5
    impact on productivity 224

employment refuge 134

Engel's Law 28, 244

enterprise management by wife 159–60

entrepreneurial style of farming 95

entry to farming 206
    problems for new entrants 206,
       262–5
environmental impact of family farming
    265–6
expansion and farm succession 207
exploitation of family labour 93, 242, 256
extended family 29–30
extensification 244

FADN 15, 47
family
    as a source of capital 18, 19, 43–4,
       55
    as a source of labour 38, 242
      variations by country 45–6
      variations by type of farming 47,
       49
    as a source of management 19
family breakdown 179, 181
    see also divorce
family business farm 74–5
family control
    undermined by capital 70
family cycle 32–4, 242
    and business objectives 95–6
    and labour productivity 128–9
    influence on labour supply 37
family discussion
    of succession process 235–7
family farm
    as a stabilizing influence 2
family farming
    as ideology 2
    regional variations 48, 67
family ideology 34
family labour
    as proportion of total labour input
      44–6
    regional variations in importance 48
    trends in OECD countries 53
    trends in use 133
family labour farm *see* family-worked
    farm
family objectives in farming
    held by farmers and wives 108–110
    and management style 104

and size of business 101
    under pressure from capital 105–7
family-owned business 18
    numbers in US agriculture 46
family relationships *see* kinship relations
family-worked farm 12, 13, 18, 44, 74–5
farm amalgamation 79, 84
farm business 24–8
farm business principal 25
Farm Business Survey 145, 150–1, 155,
    163, 181
farm diversification *see* diversification
farm household 30–2
farm housewife
    as an ideal type 170–3
    and farm succession 173
    and gender division of labour 171
    likes and dislikes in farming 108
    role in farm family business 172–3
    trends in numbers 177
farm management *see* management
farm size
    and ascent of succession ladder
      218–9
    and continuity of farm family
      business 262–3
    and farmers' objectives 100
    and marriage prospects of sons
      146–8
    and payment of wife 174
    and retirement housing 230–1
    and retirement plans 223
    and role of wife 172
    and social background of farmers
      and wives 148–9
    and succession 186
    and wife's contribution 150, 155–7,
      160–2
farm tasks performed by women 151–4
farm type
    and ascent of succession ladder
      218–9
    and use of family labour 47, 49
'farmer' gender issues 9–10
farmer's age
    and objectives 96, 101
farmer's boy as an ideal type 204–5, 260
farmers' daughters *see* daughters

farmers' sons *see* sons, marriage
    prospects
farmers' wives *see* wives of farmers
farmhouse *see* accommodation
farming system 24–5, 27
feminization of agriculture 177
Finland 128, 147, 154, 190, 193, 198, 209,
    230, 235, 245–6
fiscal framework of inheritance 198–9
flexible strategist as an ideal type 104,
    250
flexibility
    of family farming 35–6, 240, 245
    of labour inputs 119–20, 125–6
France 44, 45, 82, 84, 134, 151, 158, 183,
    189, 196, 197, 198, 200, 201, 203,
    207, 213, 217, 238, 249, 250
future of family farming 58–9, 243–67

GAEC 207–8, 213
gender
    of farmers 9–10
    and inheritance of family business
      195–6
gender division of labour *see* division of
    labour
Germany 84, 109, 134, 147, 195, 196, 197,
    203, 224, 230, 238
goals 89–90
    see also objectives
government intervention 28
    affecting family farm 77–81
    benefits larger farms 80–1
    early retirement schemes 224–5,
      238–9
    farmers' response to retirement
      schemes 238–9
    and inheritance practices 200
    in land market 82
    and small farms 79–83

hired labour 14–16, 118–19
    trends in use 51–2, 53, 133
historical predictions about family
    farming 58–9

hobby farmer as an ideal type 247, 250,
    256
horizontal integration 58
hours of work by wives 162–4
household strategies 248–50
housework 167
housing *see* accommodation

ideal types 12
    family farm as an ideal type 18
    of farm business 74
    of farm manager 102–4
    of farm wives 108
    of succession patterns 203–6
    of woman's role on farm 169–73
      implications for succession a173
    see also typology
ideology
    of family 34
    of family farm 2
    of women's domestic labour a175–6
income sources outside farming 113–14,
    22
income support 81–2
independence as a goal in farming 97–9,
    254
    and size of business 100
    under pressure from capital 106–7
indirect control by capital 67–9
industrial-type farm 16–17, 81
information access for smaller farm 81
inheritance 183
    economic influences 201–2
    impact of rising land prices 202
    and low-paid family labour 127
    partibility 191–2
    patterns 189–203
    tax 78
    timing 192–3
instrumental rewards in farming 91, 100,
    101
intensification and succession 207, 244
interaction between family and business
    1, 23, 36–9
inter-generational transfer
    as a defining characteristic 18, 23
    issues arising 39, 190–1, 255

inter-generational transfer (*contd*)
  numbers of farmers anticipating 43
  strengths and weaknesses 243
intrinsic rewards in farming 91, 97–9,
  100
investment needs of farm household 37
Ireland 7, 14, 32, 34, 67, 82, 106, 129, 147,
  150, 152, 157, 158, 159–60, 163,
  175, 178, 179, 185, 189, 190, 192,
  196, 199, 200, 201, 203, 206, 207,
  212, 218, 227, 229, 230, 235, 236,
  260
IVD 238

Jeffersonian ideal 2, 13, 21, 78

Kautsky 58
'keeping the name on the land' 185,
  189–90, 201, 260
kin
  contacts in retirement 229
  as a source of farm labour 119
kinship relations 17, 21, 29–30
knowledge accumulated in family 128

labour allocation decisions 37, 93–4,
  105–7, 122–5
labour categories 120
labour criterion 14–16, 18–19
labour productivity 125, 130–1, 244
  and business cycle 129–30
  and family cycle 128–9
  influence of management 134–43
labour quality 135
labour recruitment 93, 105–6
  and productivity 130
labour sources 118–20
labour substitution 132–3
land market 82–3
land policies 82–3
land prices
  and inheritance patterns 202, 206
landowner 53
landownership 21
  historical trends 51–2

larger-than-family farm 16
legal advisor 233–5
legal framework of inheritance 198–200
legal status of farmers' wife 160–1, 181
leisure in retirement 232
Lenin 58
lifestyler as an ideal type 104, 250
'living over the shop' 18, 22–3, 38–9,
  242–3

Maatschap 197, 205
MacSharry Plan 2, 3, 81–2
management
  approaches 4
  control fuction 27
  roles 141–3
  styles 103–4
  team 141–3, 254, 261
manager as an ideal type 102
managerial labour inputs 116–18
managerial skills 116–18
manual labour
  value attached 93–4, 106–7
  versus managerial labour 93–4,
  135–6
manual work by wife 150–1
  gender divisions 151–4
  and influence of capital 155–7
marginal cases 19–23
marginal cost of labour 120–1
marginal revenue product of labour
  120–3, 132, 134
marginal utility of farm work 122
marginalized farm as an ideal type 247,
  250
market industrialized countries 9
marriage bureaux 147
marriage prospects for farmers 146–8,
  256
married farmers 146–8
Marxist
  approaches 6, 70
  concept of subsumption 61
  predictions about family farming 6,
  14–15, 58–9
masculinization of agriculture 177, 178
Maslow's hierarchy of needs 111

mediator, wife's role as 167, 232
milk quotas 253
motivation of family workforce 139–40

neighbours, as a source of farm labour 119–20
Netherlands 45, 84, 119, 151, 152, 158, 196, 197, 203, 205, 207, 212, 224, 230, 234, 238
New Zealand 72, 103, 158, 159, 211, 213, 237, 250, 252
NFU 83
non-family farms 15, 17, 74–5
Northfield Committee 62, 264
Norway 178, 196
nuclear family 29–30
numbers of farm family businesses 43
    evidence for decline in US 49–50, 53
    trends 44–7, 49–56

objectives 88–90
    classification scheme 99, 111
    empirical evidence of farmers' objectives 97–102
    in family business 92–7
    in farming 91–2
    of German farmers and wives 109–10
    and influence of capitalism 104–7
    multiple objectives in farm family business 110–111
    of other family members 107–110
    of Wisconsin farmers and wives 108–10
occupations of farmers outside farming 22
off-farm employment
    of farmers' wives 165–6
    and local labour market 173
    and reproduction of farm business 252
office work by farmer's wife 157–8
one-man farm 22, 66
opportunity cost
    of employing family members 121–2

of family labour 93
of supervising workers 121
Overseas Experience 237
ownership
    of business, combined with managerial control 17, 20, 21, 37, 241
    of land and capital 16–17

part-time farming 13–14, 22
    and partibility of inheritance 202–3
    typologies 248–9
    see also diversification, pluriactivity
partibility of inheritance 191–2, 194–203
partnership 206–7
    as an ideal type 204–5, 261
    as a stage in succession process 215–7
payment of farmer's wife 173–5
penetration by capital 59–77
    direct and indirect 61–2
    reasons for slow penetration 64–7
    uneven 66–7
    see also subsumption of labour by capital
pension scheme 227
peripheral areas 67
persistence of family farming 59–61
personal objectives in farming 99–101
planning horizon 92–3
pluriactivity
    and farm business reproduction 252
    of farm household 255
    for survival 252
    typologies 248–9
    of wives 164–6
    see also diversification, part-time farming
polarization of farm structures 245
power within farm family 27
price support 80
primogeniture 194–6
professionalization as a household strategy 248
proletarianization 58
Protestant Ethic 94, 106

psychic costs 121
psychic income 122, 124, 222, 225, 228–9
public relations role of wife 169, 177

recognition of wife's contribution 175–6,
      180
regional variations
      in manual work by wives 155
      in methods of payment for wife's
         work 174
reproduction
      of farm business 251–3
      of farm household 253–7
         under subsumption 257–9
      of farm labour force 22, 166–9
      overlap with productive activities
         38–9
retirement 183, 222
      advice 233–5
      age of farmers 223–4
      barriers to 224–5
      housing 230–1
      income sources 225–8
      patterns 220–1, 222–3
      planning 233–5
      plans of farmers 222–3
      schemes 224–5, 238–9
      stages in process 221
      of tenants 223
rewards for wife's work 173–5
risk aversion 101, 105
rural sociologists' approaches 6, 7
      explanations of trends in family
         farming 69–72

seasonality of labour demand 115, 125
second homes 230
Self-Employed Directive 180
self-exploitation 60–1, 126–8, 131
self-sufficient family farm 13
semi-retirement 220, 222–3, 225–8, 230
separate enterprise as an ideal type
      204–5, 207, 261
simple commodity production 60, 64
single farmers 146–8
size of business *see* farm size

Small Farmer Scheme 79
Small Holders' Assistance 82
Smallfarmers' Association 11, 13, 83
social anthropologists' approaches 7–8
social background
      of farmers and wives 148–9
         and entry to farming 262–3
      of wife
         and contributions to family
            business 164
         and off-farm employment 165
social income of British agriculture 53–4
social norms
      of inheritance 200–1
      of inter-generational continuity
         184–5
social objectives in farming 99, 101
social trajectories of family farms 258–9
socialization
      for succession 211
      as a stage in succession process 217
Socio-Economic Advisory Service 234
sons, marriage prospects 146–8
stable reproduction as a household
      strategy 248
stand-by holding as an ideal type 204–5,
      206, 261
status of farmer's wife 175, 178, 181
statutory smallholdings 52, 264
strengths of family farming 241–3
Stresa Conference 2
stress in farm families 140, 169, 179, 232
subsumption of labour by capital 61,
      71–2
      empirical evidence 72–7
      versus survival 244
      and manual work by wife 155–6
      see also penetration by capital
succession 183
      as a goal 94–5, 96–7, 254
      ideal types 203–6
      ladder 211–19
      likelihood of 187–8
      patterns 203–8
      socialization for 211
      women's rights in Norway 178
successor
      identification 211

need for 184–6
 numbers of farmers with 186–8
 role in decision process 136
supervisory activities 117
supply curve for labour, backward
 sloping 124
supply response of family labour 132
supportive role of wife 149, 168–9
survival of family farming 64–5, 244–5,
 250–7
 of farm business 251–3
 of farm household 253–7
 versus subsumption 71–2
  empirical evidence 72–7
survivor as an ideal type 247

target income 123–4
technical apprenticeship, as a stage in
 succession process 215–7
technology
 and dependence on outside capital 62
 treadmill 63, 80, 244
tenant farmer 21
 security of tenure 53–4
tenant-type farm 16, 17, 18, 21
Theory of the Firm 89
Third World agriculture 9
time allocation *see* labour allocation
 decisions
training of farmers and family members
 137–9, 265
transaction costs 64, 121
transfer of managerial control 212–18
 factors making for successful
  transfer 236–7
 impact on farm business 219
 on Irish farms 212–3
 managing the process 231–7
transitional farm 74–5
tripartite structure of British agriculture
 51–2
typology
 of family commitment to farming
  257–9
 relational typology of farm
  businesses 73–5, 258–9
 see also classification, ideal type

unemployment 133–4
United States 2, 5, 7, 13, 16, 17, 21–2, 30,
 42, 43, 46, 49–50, 53, 56, 66, 77–8,
 108–10, 130, 132, 134, 152–4, 158,
 159, 167, 168, 169, 185, 189, 190,
 195, 196, 201, 229, 237
unmarried farmer *see* single farmer
unsocial hours 115–16

valuation of family labour 131, 138,
 143–4, 180
values 90
value orientations 90
 of entrepreneurs 102–3
 and management styles 104
 in work 91–2
vertical integration 58, 68, 84

Wales 7, 67, 80, 146, 150, 151, 154, 155,
 174, 175
weaknesses of family farming 241–3
Weber 58
welfare status of wife 180
west room 230
wives of farmers
 contribution to family business
  149–57
 hours worked 162–4
 numbers doing farm work 150
 payment 173–5
 role in decision-making 136
 work experience 148–9
 working off the farm 22
will
 importance in planning succession
  235
woman farmer
 and farm succession 173
 and gender division of labour 171
 as an ideal type 170–3
 likes and dislikes in farming 108
Women's Farming Union 83–4, 169
women's work 22
working farmwife
 and gender division of labour 171
 as an ideal type 170–3

working farmwife (*contd*)
    likes and dislikes in farming 108
    trends in numbers 177
working relationships in farm family
        business 140–1

Yankee farming patterns 189
Yankee goals in farming 95, 104
yeoman goals in farming 95, 104, 184–5

'Z' goods 123, 125